metal cowboy

ten years further down the road less pedaled

JOE KURMASKIE

BREAKAWAY BOOKS
HALCOTTSVILLE, NEW YORK
2010

This extended roadtrip and the words that followed would not have been possible without the help of my parents, Claire and Joe, my sister Jennifer, and brothers, Dan and Tim (thanks for all the free room and board, ya'll). Thank you to Beth and Quinn.

I'd also like to thank the gang at The Silver City *Daily Press*, which first published some of these essays in column form—especially Tauna Gallagher, Richard, Bill, Neva, Wayne, and Steve. Jim Owen gets a special salute for inspiration and for his own brand of motivational technique. ("Let's go walk in the woods, Joe. Work can wait.").

A thank you to all the Biaginis, Willie and Kat Weir, Joy and Mike Garcia, Albert Pantone, Matt Siegel, and all the vibrant souls found in the pages of this book . . . and in tales not yet told. You gave me friendship, laughter and something real and unpolished to write about.

I've saved my pubisher, editor, and friend, Garth Battista, for last. Deepest thanks for believing in me and this book, and for helping it onto the road.

—J. K., July 1999

Metal Cowboy: Ten Years Further Down the Road Less Pedaled
(A tenth anniversary reprint of the original, with new material)
Copyright 1999, 2010 by Joe Kurmaskie

ISBN: 978-1-891369-86-5
Library of Congress Control Number: 2009940011

Published by Breakaway Books
P. O. Box 24
Halcottsville, NY 12438
(800) 548-4348
www.breakawaybooks.com

Visit **www.metalcowboy.com**

contents

For Beth,
who took a chance on a guy with only a bike,
some camping gear, and a few tattered journals.

Introduction to the 10th Anniversary Edition

I'VE BEEN THE METAL COWBOY FOR A FULL DECADE NOW?

Can we get a ruling on this?! Okay, my lawyer says it's official. You don't argue with the suits, not when you wear lycra and Hawaiian shirts. A decade though, that's a healthy chunk of my time on this planet. Substantial . . . *legitimate*, even. I could be mistaken for "The Man."

Life sneaks up on you sometimes and sometimes it's a blind old rancher who wanders into it for a few moments that changes everything. Technically, I was christened back in 1990, when that bent and broken down old codger wandered out of the mist, worked his cane over the entire endeavor and branded me; so really, the Metal Cowboy thing has been floating around for twenty years, but it wasn't until this book hit the market, that it found a life of its own.

What began as a sprawling manifesto found its footing when I tore each story down for a weekly column at a newspaper where I was working. I would feel my way through to the essence of the adventures.

When I decided to put artifice aside and just take readers out there, give them a saddle-top view of what it means to be young at heart and fresh in the legs, to test the wild roads less pedaled, to let people and events in and the miles set me free or break my heart, that's when this book turned into something that would hold up ten years later.

Metal Cowboy brought together a cast of characters too real and raw for fiction, from old men still pedaling up hills with little more than a frying pan, a parka, and the will to carry on, to a band of second-rate Elvis impersonators celebrating excess for at least an hour after sundown; an Italian barber trying to win the Tour de France and a rockhound trying to save a pile of scarred stones in the desert. I rode into eco-wars and small town parades. I joined up with folks finding the first moments of independence and stood beside shattered remains of others losing everything they loved or cared about. Beginnings, endings, and the messy, vibrant in-betweens.

In short, I found meaning in the miles; humor, hurt, physical limits and how to push beyond them, and what happens when you jump the track, on purpose to see what there is to see.

In this tenth anniversary edition all the original tales are here and a few new ones. The question I've been asked repeatedly over the years is whatever happened to this or that person or situation. This edition includes an "Updates" section. *The rest of the story,* to steal a famous tagline. Read it only when you are prepared to jump the tracks with me once more, to feel the heartbreak and quiet heroism, along the road less pedaled.

Oh, to Be Young and Go Very, Very Fast

IT WAS 5:30 A.M. IN POCATELLO, IDAHO, A THIN SHEET OF ICY RAIN masked sunrise, and I wasn't quite sure I was up for my latest bicycling adventure.

Coasting through the nearly deserted streets of this small western town, I found myself poised at a stoplight. An ingrained obedience to traffic laws coupled with a sleepy hangover from the long train ride kept me anchored in place though there wasn't a car in sight.

As I waited, an old rancher ambled up to the intersection. The fur collar on his long coat was tattered, crusted with tobacco stains, and faded. As his cane tapped its way over my bike, I noticed for the first time that he was blind. One eye drooped shut like that of a tomcat that had seen too many late-night brawls, while the other, still open, was cloudy and distant. That eye reminded me of an African tribesman seen in the pages of *National Geographic* who suffered from river blindness.

The old rancher continued to work his cane over me, tapping as he went. And though the light changed from red to green several times, I remained frozen, allowing this slow survey of my person.

The moment felt intimate and awkward, but I did not break it.

When he was done, the old rancher stood back, grinned through a ruin of teeth, and said, "Ah, metal cowboy."

I was dumbfounded; first, that he had spoken at all, and more importantly, that this battered husk of man had hit upon a perfect description of me at the time, and my story. Though I looked more like a surfer, or a guy on a fool's journey, to him I felt like a metal cowboy, the bike my horse, and the asphalt my trail.

"Keep the wind at your back, and find where the innocent sleep," he added. Then, without fanfare, my rancher crossed the street and dissolved into the early-morning mist.

A chill passed through me.

I have thought about that old man many times during my travels. He was right about the wind, and as for locating where the innocent sleep, I want to believe he meant to look for the best in people along the road, and that's what you will often find.

My bicycle has also brought me to the innocence and the best in myself. Collectively, my travels have been the antidote for the cynicism that can gather at the feet of complacency and grow in even the most useful and noble life.

I remember the crusty old rancher tapping the back of my bike gently before he crossed the street into the rest of his life. That little push has kept me rolling right up to the edge of the millennium.

But every cowboy's story needs a beginning. Mine started the moment I learned to ride.

Until the day I met the woman I would marry, the love of my life was a bicycle. Just a collection of metal, rubber, grease, and gears to the untrained eye, to me that two-wheeled contraption has always represented something more.

It has to do with possibilities.

In 1970, my sister began her bug collection in earnest, so, at the ripe old age of five, I scooped up her bike and decided to teach myself to ride.

How hard could it be?

I skipped right past training wheels and took a couple of nasty spills. My five-year-old brain registered that this was going to take some effort, but I desperately wanted to learn.

Never mind that the vehicle in question was a powder blue, one-speed tank with a pink polka-dot banana seat, ape hanger handle-bars, and pompom-style streamers fluttering from the bars' grips. The flower-covered basket attached to its front and a pinwheel twirling in the wind from its rear completed the look.

Macho was not in my vocabulary back then.

But by dinner, I was circling the block, growing more confident with every pedal stroke. My sister lodged a complaint with the parental authorities, but by the time they came to investigate, I was gone.

Freedom.

That's what I felt my first day balanced on two wheels, and through all my years of riding, that feeling has remained. Sure, I love the wind in my face, the sound of my beating heart as I work up a hill, but the simple, clean rush of freedom was what hooked me. Pedaling along, playing the gears like a concert pianist battling through Rachmaninoff, you feel like the hero of a tale that's being written where the rubber meets the road.

When my parents tracked me down that evening, I was six blocks away, hanging out by the elementary school fence with some rough-looking second-graders, future Hell's Angels who had whole suits of playing cards attached to their bicycle spokes.

I think they respected the fact that I would even approach them sporting a bike that looked like my sister's.

"Kid must be fearless," they probably thought.

I rode my sibling's cycle straight through winter. Nothing could stop my daily escapes. My parents huddled together, and because there were no official holidays or birthdays on the horizon, they did something unheard of in the history of my childhood: They bought me a bike simply because I wanted one—and not just any ride, but a black-and-gold Schwinn with a functioning speedometer.

The speedometer was my parents' one mistake. The expression "speed kills" comes to mind every time I think of that device. We lived at the bottom of a rather steep hill, a hill that needed conquering.

Oh, to be young and go very, very fast.

Speed didn't kill me that day, but, with my left arm snapped in three places, I was a few steps farther along the road to understanding a body's limitations.

Before the plaster on my cast had even dried, I was back on the bike, waving to neighbors and friends as I pedaled along the route of the accident, like a homecoming king in a small-town parade, the fallen hero rising from the ashes. I was blind to the occasional head-shaking and sagelike finger-wagging of parents sitting on porches.

Little did I know then that as an adult, my story would include numerous bicycle adventures around North America, an odyssey across Australia and New Zealand, and even a few seasons spent managing a bicycle-and-canoe touring company in the backwoods of Florida.

My love for cycling has helped shape who I am today. That old rancher knew the score. With a few taps of his cane he'd glimpsed this collection of lessons, experiences, and moments of absurdity gathered while atop a bike.

Metal Cowboy. My name came looking for me that morning in Idaho—and I found the rest of the story.

Oh, to be young and go very, very fast!

Finding Sanctuary
in a Wild World

To sleep, perchance to dream. —Shakespeare

THE LONG-DISTANCE CYCLIST PEDALING THE OPEN ROAD IN SEARCH OF adventure is, by default, also on a quest for sanctuary, a safe and relatively comfortable spot to lie down and recharge the engines each night. This often can be a daunting task. Some evenings, after a grueling day's ride, I knew exactly where I would end up: a state park with camping facilities or my relatives' homes.

I'd accept an invitation from a newly acquired or longtime friend to simply drop in, or, when I was in vast, unfettered territory like the Olympic Peninsula, the jungles of Venezuela, or the Australian outback, it was a matter of merely deciding that I'd had enough and pulling off the road. (I use the term *road* loosely when recalling the jungles and the outback.)

But on other days, locating sanctuary was just a bit more challenging. During my earliest adventures, the ride from Maine to Florida, especially, I gave camping arrangements and possible destinations far too much of my time and energy.

With the concentration of an engineer, I would sit by the side of the road with maps unfolded, or spread them across the booth of a coffee shop, plotting wind speed, weather conditions, planned stops, the average miles per hour I was maintaining, and other complicated factors. Through much effort, since math has never been my strong suit, I'd pinpoint where I thought I'd arrive by nightfall. My calculations were right less than half the time. I chalked it up to my gregarious nature, always getting sidetracked in conversation with compelling people or detouring to check out some eye-catching architecture high on a hill or tucked away along a back road.

It wasn't long before I adopted the Buddhist saying, "Don't push the river," as my operating instructions. If there were definite camping possibilities close by, I would shoot for them; otherwise, I relied on ingenuity and no small measure of resourcefulness.

The results were often amusing. I've slept in playgrounds and church courtyards, and on beaches. Once, I awoke to find that I had set up my tent in the middle of a construction site. I beat a fast path away from the hammers, nails, and shouts of workers that morning.

My selection of certain makeshift campsites often led to other adventures. The night I thought I'd nestled myself in a wooded park was clarified in the morning when the rattle and whoosh of the amusement park's roller coaster brought me out of sleep. The attraction was closed for the season, but workers were testing the ride for weak tracks and rotted planks. That was the morning I got to take a ride on a roller coaster before breakfast.

Then there was the time I rose to the aroma of pancakes cooking in a church vestry. I thought I'd gotten my gear packed up without detection, but when I took my stack of flapjacks and placed my donation in the pastor's hand, he winked and asked if I'd slept comfortably under the willow trees.

Things didn't always end as pleasantly. My little tent was low enough to the ground that I could hide behind a collection of rocks, or even in depressions and culverts. This made me, when fatigue took its toll, a little too quick to pick a spot and call it home.

In coastal Georgia, I pulled off a desolate road and set up shop in what I thought was a quiet ravine. About three in the morning the gray water from a sewage plant made its way rapidly through my tent en route to the ocean. "Rude awakening" does not begin to cover it. I spent half the next day in a laundromat trying to clean up my possessions.

And never, *ever* try renegade camping in Humboldt County, California. At the time, I was not aware of this region's reputation as marijuana cultivation central. I rolled out my sleeping bag one evening in the pastoral setting of a tranquil valley only to have the sound of a pump-action shotgun being loaded freeze me in place. The briefest of conversations followed and, though darkness had settled in around me, I considered myself lucky to be back in the saddle and on my way.

My final resting spot that night was a roadside attraction called Snake City. The owner was more than happy to let me put up my tent, but didn't I want to visit with some of his pets, first? The twenty-foot python named Stretch looked hungry.

"Do they ever get loose?" I asked casually.

"Rarely" is not the answer I was searching for, but it was already the middle of the night, so I took my chances.

But hands down, I discovered, one of the best places to make camp for the night is a cemetery. Maybe that sounds sacreligious, but consider this: As long as you're not the type of person who gets creeped out easily, it's a quiet, safe night's sleep; a spot where you won't be disturbed by anyone else getting up to use the bathroom.

Once, at daybreak, I crawled out of my tent to help a worker unload and steady a pair of headstones. He said the couple, married nearly sixty years, had died within days of each other. We should all be so lucky. Her stone read, YOURS, and his, FOREVER.

I considered my scant efforts a form of payment for the evening's stay. Often, I lingered in those graveyards wandering the rows, reading headstones and pondering stories like the old couple's, and many others only hinted at through a few words carved in marble.

Rather than causing me to experience melancholia or tumble into feelings of helplessness over the nonnegotiable finality that is death, cemeteries will always represent a gathering of our collective histories, as well as a comfortable spot outside where old friends come together one more time.

And a few hours after sunrise on the outskirts of Beaufort, South Carolina, a small country cemetery became the site of one joyous celebration. I thought I was still dreaming: The voices harmonizing gospel reached my ears like a gentle kiss. When I unzipped my tent, a sea of black faces confronted me. They were clutching garbage bags, rakes, and brooms. The fact that I was camping on their property caused my foggy brain to register fear. I'd overslept, a rare occurrence on the road. An apology for being there began to form on my lips.

"Shoot," one older woman said, barely containing her laughter.

"You're camped right next to my granddaddy, Roger Henry. He liked to sleep late on the Sabbath and skip church as much as possible, so I'd say you're in good company."

The cemetery was part of a larger park and church complex, which members of the congregation cleaned on Sundays before they got down to some serious worshipping around noon. When the final Amen was declared and the last note on a steel lap guitar sounded, they asked me to partake of a spread of food assembled atop picnic tables in the shadow of the afternoon.

Children dashed through the cemetery, playing hide-and-seek among the headstones of their relatives, and I enjoyed some of the best eats, stories, and fellowship on record. I slept indoors that night, my quest for temporary shelter taken care of by none other than the Henry family.

The next morning I would ride off into the wilds of another day, and by nightfall there was no telling where I'd lay my head, but for the moment I was among friends, free to sleep, and, perchance, to dream.

If You Can't Run with the Big Geese, Stay on the Porch

THEY SAY THE THRILL IS IN THE CHASE, AND IT MUST BE TRUE, BECAUSE I've been pursued by all manner of beast and man during my bicycling adventures around the globe, and lived to tell the tales. But there were a few rather close calls.

Every breed of dog has tried to run down both me and my fully loaded touring bicycle. Some of them have made truly valiant attempts.

An especially enthusiastic trio, two Doberman pinschers and a rottweiler, nearly caught me on a remote stretch of highway in Texas. These wild dogs had a serious look of hunger in their eyes, and I was facing a slight incline. It was touch and go until I crested the small hill. Then, just when I thought I could relax, a fourth member of their pack, an angry-looking mutt with dinner on its mind, broke out of the tall grass a few yards from my front wheel, forcing me, nearly exhausted at that point, to pedal for all I was worth.

The Public Broadcast Service aired a program about such hunting methods perfected by wolves in the tundra. I guess dogs in Texas watch more public television than any of us suspected.

But I hold no grudges. It's hardwired directly into a canine's brain to break into a sprint at the slightest hint of a freewheel spinning or a derailluer shifting within its territory.

Of course, people are a different story.

More than a few have targeted me for sport. Though I want to believe most individuals have more sense than their pets, I've been proven wrong on several occasions.

There were those rednecks gunning a pickup truck at me in Georgia, and a few good-old-boys in a king cab near the Utah state line who thought I'd make decent roadkill, and I can't forget the carload of laughing teenagers in Pensacola who chased my bicycle through three red lights so they could pelt me with a bag of half-melted M&Ms. Just another summer afternoon in Florida, I suppose. I blamed the incident on the heat, but recall that my donations to Amnesty International began around that time.

Atop my bike, I've been chased by buffalo in Montana with only a few scraps of barbed wire separating me from certain death, and I've been knocked off the hardtop by several reckless logging trucks along the Oregon coast. Fortunately, pine needles and moss along the Pacific Northwest roadside make for a fairly soft cushion.

Pursuit is not limited by national borders. Old bus drivers in Latin America have no respect for human life; the wind in Aruba actually knocked me to the ground; and I swear that more than a few kangaroos shot me menacing stares during my odyssey through the Australian outback, but thankfully, they never gave chase. An adult kangaroo is a fierce-looking creature—sharp claws, bared teeth, and an average hopping speed that would put Deion Sanders to shame.

The most unusual chase, though, involved a gaggle of guard geese in rural New Hampshire. Where a garden-variety pack of dogs will usually give up the race in a couple of minutes, tops, I'm here to testify that geese know something about commitment.

It was an easy mistake to make, but a regrettable one. I had hastily taken down the address of a friend's cabin while crammed against the wall of a phone booth in a loud bar. A napkin probably wasn't the best surface to write the address on, but my choices were limited at the time. It was a long-distance call and I already felt bad about reversing the charges, so I didn't ask him to repeat it.

That is how I found myself a quarter of a mile down a private road on a chilly New England afternoon, searching for a quaint log cabin I'd been told overlooked a placid lake. What I found was a double-wide trailer, at the bottom of a muddy hill. Truck parts littered the yard.

The first goose waddled around from the backside of the double-wide and began squawking at a remarkable decibel level. It reminded me of the petting zoo from my childhood. I began to laugh.

Apparently, geese don't like to be taken lightly. Several more of the flock appeared from behind a rusted-out Jeep, hissing and bobbing their heads like out-of-control windup toys. My laughter faltered. In all, six geese materialized before I had my bike pointed toward the exit.

I never made it.

In a scene that would have warmed Hitchcock's heart, the birds reached me before I even had my feet in the toe clips. My bike abandoned, I fled for the nearest tree, thick orange beaks pecking me as I went. I remained in the high branches for the next hour, treed by geese in New Hampshire.

If you've ever witnessed the damage geese can do when they work themselves into a lather, you understand why I felt no shame clinging to my treetop refuge. Okay, I've never actually seen the aftermath of a goose's fury, but I heard somewhere that a goose once knocked a man from a horse, killing the poor fellow in the process. And they did peck me pretty damn hard.

My web-footed captors kept watch at the base of the tree until their owner arrived home from work and called them off, whistling at them like family pets.

Cold, humble, and still watchful for quick flashes of feathers and beaks, I apologized for trespassing, and planned to move on in rapid fashion. But Becker, the geese's owner, would hear nothing of it. He knew my friend well, and with a phone call the three of us were eating a tasty dinner on the back porch of his trailer, feeding the leftovers to the now rather docile geese.

That's how so many of my days on a bicycle went. One minute I could be treed by ferocious geese, and in the next I might be sitting pretty—fat and happy in the company of friends. My travels taught me the art of rolling with the punches, a skill that has served me well.

For better or worse, life often boils down to this: If you can't run with the big geese, stay on the porch.

It's a Good Day to Ride!

SOME MORNINGS THE BICYCLE JUST HAS YOUR NAME WRITTEN ALL OVER it. You can't wait to pull up those tent stakes, stuff the last bit of gear into your panniers, grab the handlebars, and take off down the road from a running start.

This was not one of those mornings.

At dawn near the Colorado border in late September ice forms a protective layer over the ground. I stuck my hand against the side of the tent and a slab of it broke off. Earlier that week the guys in the guns-and-ammo section of Acker's Sports in southern Idaho told me to watch for snow when I got closer to the high country. They also commented that cycling over the Rocky Mountains at this time of year was a novel idea. *Loco* was the word their upbringing wouldn't let them utter, but I caught their drift in the tone of their voices. One of them, who said he volunteered for Search and Rescue, tossed me a sun-faded but functional fleece pullover. "No charge," he said when I began to put it back.

Not a morning person by nature, I've used lesser excuses than chunks of frozen water on a rain flap to keep me anchored inside a sleeping bag. There's no better feeling than avoiding the elements through inertia, and few things more easily accomplished. But I felt certain it wasn't the coldest morning I was going to face. If I didn't take advantage of the relatively good weather now, I might find myself cycling through snowbanks. I might anyway, but it was an argument that dragged me out of the tent.

A voice in the back of my head kept grousing about the stupidity of taking on the Rockies so late in the season. "Heard of the Donner Party?" it whined. "That was the High Sierras, an entirely different mountain chain!" I volleyed back, then packed up my gear and hit the road before more doubts could find the speaker's podium. Completing four solo long-distance bicycle adventures is a double edged sword. The upside is you feel like you can do anything. That's also the downside.

By noon my joints were still tight; long gone was the spike of energy a breakfast bar provided. A light, sleety rain had begun slicing almost horizontally across the road. I dug in and reminded myself that the worst day of cycling is always better than punching a clock somewhere. That's when Gordy blew by me. From the quick glance I got, Gordy had to have been cashing social security checks for years already, but then the elements can weather a man like a piece of barn wood. Maybe he wasn't that old. His spindly legs sure were moving him along at a nice clip.

My competitive juices started to flow. It's a sad day when a man in his twenties sets his sights on the rear wheel of a senior citizen. I searched around for another Power Bar, gave up and pedaled with a vengeance.

It took a good-size hill to slow Gordy down, and that's when I made my move. I pulled alongside him and tried to keep my breathing steady. My plan was to appear relaxed, smile, maybe offer a few words of encouragement before taking the summit first. Pathetic.

Only Gordy wouldn't behave. He matched my cadence over the next quarter mile. The sound of my labored breathing was broken by the piddling taps of rain on my windbreaker. To the right, Gordy was as silent as a monk.

At least he had the civility not to pass me as we crested the hill. Somehow we knew it was time to stop and make introductions.

"The knees gave out on me back in the 1970s," Gordy said in a matter-of-fact tone. "I work the flats as hard as I can 'cause I know the climbs are going to slow me down."

Gordy offered me a Lifesaver.

"If you want to call that pace slow I suppose you can, but it felt pretty solid to me."

Small miracles: I found that Power Bar. The Lifesavers seemed to be all Gordy was carrying in the way of food. I offered him half of the bar but he waved it away like I was trying to pawn an old shoe on him.

"No," Gordy replied. "I just crawl over the hills now. Back in the 1950s I owned these climbs." He nodded, drifting proudly inside himself for a minute to peek at the glory days. "In my prime . . . I was a bear."

I'm not sure what that made me, but he was still something to behold. Even older in the face than I'd first surmised, Gordy's body resembled a tough piece of jerky. He sported a short, gray crew cut and a hint of stubble a shade darker on his cheeks. Wrapped in a military parka, loose shorts with dark thermals under that, Gordy was a cross between a deranged Eskimo and a fashion trendsetter for the Seattle grunge movement. The bike he was riding, a no-name rig with a few upgraded components, was devoid of panniers, a front bag, anything really, except for a tarp and a small satchel bungeed to a narrow rack. One water bottle and a minute pump decorated the frame. He saw me surveying his setup.

"After the knees went, I had to make a choice. Give up touring or cut back on the amount of weight I would carry." Again his face filled with pride.

I was looking at the equivalent of prison camp conditions to a touring cyclist, and the old man was beaming about it. No tent, sleeping bag, maps, camera, spare clothes, or space to carry anything. Nonplussed in the same way people are when suddenly confronting the aftermath of a car accident, or some freakish anomaly in nature, I began to wonder just what he did have aboard. For a moment I thought he could be one of those Howard Hughes types, carrying a credit card with a zillion-dollar limit, or being trailed at a safe distance by a caravan of men in dark suits and a forty-foot RV.

Gordy popped another Lifesaver into his mouth and pulled at the back end of his thermals.

If he was a wealthy tycoon, Gordy had his cover firmly in place.

"I've got a tool bag under the tarp, a compact rod and reel, and a little pan for cooking those fish, or maybe flapjacks. When I sleep outside I roll myself into the tarp and drop right off like a baby. There's a hat and gloves in the bag but it's not cold enough for them yet." He looked around like he'd forgotten something. "And my toothbrush. At seventy-eight years old most of these are still factory issued."

He did have a nice set of chops.

I gave Gordy the *Reader's Digest* version of my life while he rubbed his knees.

"Hell son, with that much mileage racked up, you might catch me in, say, three decades or so. I've tapered off to a couple rides a year now. The people at work are rather understanding."

Work?

"I'm a short-order cook at a truck stop. It's one of two things; either good help is just really hard to find, or I still whip up a decent breakfast special. Either way, they let me ride off for a couple weeks at a time, sometimes a month. Knees won't let me go much longer than that, anyway."

In the course of five minutes, Gordy, a rarefied creature among the touring cyclists' tribe, had humbled me. If even half his story was true, he'd cycled the distance of the globe a dozen times. The man had witnessed the building of an industrial nation. Most of North America's highways and dams didn't exist when Gordy first took to the road.

"Don't like to leave the western half of the country anymore," he added. "Too much traffic on the other side of the Mississippi. But I biked to New Orleans a few years ago. Did the whole Fat Tuesday party down there. Quite a hootenanny."

He got back on his bike.

"They make a mean breakfast in the French Quarter, 'cept it's more like a snack before bed for most of them." Gordy pocketed the rest of his Lifesaver roll. I hadn't seen him drink any water yet.

"Shall we ride?" he said with a grin.

"I'll try to keep up with you."

Gordy got a kick out of that.

It was about 4 P.M. We'd been talking and drafting each other all afternoon.

"You want to camp indoors tonight?" Gordy asked.

On the surface, the logical answer to that question should always be yes. But I've learned the hard way that all indoors are not created equal. The big outside is often preferable.

"What did you have in mind?"

"I've got friends all over," Gordy said.

Not surprising, I thought.

"There's a one-room schoolhouse a few miles from here. I have a standing invitation to bunk there as long as I'm gone before classes start in the morning. The key's hidden inside the bell."

By dinnertime the rain had stopped. I spread out the contents of my food pannier, standard cycling chow: a few odds and ends taken from condiment racks at fast-food restaurants, as well as rice, pastas, some canned meat, and a couple of vegetables I'd picked up at a roadside stand the day before. Gordy looked giddy. "I can work with this," he kept whispering.

I went down by the creek to relax and wash up for what I thought would be a plain but filling meal. The schoolhouse had a chapel feel to it; old wood, and windowpanes that had been in place so long they'd begun to run. A nun once told me that was God crying. In the fading light it looked beautiful.

Maybe it was the residue of foods built up over the years on Gordy's skillet, but my supplies never tasted so good. During my travels I readily shared my food with riding companions regardless of what they were able to contribute. In Gordy's case, his culinary skills were worth far more than my scraps of rice, onions, and canned ham. If we'd been in a diner I'd have left a healthy tip.

"Whenever I break bread with a new rider it's custom to share a true story of some importance to me, and vice versa. Are you game?" Gordy asked.

"Sure."

"There's a catch. We pick each other's topics," he added.

Leaning over the campfire, Gordy took on the appearance of an old sage around the council circle.

"You want me to go first?" I asked, cocky. I was never at a loss for words.

Gordy smiled. "Tell me a story about . . . old people. I like to keep tabs on my peers."

That knocked me back. The only old people I knew were my grandparents, whom I saw every couple of years if all the stars were aligned properly. There was that bent-over man who lived in the apartment across the courtyard during college. Except for the trash outside his door each week and the sound of his television at all hours of the night, I wouldn't have known he was alive.

Gordy hadn't given me much to work with.

Wait. I remembered something. The two months I spent lifeguarding last winter at a "planned retirement community" in Florida. A glorified nursing home, the place needed a lifeguard like Italian drivers need rearview mirrors. My job consisted of sleeping by the pool each morning until the occasional resident wandered into the water around noon. There were a couple of regulars right after lunch. I guess they figured they'd lived this long; why should they have to wait a half hour after eating before going in the water? No one used the deep end anyway. And there were clusters of women who came out to play bridge and canasta under the umbrella tables.

My campfire pal offered a pained nod. "Don't worry, Gordy. You're never going to have to see the inside of one of those places."

"You don't know, first it's the knees, then. . . . But I'm not going without a fight."

Well, the fight seemed to be out of everyone in this place. Or that's what it felt like at first. Then Lou, a retired policeman from Boston in his mideighties showed up and turned the pool area on its head. A rowdy Irishman, he was using his sister's apartment for the winter. Lou forced me to take a closer look at the clientele. Cannonballs, liquor in the pool area, harmless chatting up of the canasta girls.

One of the residents told me Lou's children passed him back and forth every couple of months; then, when they were at the end of their collective ropes, shipped him south for the winter. That sort of nomadic life had to eat a guy up inside.

Management informed me his name was popping up too often in the complaints box. I asked Lou to hide his liquor in soda cans and cut the gals at the umbrellas some slack. We began laughing halfway through my little reprimand speech. Long as the guy didn't drown anyone, what did I care? These people had been adults for a quite some time.

His answer was to bring a boom box down to the pool, put on a bow tie that didn't remotely match his swim trunks, and tell each woman in the area that there was one more slot left on his dance card. Exasperated, Lou dropped the piece of paper into the pool and lay across the diving board.

"If you hadn't noticed, we're not dead yet," he hollered to everyone in particular.

Rose, a lump of sadness who sat zombielike each day in a corner lounge chair, began to cry. "It won't be long," she sniffled.

"Christ!" Lou said, fed up.

"I'll dance," a voice called from behind me.

I turned to discover an elegantly dressed elderly woman standing by a car near the gate.

"Not here, or now, but if you take off that foolish tie and show up sober at the social tomorrow night, you might get a dance." The mystery woman then said something to one of the canasta girls before turning on her heels and driving out of the retirement community gate. Lou did a cannonball, surfaced, and toweled off.

"Someone want to tell me who that was?" he asked. "She owns a car, which makes her prime real estate."

I don't know if Lou ever got his dance, but I did learn who the mystery woman was. Beatrice Alco was a piano teacher all of her life. She hated canasta but started coming out to the pool to sip Frescas.

She launched into an animated discussion about music theory one afternoon. When she asked if I'd come back to her apartment so she could play me what she was talking about, I didn't have the heart to refuse. Her place was stuffy, with loud-colored shag carpeting and framed photographs and portraits everywhere. Along the piano were a few snapshots of famous-looking musicians standing next to a much younger Beatrice. I reasoned the guys were famous because the snapshots were posed outside of places like Carnegie Hall and the National Cathedral.

"Did you ever play the big halls?" I asked.

"Never. But I taught some of the best who did."

Her playing was beautiful. Sitting there, I had a revelation. Some of us, myself included, need an audience to bring out the richest stuff that's inside, and others would reach their potential even if they lived on the dark side of the moon. The ones who don't need the spotlight often have the most to teach.

"You've got better things to do than hear an old woman play badly," she said, but we both knew her music was still powerful.

When I said goodbye to Beatrice, I could hear her piano kick into action almost immediately after the door closed.

Management asked me if I'd be Santa at the Christmas party. It was a sweltering experience inside a wool suit, and passing out gifts in the constant-care wing disturbed me more than it should have, but when I came to some of my regulars from the pool, I was glad I did it.

At the end of the day, Lou sat heavily on my lap, the bastard, and told me he was heading north for the rest of the holidays. He looked pleased as he handed me a bottle of whiskey.

"People are always leaving you cookies and milk. You're a grown man, for Godsakes, enjoy!"

"Gordy, I don't know if being around those people made the thought of getting on in years any easier, but it taught me there are a lot of different types of old. I'm shooting for old like Beatrice, with a pinch of Lou on the side. Definitely your kind of old."

"But with better knees, son," Gordy piped in.

We watched the fire.

"I . . . I just want a few more rides before I let go," he said softly.

"Tell me why you started touring the country on a bike," I said.

He came back from his thoughts.

"There's no drama in that one. Wasn't running to or from any-thing. Not off on any great quests or wrestling demons. Truth is I saw the bike and got on."

Gordy shrugged.

I couldn't contain my laughter. Sometimes it's that simple.

"Why don't I tell you about the Navajo cyclist I toured with once? Now that one's got some spice."

Hey, at seventy-eight years old, if Gordy wanted to change the rules of his game, I wasn't going to stop him.

"You don't see a lot of Indians touring around on bicycles, do you?"

He had me there.

"Well, twenty years ago there were even less. Jonathan Blackhorse was the only one I've ever met. He pedaled up to the truck stop with so much desire that I decided to accompany him for a few miles. Now this was a man on a vision quest. Growing up all he'd heard about was how the white man had ruined everything and the elders warned that the destruction wasn't over.

"Jonathan decided it was time to leave the reservation. It felt better than waiting around for things to get worse. He'd never learned to drive a car so he got a bicycle, taught himself to ride, and struck out for the territories.

"It was the 1960s. We hooked up with some rainbow gatherings, attended antiwar rallies, and even heard Hoffman speak on the campus, I think in Missoula. I stayed away from my job for months that time."

Gordy regaled me with some of the adventures they'd had. I was amazed not only by these tales, but because Gordy was middle-aged when they took place.

"By the time we said goodbye, Jonathan was genuinely excited about the future. He was so sure from what he'd experienced that the younger generation was getting it.

"'It's a good day to die!' I said at a fork in the road where we were going to part company. 'Isn't that one of the ways you folks say farewell?'

"Jonathan smiled. Straddling that bicycle was a man who'd become addicted to the pedal stroke and the feeling of two wheels rolling under him. He was hooked.

" 'I think I have a better one for this occasion, Gordy. How about: "It's a good day to ride!"'

"Don't exactly know what became of him, but I hope he managed to help his people in some way. And I do hope Jonathan kept riding."

Gordy stayed up with the fire after we said good night.

The sun shining in through the runny windowpanes woke me. For a few moments I couldn't remember where I was. Gordy wasn't inside the schoolhouse and I foolishly worried for an instant that maybe he'd stolen into the darkness with my bicycle and gear. God knew he could use it.

I found him wrapped in his tarp beside the smoldering ashes, a bit of frost clinging to his stubble.

"Got so comfortable I just fell asleep out here," Gordy said, rubbing his eyes. "I'm gonna loop north through Jackson Hole and be tucked inside the truck stop before winter settles on us."

I nodded.

"My plan is to outrun winter over the mountains and coast into the deserts of New Mexico. Your fortitude has inspired me."

Gordy shook his head. "Bad plan, son. Sometimes winter shows up in July over those peaks. Go by way of Utah. You'll stay warm and see some sights God saved just for that spot on the map."

Considering I met my future wife by taking Gordy's advice, this was one time I'm glad I listened to my elders.

It took Gordy all of thirty seconds to break camp. My gear was still spread everywhere.

"Drop by the truck stop. I fix a nice plate of flapjacks."

At the top of the path he paused to rub his knees. I knew exactly what Gordy was hollering before he disappeared over the hill. If I learned nothing else from that old cyclist, I learned this: "It's always a good day to ride!"

Heartbreak Hotel:
The Day Elvis Took My Bike
for A Spin

EARLY ONE FRIDAY IN ST. GEORGE, UTAH, BACK IN THE FALL OF 1990, Elvis Presley took my touring bicycle for a test drive around the parking lot of a second-rate motel. It was a glorious morning, and as it turns out, The King's not a bad cyclist for a dead man.

Now, before you begin speculating about whether, in the not-so-distant past, I went over to the dark side and did a stint of writing for the *National Enquirer,* allow me to explain the circumstances surrounding my bona fide Elvis encounter.

I was almost through the state of Utah, and it had been quite the wild ride. The red rock canyons, otherworldly geological formations, harsh, windswept mesa tops, snowcapped mountains, and desert basins of the region had been as exhausting to pedal through as they had been awesome and inspiring.

Nature, on that scale, takes no prisoners and humbles all completely. And though I was more than a month into that particular cycling adventure, finding myself in increasingly better shape, not to mention on an adrenaline high from my encounters, Utah had temporarily sapped my physical strength.

A brief respite from the road was all I really needed: a bed and some serious air-conditioning, and maybe a pool or, ah yes, a hot tub to soak my tired bones.

But when a young long-distance cyclist decides to spend precious resources on a hotel room, he must be quite selective about the accommodations. A treat of such magnitude should not be squandered on the first VACANCY sign that comes along.

That's why, with momentum built up from the downhill run out of Zion National Park, I decided to coast through the length of town, bird-dogging the hotels and motels along the city's main strip.

Though nothing I could afford looked like the Taj Mahal, there were a few strong possibilities in my price range: a relatively new Best Western and a Motel 6 that appeared to be far enough off the highway for some peace and quiet. Both had pools with relatively algae-free water in them.

Coming to the outskirts of town, I made a U-turn in the parking lot of a no-name, mom-and-pop motel that looked like it hadn't seen many capital improvements since the 1970s. After passing the office, I came abruptly to a halt. I fully intended to pedal back to the Best Western, but what I was witnessing deserved a few moments of contemplation. Elvis was everywhere.

By the pool—which was filled with water a touch on the cloudy side—was The King in every shape, size, age, and gender; sunbathing, smoking a cigar in a decrepit lounge chair, and doing cannonballs in the deep end.

Elvis was also standing patiently by the ice machine, and there he was again in a karate outfit performing a few moves outside of a no-smoking room. He nodded at me from the balcony and gave me that famous fingers-first wave as he unloaded luggage from the back of a pink, mint-condition 1957 Cadillac.

I took a long drink from my water bottle and splashed some on my face for good measure as I considered the possibility that I was suffering from sunstroke. Then my eyes caught sight of the lettering just above the VACANCY sign. Faded, weather-worn words—WELCOME, ELVIS IMPERSONATORS, NEXT STOP VEGAS!

As a budding journalist, my fate was sealed. Comfort would just have to wait. I turned my rig around and headed for the office, praying the dump still had a room for rent.

"Let me introduce you around," a middle-aged Elvis with a fatherly smile said. I was in a coffee shop across the street from the hotel with no fewer than two dozen Elvis impersonators, many of whom were partaking of the daily special, chicken-fried steak with a mountain of mashed potatoes on the side. The King would have been proud.

Everyone in this formidable tribute caravan had left his or her civilian name behind for the duration of the tour. They referred to one another by the type of Elvis they had chosen to emulate.

For instance, the fatherly Elvis who was making the introductions called himself Comeback Elvis, in memory of The King's Hawaiian comeback concert of 1973. There was Little Elvis, a dwarf with a nice head of King-like hair; and Oldest Elvis, who, at eighty-four, was still dying his locks jet black and sporting an oversize pair of shaded prescription sunglasses with Coke-bottle-thick lenses. Biggest Elvis, who looked to be about 350 pounds, was sitting next to Magician Elvis, who was talking to Animal Elvis.

Every era of The King's career was represented, as well, from the spry Elvis-the-Pelvis days to the "Elvis in the Army" period to his final years. In all, almost three dozen devotees crowded the restaurant.

You could tell that the spouses of some of the Elvis impersonators had gotten into the spirit of the thing. A number of Ann-Margrets and Priscilla Presleys were in attendance. And off in a corner booth, keeping a watchful eye on the proceedings, was a gentleman bearing a striking resemblance to the Colonel, Elvis's manager.

Something told me this wasn't the A-list of Elvis impersonator tours, but no one in the group seemed to care. They were having a good time and there was a real family vibe in the air.

"Some of us make a living at this—Magician Elvis, a few of the younger Elvises with decent singing voices and stage presence—but most of the caravan gets together a couple times a year for these conventions out of love for the greatest man to ever walk out of the woods of Mississippi," Comeback Elvis explained.

"But why are you guys staying at that no-name motel?" I asked. "Why not just go straight to Vegas?"

Comeback Elvis informed me that the convention didn't begin until the weekend. Impersonators from around the country liked to make big entrances on Friday afternoon.

"As for why we stay across the street every year," Comeback Elvis paused, and lowered his voice to a whisper, "because it was one of His favorite hideaway stops."

Of course.

That night, and over the course of the next day, I spent quality time with a handful of Elvises.

One of the standouts of the group was Animal Elvis. If you set aside the fact that she was, well, a woman, Animal Elvis looked more like The King than almost anyone in the group. What took Animal Elvis to the next level, a state of absurd grace, was her menagerie of pets. She had a standard poodle named Hound Dog, with fur that had been styled to resemble the Elvis look. The poor dog wore sequined clothing and could bark out what Animal Elvis swore was "Love Me Tender." There was an Elvis ferret running around the room somewhere, and a cat that wanted nothing to do with Elvis Presley.

Animal Elvis said something about cats being independent like that and moved on to her greatest Elvis creation, a large African gray parrot confined to a cage filled with bird droppings, ornate little furniture, and mirrors everywhere.

"It's a miniature version of the Jungle Room at Graceland," she proudly announced.

At that moment, I realized the true meaning of the word *obsession*. The parrot's name was Memphis, and, when Animal Elvis clipped a velvet cape onto its back, the bird started mimicking a bunch of Elvis catchphrases: "Lord have mercy," "Are you lonesome tonight?," "Thank you very much," stuff like that.

The parrot got off track a couple of times, mimicking lines from shows like *Kojak, Fantasy Island,* and *Hawaii Five-O.* Animal Elvis shrugged her shoulders, saying the bird had been exposed to a lot of network television in the 1970s.

Late into the second afternoon, sitting by the pool with an eclectic collection of Elvises, I asked a Barbara Walters–type question.

"In one sentence, sum up what Elvis Presley added to the world."

Most of them, overwhelmed by their feelings for The King, couldn't distill it into an encyclopedia, let alone one sentence. It was Oldest Elvis, on his way to bed at five in the afternoon, who rose to the occasion.

"Elvis was a hellcat of a man-child with a voice handed down from heaven, and when he opened his mouth, the world made sense for a few moments."

As the sun sank below the desert floor, the caravan sat around listening to songs by you know who and catching up with one another's lives. What these people had managed to form was something of an extended family and it touched me to have gotten a chance to slip into their world for a while.

When "Fools Rush In" began to play, the courtyard seemed to swell with voices. It was a full-fledged Elvis campfire circle. Somehow everyone knew to stop singing and let The King solo the last verse, but then, I guess families know those sorts of things.

The next morning, before the caravan pulled out for Vegas, Karate Elvis, a Hispanic man who looked more like Tony Orlando on steroids, asked if he could take a little spin on my bicycle. How could I refuse the greatest showman who ever lived?

Packing the last of my gear into my panniers, I watched the caravan drive out of sight and couldn't help yelling after them, "Elvis has left the state of Utah."

I rode my bike toward Arizona with plans to climb down one of the largest canyons on Earth until I was miles from any other human being. I guess we all have our obsessions.

Long live The King, and those who love him.

Making Music with the Button Boy of the Delaware Water Gap

A LONG TOLL BRIDGE NEAR THE DELAWARE WATER GAP HAD BEEN raised to let several sizable sailing vessels navigate under it. This event forced me to bring to a stop the fully loaded touring bicycle I was attempting to ride from Maine to Florida. Now I would have to try to enjoy the sights and sounds of a brisk morning along the eastern seaboard. I should have seized the moment as a chance to stop and smell the roses or, in this case, the cherry blossoms along the river.

The problem was, I had just managed to coax my sore legs into a steady cadence for the first time that day and wasn't exactly thrilled about the holdup. It's hard to get away from routines and schedules, even on an adventure. But one cursory glance at my surroundings revealed that I would most certainly have stopped dead in my tracks, no matter what condition the bridge had been in that morning.

Sitting atop a three-wheeled contraption—which had once been an oversize tricycle of the sort many retirees along Florida's Gold Coast gingerly pedal to and from the store in the afternoon heat— was a shocking aberration of a man.

From his scalp, a stalk of red hair grew wild in every direction, like an abandoned rose garden sprawling over an old mansion. His face, starting to wrinkle in places, was that of a boy. A broad set of shoulders supported a ragged blue pea coat, the type worn in the navy, but this one was far from standard issue: Pinned to every inch of the garment were buttons—hundreds upon hundreds of buttons.

Buttons advertised everything from Bazooka Joe bubble gum to Marlboro cigarettes, Delta Air Lines to Dunkin' Donuts. Some buttons had cute slogans and pop-culture sayings like MAKE MY DAY, ONLY THE SHADOW KNOWS and WHY BE NORMAL? Others depicted cartoon characters, movie stars, and political figures. Gumby was smiling next to Marilyn Monroe on one sleeve while Malcolm X was pinned beside a Mouseketeer on the jacket's lapel.

One thing was certain: The full spectrum of political and social beliefs was represented. I tried to figure out if there was any sort of pattern to the assortment of buttons—a method to this burly man's madness. Was the smiley face exhorting people to HAVE A NICE DAY placed next to the National Rifle Association membership pin for a reason? And what did a picture of Gandhi have to do with a cartoon bubble button above him, saying, DON'T WORRY, BE HAPPY"?

Studying the man's attire was similar to pondering a stunning piece of modern art, while its creator still inhabited his work—like a mollusk within its shell. Button Boy's rig was no less amazing. It resembled some sort of Frankenstein marriage of a shopping cart, a tricycle, and a chopper. Modifications to the tricycle's frame included replacing the original saddle with a bucket seat from a 1965 Mustang fastback. The red vinyl chair even reclined, which was the position Button Boy had it in when I pulled up. He might have been sleeping for all the response he gave to my arrival. Metal baskets had been welded or otherwise connected to the trike and were filled with every imaginable item, from musical instruments to board games. A wooden platform had been assembled across the back of the vehicle to accommodate even more gear. It looked like someone had emptied his closets of random possessions just before the house burned down.

Button Boy had to be lugging a couple of hundred pounds of extra weight. As I grinned at my good fortune to be carrying less than a tenth of that on my own rig, the button-covered coat spoke.

"Are you enjoying your ride?" he asked through a thick Irish brogue.

This was an interesting choice of questions. Why not ask me where I was coming from, how many miles a day I averaged, if I got lonely on the road, or what my final destination would be? These were all standard queries I had grown accustomed to from curious well-wishers.

The question caught me off guard, and while I gave it some thought, two fresh-faced Mormon cyclists arrived on their matching bikes to wait for the bridge to go down. I shared small talk with the two guys, suggesting to them that they think about wearing helmets, then listened quietly to their message about the Mormon religion.

"I believe in God!" Button Boy bellowed, bringing his bucket seat to a full, upright, and locked position. His presence came as a shock to the Mormon gentlemen, who up to that point must have thought the tricycle was abandoned. They flinched as the hulking mass of red hair and buttons continued: "Sure do. Most days I know he's around 'cause I can hear him having one big laugh at the rest of us!"

Button Boy looked like he was going to jingle harmlessly back down in his seat, but then the guy nearly lunged from his trike in an effort to finish his thought.

"But I got the big man's number, 'cause some days . . . I laugh back!" And, of course, he began hooting and cackling to the heavens.

The Mormons went quite pale and I must admit to a bit of an adrenaline rush when I realized I was within striking distance of the burly man. But the mood quickly changed when this fiery guy announced, in a most endearing Irish accent, that we should try to make some music to show God what a glorious morning we thought it was. No one said a word.

But Button Boy's eyes glistened with such sincerity that resistance was futile. He mumbled softly as he searched the trike's compartments and lower holds, then pulled out enough instruments to outfit a full orchestra. When the band was assembled, Button Boy was gripping the neck of a fiddle, one of the Mormons was in possession of a worn but nicely tuned guitar, while the other missionary and I formed the percussion section.

Button Boy led the group, fielding requests, but honoring none of them. He would count to four then launch into a lively jig or a soulful ballad, and we'd try our best to keep up. He was rather patient for a madman, and the Mormons found his style and tempo a few bars into each song. I did what I could, but was under no misconceptions that I was born with rhythm.

As we sat together on a low wall overlooking the river, our music connected us to the moment and one another as few things can. What none of us was prepared for was the voice that came from a place buried but unguarded inside Button Boy when he broke into a rendition of the gospel "Deeper River."

Think of Celtic spirits embracing a powerful baritone who has been quietly biding his time in the back row of a gospel choir. For a few minutes, the Button Boy of the Delaware Water Gap let his Technicolor coat fall to the ground while he found the strength to laugh with his Creator through the notes of a song. The experience left a hole in my heart that fills in only temporarily when the right combination of voice and music meets.

I hung around for a while after the bridge was lowered. A few tattered photos of family portraits taped to the trike's handlebars hinted at a life interrupted. Button Boy said he was thinking of heading out west, maybe finding a little more space. That was over a decade ago, but I still keep one eye out for the big man, if only to give him an answer to his question. Yes, I am enjoying the ride.

The Touring Cyclist's Diet: Anything That's Not Nailed Down

I like mine with lettuce and tomato, Heinz 57 and french fried potato,
big kosher pickle and a cold draft beer . . . Good God almighty
which way do I steer . . . Cheeseburger and Paradise!
—Jimmy Buffet

FOR ALL THE CRUEL AND UNIQUE WAYS A LONG-DISTANCE BICYCLE TRIP can punish a person's muscles and bones and, yes, shake his emotional core, there is one miraculous benefit the cyclist can always count on, one delicious upside to pedaling over the sides of mountains and through stretches of desert, and battling the forces of nature along windswept coasts.

It's the complete and unfettered disregard one is allowed when it comes to food intake. A few days into a bike adventure traditional rules involving calories no longer apply. Trust me when I say, "You can eat everything!" Actually, three or four of everything and anything—and still be shedding pounds at each turn in the road.

It's astounding and a little unnerving at first, but once you realize it to be a truth along the lines of gravity or the Earth revolving around the sun, then the fun begins.

Invite a long-distance cyclist into your home sometime for dinner (if for no other reason than to feed the traveler, which is, in many cultures, an act of spiritual renewal) and you'll discover what it must have been like sharing a table with Conan the Barbarian.

Even the most petite women turn into ravenous eating machines after pedaling a loaded bicycle all day long. Picture the training table of a professional sports team in the midst of trying to bulk up.

Once, in North Carolina, I was graciously welcomed for dinner into a bicycle repairman's humble home. Three children and his wife greeted me with smiling faces as we took our places at the table. After a quick grace, I was, as the guest in a southern setting, given first crack at a pot filled with some beef-and-macaroni concoction. In the real world, macaroni is no delicacy, but to a hungry cyclist—manna from heaven, sports fans. Maybe it's the body craving carbohydrates, but mac and cheese is to die for at the end of a long day of riding.

I confess to getting a little carried away with the serving spoon that evening. It would not be exaggerating to say that my eyes bonded with the noodles, cheese, and beef, causing a trancelike state wherein my hand couldn't stop shoveling the food onto the plate.

It wasn't pretty. I can't actually remember the moments of contact between pot, spoon, and plate. When the sauce finally settled, shame washed over me. I set down my spoon and looked up into the faces of five, count them, five other people at the sparse table. It appeared they were trying to maintain their smiles in light of a nearly empty pot.

These were not the Kennedys I was dining with. No armada of courses was going to be wheeled in on silver carts from the kitchen to amaze and astound our taste buds. A painful silence descended. It was a moment in which I searched for guidance out of this awkward situation, and I suspect they prayed that the spandex-clad stranger at their table would just give them back their dinner and pedal quietly away.

"Would you look at that," I said in a surprised tone, as if the exorbitant mound of food on my plate was some wild animal that had leapt from behind the couch and into my meal when I wasn't looking. "That's way too much food for me" (an outright lie).

I extended my hand to the closest child, calling for his plate in an Oliver Twist–type scene. I imagined the child whispering, "More porridge, I mean Hamburger Helper, please."

While dishing equal portions to the group, I felt like I'd recovered nicely, that is until I inhaled what was left on my plate in less than a minute, leaving the rest of the meal to savor my Kool-Aid and ponder the concept of seconds. I found myself watching everyone's plates and daydreaming about food even while we discussed my adventures.

Buffets and smorgasbords in small towns never knew what hit them as I'd pedal out of the parking lots. Milk shakes were a standard at any meal, and I once nearly finished off a five-pound bag of potatoes waiting out a storm while in my tent along the Olympic Peninsula. There were more chicken wings consumed, dark beer drunk and games of pool lost along the road than I can fathom, and still the scale never inched up.

Carrying enough food in my panniers to keep me satisfied was one of the biggest logistical challenges of my trips. Somewhere in the swamps of Georgia, far from any store, I realized I was carrying only a can of Dinty Moore stew and a handful of sugar substitute packets. Hunger enveloped me to the point that I squatted caveman-style and ate the stew cold as soon as I had enough of the can pried open to scoop it out. And the sugarlike substance made a fine dessert.

I'm not exactly proud of these memories, but they help me understand how the survivors of shipwrecks and plane crashes overcome certain culinary taboos. Hunger is a powerful thing.

But the fellowship that accompanied many of the meals over the course of my travels was often stronger. Eating some tasty but better-left-unidentified meat with a group of Aboriginals in the outback was the start of an incredibly moving evening.

That night I learned that certain people on this planet believe with all their heart that the universe was sung into existence; that only music could have gotten the cosmic ball rolling. You just can't beat the beauty of that concept.

Then, as if to prove—no, celebrate—this truth, they sang some of their stories. The stars crowded the heavens, the desert stood still, and, as the fire burned, I really heard the world for the first time.

Back in this hemisphere, I remember savoring Hershey bars and glasses of wine drunk from camp cups at a picnic table in Yosemite.

The couple told me they were on the final leg of an around-the-world adventure. The journey had taken them twenty years to save for and less than three to complete.

"We'll be broke when we get back to Wales," the man said with a wink. "But we'd have been broken for the rest of our days if we hadn't done this."

I drank to that.

There's one particular meal that sticks with me like an anthem, though I can't even remember what it was we ate that evening.

I'd reached a point on one of my rides where boredom, fatigue, or just plain lack of character threatened to capsize the adventure. It happens on every tour. You start asking yourself what you are hoping to accomplish. What in the name of all that is comfortable and easy are you doing pedaling the back roads of the planet?

When this sort of mood blanketed me, I usually lashed out at things beyond my control: global warming, man's inhumanity to man, voodoo economics.

That's when Norton Bloom pulled alongside. His panniers were full and his smile was wide. We rode together most of the day. He let me rant about the injustices of the world while I enjoyed the free-doms of being a healthy, young, white man on a bicycle in the richest country on Earth, during the most prosperous time in history. The irony of the situation escaped me while I raged loudly against the machine.

A little café boasting an all-you-can-eat special caught our atten-tion. When Norton got off his bicycle, his legs seemed a tad stiff. I mentioned this, but he said it was nothing he could feel. We laughed at what I thought was an understanding between touring cyclists regarding the price of the ride.

As we stared down at plates heaped with food, Norton said a quiet grace. I didn't think the creative powers of the universe wanted a piece of my mind at that moment, so I skipped right to the eating portion of the program. Out of the corner of my eye, I noticed Norton fiddling with something. He was detaching his legs at the kneecaps, first the left, then the right, before placing the artificial limbs inconspicuously under our table.

He smiled sheepishly at me. "Didn't mean to shock you, but after a ride like today, I need to give the connecting joints a break."

I would have looked less stunned had Norton bopped me over the head with one of his legs. I stopped eating, bowed my head and counted, truly counted, my blessings for the first time on that trip.

"Are you all right?" Norton asked.

Looking over at him, the universe sang itself back into place. I smiled and lifted a glass in his direction. We clanged rims and drank.

"Never better, Nort," I announced, "never better."

Cutting Corners

ROBERTO CARRIED HIS SCISSORS EVERYWHERE HE WENT. THOSE custom-made blades, a barber's razor-sharp shears, were on board the Bianchi racing bicycle he'd modified in slightly unnatural ways for the purpose of touring around New Zealand. We met beside an impossibly green field dotted with dandelions at the bottom of a short hill. Sheep wandered about this pastoral setting, which was tucked along the southern coast. Sheep outnumber people something like twenty to one on this island nation, but those sweaters-with-legs seem perfectly content to let us run the place, for the time being.

When I coasted up to Roberto, balding, pushing fifty, but in fine shape, he began talking to me like we'd known one another our entire lives and that this was the continuation of an earlier conversation.

"I enjoy lamb when it's seasoned well, and served over polenta, or maybe with a few potatoes and a side salad." He used his hands a lot when he spoke. Roberto's English was clear considering Italian was his first language. The accent didn't distract, and, at times actually emphasized what he was talking about. "But I wouldn't order it on my own, no." He shrugged one shoulder. "I suppose I enjoy fish too much."

"Hear that?" I remarked to the closest sheep. "You're safe with this guy. He's a surf-and-surf man."

I shifted my water bottle to the other hand and we shook.

"Is mutton lamb, or is it some other animal?" I asked. "I can never keep that straight."

When he laughed, Roberto turned his head to one side. Only later would I realize this idiosyncrasy was related to his barbering profession. How many people want a barber who laughs right into the back of their head?

"It's an adult sheep, of that I'm sure. But, you know, there is a fish they call mutton, the mutton snapper. Now that I would order!"

We took the next fifteen kilometers at a solid pace, nothing I couldn't handle, but it was satisfactorily brisk. I guess Roberto wanted to show me that he might have lost all of his hair, but the legs were still present and accounted for. (After weeks in New Zealand, I was on the verge of thinking about distance in terms of kilometers, but I still did the conversion to miles in my head.)

We pulled over at a café and ordered warm drinks. Tea for me and coffee for Roberto. He lamented the fact that Kiwis wouldn't know a real cup of coffee if it ground and brewed itself right there for them.

"Not their fault," he added, pointing to my drink. "It's a country of tea drinkers."

I took a sip. "But the tea really is quite good."

He sat back. We would take many such breaks during our time together.

"Sheep and tea," he said softly. "I'm a long way from home."

Home for Roberto was a barbershop along the Italian coast near Naples. He said he'd been away from the place for a few months, cycling the North Island first, with a break in Christchurch. Now he was pedaling his way down the South Island.

"What about your customers in your absence?" I asked, knowing that for many people, once they land someone who can properly cut their hair, it's a crisis when he isn't available. A good barber is almost like a fireman or a physician to many people.

Roberto shook his head, offered a rueful smile, and set his hands on the table for my examination. They looked fine to me. The only thing out of the ordinary was all the extra padding around each wrist.

"Some people spend their whole lives searching for what they want to do, no? I fell in love with a pair of scissors and oh, did they love me back. If I cut your hair once, I promise that you would be my customer for life. It's a gift—but then I strayed, and paid a big price." He leaned back and ordered another coffee.

I leaned forward and said, "What the hell are we talking about here?" We'd moved from hair to adultery without a beat.

"Carpal tunnel is the medical term for it, but. . . ." He tossed me that one-shoulder shrug, what came to be known in my mind as the Roberto response. "It's a simple case of betrayal. I cheated on my love of the perfect haircut with my love for . . . bicycle racing."

He drank the second cup like it was an espresso, one quick shot, leaving behind what wouldn't go down in a single, healthy gulp.

"I will tell you the whole, sordid story, but first we should knock off some kilometers, no? That ride in was a nice warm-up!"

Uh oh.

Turns out Roberto chased the yellow jersey in an annual little race the French cooked up a few years ago. For the rest of the week I worked my way over the rolling hills of New Zealand with a onetime Tour de France contender. He denied ever really having a shot at the jersey, saying he was more of a pacesetter for some of his fastest countrymen.

"But there was a time," Roberto noted, a hint of nostalgia in his voice as we pedaled along, "a time when some believed I had what it took. I came to believe this as well. More training was added to my schedule. I hardly noticed the expressions of reproach customers flashed when I would ride up to the door of my shop more than a few minutes late. My customers are like family, no? They wanted me to bring fame and recognition to their town, sure. But they wanted a nice trim and a close shave even more."

Roberto pedaled his Bianchi straight and hard along the quiet country roads of New Zealand, but his stories tended to meander all over the place. That was fine with me. His voice was hypnotic. It kept me focused on something other than the fast pace we were setting. Needless to say, Roberto took most of the afternoon to get to the part of his story where things fell apart.

"You can cheat on your true love a little, and she may take you back, but if you throw it in her face, she'll make you pay!"

I perked up. We were getting down to it now.

"Fillip was the first to notice the tremor. A little muscle twitch in the wrist of my scissor hand. So slight I couldn't really feel it at first, but Fillip is a jeweler with the eyes of a cat."

Roberto pulled us over near a little hollow. We faced each other, resting against some trees. I peeled an orange while he drank from a small silver flask he kept in his front bag for special occasions. I offered him the last section of orange but he waved it off.

"I ignored the twitches for as long as I could, sure, but a barber needs steady hands. It's not an option." He opened and closed his gloved mitts. Unconsciously, I did the same.

"Maybe the gloves I wore were too thin, or was it that for years I didn't change my hand positioning enough during races. Who knows? I tried everything, but the spasms got worse. The problem abated only by cutting back on my barbering duties—or laying off the extra training." Roberto paused, expelling a deep sigh.

"My lovers had discovered each other, and were in a battle for my attention. They would not share. I was being forced to choose."

"Your job was your passion, man. To make a living at something you enjoyed, shouldn't that have been enough? Hell, that's all I've ever wanted," I revealed.

Roberto capped his flask. "But it's never enough. We have hands so we can reach, no?" He shrugged. "But there is something about racing that you can only understand from the inside. No offense, you're a sturdy rider, actually one of the few people on this island to keep up with me for a decent stretch, but you're not racing material."

It was my turn to shrug.

"I couldn't walk away from the biggest race in the world at the height of my powers," he noted, getting excited now.

"So you took your shot, and win, place, or show, you went back to the barber's chair when it was over, right?"

I wanted a happy ending here. Roberto held up his hands again.

"The race finished them off, I'm afraid. My scissors never moved the same in hands that attempted to grip their way all over Europe faster than any other racer in the world. People said they couldn't tell a difference, but when I ran my hands through their hair after what should have been the final snip, I knew, I knew, so . . . *finito!*"

We enjoyed the cool, moist silence of the afternoon for a few moments.

"You quit the profession?"

"I run a resort with my brother now," Roberto said.

"But I thought you said home was a barbershop along the coast?"

He smiled. "I still own the shop. But I rarely cut hair there. I went out and found someone whose only love is the blade. He's quite the ladies' man, but when it comes to work, he's a priest and my shop is his church. We're partners. I go over there all the time in the off season. Those people are family, no? But when I do cut someone's hair, I don't accept payment. It wouldn't be right."

"That's a little harsh, don't you think?" I protested.

"I never cut corners—not racing, and not when working on someone's hair. They get my best performance, or they get it free."

I searched for a silver lining.

"How'd you do in the race?"

"The French Alps broke me. I finished . . . middle of the standings."

He was killing me.

"At least you finished. At least, you reached!" I said with a nod, knowing I finally had him with his own words.

He nodded back, smiling. We had come to an understanding. As we got onto our bikes, I noticed him studying my head.

"I'd like to cut your hair. Quite a challenge, that light, straight hair. Any mistakes and it shows, yes?"

I did need a trim.

"How do your hands feel today?" I asked.

"No, that hair needs fresh hands. I let you know when I'm able, then you can decide if you want to chance it."

Around lunch time the following day, we were sitting outside a small café talking to a sheep farmer. The term *sheep farmer* is not very descriptive in New Zealand since most of the population, at least in the rural areas, tends a certain number of sheep. But the gentleman we were talking with ran a fairly good-size operation.

"It's an hour inland by bike, but you're welcome to stay over. And you're in luck if you want to try your hand at shearing sheep," the farmer said before getting into a truck that had to be thirty years old. People who live on islands don't discard things just because they get on in years.

I was excited, but Roberto seemed thrilled. The chance for a retired barber to get his hands on that much hair was too much to pass up. The farm was glorious. It made me want to park my bike for good and plant corn somewhere for the next fifty years; get up with the sun and drink lemonade on a porch swing in the late afternoon. Sit back and survey all my hard work. Do something of value.

The actual shearing of sheep was more fun in the abstract. They don't always behave; there was dust and hair and pollen that had been trapped in the hair flying everywhere inside the barn. And you really have to push those shears at times. There's a certain art to the whole affair that I never quite mastered. But Roberto—we couldn't get him to stop. The crew asked if he wanted a job. My guess: The lack of good coffee was the only thing that kept him from signing on.

"I can spot the sheep you worked on, Joe," Roberto teased good-naturedly as we lounged around our campsite not far from the barn.

"Well, Roberto, they have my apologies."

We found a barbershop on the last day of our travels together. I insisted that he cut my hair in a real chair, with those adjustable handles, wall mirrors, the whole setup. We'd been on the lookout for such a place all week.

With the care afforded an infant, he removed his blades from a beautiful leather pouch. The shop owner, a tall man with a narrow goatee, was thrilled to accommodate us. Roberto pointed out that good barbers are a rather easygoing lot.

"And we're wonderful conversationalists, no? If you want to cut hair properly, you learn how to tell an interesting story, it keeps your customers engaged while you find the lay of their hair," Roberto said, adjusting the chair to fit my height in one skillful move.

"Don't forget our listening skills," added the Kiwi barber. "With all these mirrors to watch us in, we wouldn't dare ignore what people are saying. They'd spot us, right off."

I felt a little like the odd man out, which was just fine. Roberto and the shop owner spoke the language of their profession. Hair tonics, shaving creams, comb teeth widths, and clipper settings. I enjoyed watching my friend court his old love. He would touch the counters and study the various scissors arranged just so, with such a tenderness in his eyes.

Interrupting this meditation, I chimed in with: "Hey, I just thought of something. Do either of you sing in a barbershop quartet?"

Quaint images of Roberto dressed in a candy-striped shirt harmonizing with his pals on a beach, and the Kiwi standing with his quartet behind his barber chair came to mind.

"I can't sing a note," Roberto informed me.

"My voice has been dreadful ever since it dropped," said the shop owner.

It didn't matter to me whether Roberto delivered a once-in-a-lifetime haircut. Any touring cyclist worth his salt spends as little time on the do as possible. Helmets put the brakes on attempts at vanity. As long as my hair didn't start dropping out in clumps, I basically ignored it. Roberto, on the other hand, took the task quite seriously. He kept me turned away from the mirrors.

While he worked, my Italian barber talked about my hair like it was another person who had just arrived. He explained why the cowlick on the back of my head was different from the one on the left side of my part.

"The one in the back, it's not a problem, but the other, it must go," he said, not waiting for my opinion on the subject.

Roberto clipped and snipped, keeping the conversation light and lively, while his eyes concentrated on my scalp. A paying customer walked in, and after the shop owner ceremoniously brushed the other chair of stray hair, he took a seat. Now Roberto had something of an audience.

"You know, there's a joke about barber chairs in Italy. We set them farther apart to accommodate the way we're so fond of talking with our hands." He winked at the man in the other seat. "There's a one-eyed gentleman wandering around Italy with very long hair. I think he's the one who helped start this tradition."

I wondered how many times he'd told that joke. It broke them up in a little shop in New Zealand.

Roberto lingered over his work. Like an old sweetheart you see once every ten years at the high school reunion, he wanted one last look. I thought I was prepared for anything. He talked like a barber, he carried his own scissors, what other credentials does a man need?

It did cross my mind right before he turned the barber's chair, allowing me to gaze upon his craftsmanship, that I could haul around a bullwhip and a chair, but that wouldn't make me a lion tamer.

My hair was perfect—shorter than I usually wore it, but maybe that's what had been wrong all these years. Roberto dragged my look out of the 1970s, and for that I will be eternally grateful, or at least until I go bald and stop caring about such things. When I say it was perfect, I mean screen-test perfect. And I would discover, too late to thank Roberto, that it was one of those cuts that magically lasts as the hair grows in.

We hung around the shop for a while soaking in the atmosphere as the lunch crowd came by for trims. When I told Roberto of my plans to head for the high country, maybe try to find a kayak to rent on a lake, or do some skiing, he looked a little disappointed. We'd fallen into a nice groove, eating up the kilometers and stopping for coffee and tea when it suited us, or when the wind and microbursts of rain got to be too much.

"One more drink before you go?" he asked.

Roberto would not accept money for the haircut—he didn't need it, and it wasn't part of his code—but I managed to slip an envelope with a ten-spot into his pannier without him seeing. A symbolic gesture, the note I enclosed read: "To my real life Barber of Seville, who can't carry a tune, but holds the steadiest scissors I've ever seen, no?"

As we sat together that last time, Roberto brought his little silver flask out and topped off my tea with a healthy shot. We clinked our mugs together in a silent toast.

Somewhere in that silence were things Roberto knew too well, and I was just beginning to comprehend.

Rough Road Ahead:
Do Not Exceed
Posted Speed Limit

FORGET THAT OLD SAYING ABOUT NEVER TAKING CANDY FROM strangers.

No, a better piece of advice for the solo cyclist would be, "Never accept travel advice from a collection of old-timers who haven't left the confines of their porches since Carter was in office." It's not that a group of old guys doesn't know the terrain. With age comes wisdom and all that, but the world is a fluid place. Things change.

At a reservoir campground outside of Lodi, California, I enjoyed the serenity of an early-summer evening and some lively conversation with these old codgers. What I shouldn't have done was let them have a peek at my map. Like a foolish youth, the next morning I followed their advice and launched out at first light along a "shortcut" that was to slice away hours from my ride to Yosemite National Park. They'd sounded so sure of themselves when pointing out landmarks and spouting off towns I would come to along this breezy jaunt.

Things began well enough. I rode into the morning with strong legs and a smile on my face. About forty miles into the pedal, I arrived at the first "town." This place might have been a thriving little spot at one time—say, before the last world war—but on that morning it fit the traditional definition of a ghost town. I chuckled, checked my water supply, and moved on. The sun was beginning to beat down, but I barely noticed it. The cool pines and rushing rivers of Yosemite had my name written all over them.

Twenty miles up the road, I came to a fork of sorts. One ramshackle shed, several rusty pumps, and a corral that couldn't hold in the lamest mule greeted me. This sight was troubling. I had been hitting my water bottles pretty regularly, and I was traveling through the high deserts of California in June.

I got down on my hands and knees, working the handle of the rusted water pump with all my strength. A tarlike substance oozed out, followed by brackish water feeling somewhere in the neighborhood of two hundred degrees. I pumped that handle for several minutes, but the water wouldn't cool down. It didn't matter. When I tried a drop or two, it had the flavor of battery acid.

The old guys had sworn the next town was only eighteen miles down the road. I could make that! I would conserve my water and go inward for an hour or so—a test of my inner spirit.

Not two miles into this next section of the ride, I noticed the terrain changing. Flat road was replaced by short, rolling hills. After I had crested the first few of these, a large highway sign jumped out at me. It read: ROUGH ROAD AHEAD: DO NOT EXCEED POSTED SPEED LIMIT.

The speed limit was 55 mph. I was doing a water-depleting 12 mph. Sometimes life can feel so cruel.

I toiled on. At some point, tumbleweeds crossed my path and a ridiculously large snake—it really did look like a diamondback—blocked the majority of the pavement in front of me. I eased past, trying to keep my balance in my dehydrated state.

The water bottles contained only a few tantalizing sips. Wide rings of dried sweat circled my shirt, and the growing realization that I could drop from heatstroke on a gorgeous day in June simply because I listened to some gentlemen who hadn't been off their porch in decades, caused me to laugh.

It was a sad, hopeless laugh, mind you, but at least I still had the energy to feel sorry for myself. There was no one in sight, not a building, car, or structure of any kind. I began breaking the ride down into distances I could see on the horizon, telling myself that if I could make it that far, I'd be fine.

Over one long, crippling hill, a building came into view. I wiped the sweat from my eyes to make sure it wasn't a mirage, and tried not to get too excited. With what I believed was my last burst of energy, I maneuvered down the hill.

In an ironic twist that should please all sadists reading this, the building—abandoned years earlier, by the looks of it—had been a Welch's Grape Juice factory and bottling plant. A sandblasted picture of a young boy pouring a refreshing glass of juice into his mouth could still be seen.

I hung my head.

That smoky blues tune "Summertime" rattled around in the dry honeycombs of my deteriorating brain.

I got back on the bike, but not before I gathered up a few pebbles and stuck them in my mouth. I'd read once that sucking on stones helps take your mind off thirst by allowing what spit you have left to circulate. With any luck I'd hit a bump and lodge one in my throat.

It didn't really matter. I was going to die and the birds would pick me clean, leaving only some expensive outdoor gear and a diary with the last entry in praise of old men, their wisdom, and their keen sense of direction. I made a mental note to change that paragraph if it looked like I was going to lose consciousness for the last time.

Somehow, I climbed away from the abandoned factory of juices and dreams, slowly gaining elevation while losing hope. Then, as easily as rounding a bend, my troubles, thirst, and fear were all behind me.

GARY AND WILBER'S FISH CAMP—IF YOU WANT BAIT FOR THE BIG ONES, WE'RE YOUR BEST BET!

"And the only bet," I remember thinking.

As I stumbled into a rather modern bathroom and drank deeply from the sink, I had an overwhelming urge to seek out Gary and Wilber, kiss them, and buy some bait—any bait, even though I didn't own a rod or reel.

An old guy sitting in a chair under some shade nodded in my direction. Cool water dripped from my head as I slumped against the wall beside him.

"Where you headed in such a hurry?"

"Yosemite," I whispered.

"Know the best way to get there?"

I watched him from the corner of my eye for a long moment. He was even older than the group I'd listened to in Lodi.

"Yes, sir! I own a very good map."

And I promised myself right then that I'd always stick to it in the future.

Doing the Hokey-Pokey

You put your whole self in, you take your whole self out.
That's what it's all about.

I MISSED MY SENIOR PROM.

I'm not sure why. I suppose I just didn't have the strength to keep up appearances any longer. My high school experiences had been placid enough on the outside, but underneath, where it counted, not so good. It seems emotionally I had vacated those halls of learning months, if not years, earlier.

Also, one of my friends said the fish would be biting something fierce the entire weekend just south of Old John's Pass, and, after calculating how much money I would save on dinner, tux rental, limo ride, and the like, I bought a top-of-the-line rod and reel, some fresh bait at the Crab Shack, and never looked back.

And that's how my prom-night memories would have remained, had I not cycled up to Ranada O'Ryan KirkPatrick in the Chevron station parking lot along a back road in Pennsylvania's rural hill country.

My intentions were to level out the air in my front tire and add a few pounds of pressure to the rear, then be on my way.

By Pennsylvania I had developed my own riding style. I felt comfortable on my bicycle and in the role of the errant adventurer taking the road less traveled. Posing beside my bicycle became something of a game, as well. It never took long for someone to give me a curious nod and ask where I was headed.

That morning, I had time to study the young woman using the air hose to fill the tires of a brand-new Jeep. The way she kept looking me over, I was confident she was going to strike up a conversation. That or I had food on my jersey left over from breakfast. Detailed hygiene was not a priority while on the road.

Her strawberry blond hair curled across her shoulders. She had a healthy look—strong, with the last vestiges of baby fat left over from childhood.

"I didn't mean to hog the air pump," she announced as she handed it to me. "I guess I was spacing out thinking about how great it must be riding a bike like yours anywhere you want to go."

She introduced herself and we talked in the parking lot for a while. I found out that to help support her family she'd quit school a year early, gotten her G.E.D., and started working in the box factory where other family members had labored for years. Every time she mentioned the factory, her shoulders would sag almost imperceptibly.

"Yeah, my mom worked there until she couldn't stand on her feet anymore; so did my sister until she got pregnant with this semipro boxer down in Atlantic City. Now she just lays around our house waiting to be a mother while he works on his big comeback."

Ranada shadowboxed in my direction and laughed to cover the desperation. I put up my hands in mock defense and smiled.

"Sometimes my sister talks about the factory like those were some of the best times of her life. Pretty pathetic, huh?"

Leaning against her Jeep, the young woman wanted to know where I ended up at the close of each day of riding. How did I keep going? Was it always a new adventure wherever I went? Did I get worried that someone might mess with me or my stuff? What sort of amazing country had I ridden through? The questions came at me like bullets.

But how could I impart the good and bad of life on the road in a two-minute exchange off in one corner of a Chevron station, when I was still learning about it for myself? Her face pleaded for something—anything—that would snatch her from the monotony of inspecting boxes all day long two floors up in a windowless factory.

"At least I've got this nice Jeep, even if it sits in the parking lot most of the time," was her parting statement. I gave her the thumbs-up sign and rode away with a heavy heart.

It wasn't that I condemned the lives of people doing honest work in factories, but searching Ranada's face, I felt she'd been yanked into the grind too soon.

Life on the road is about forward motion and I soon had my sights set on a new destination. The sign indicated that the orchard gave daily demonstrations on making apple and peach cider, as well as maple syrup. It was a substantial loop ride to the north, but I had nowhere else to be, so I took the detour.

I will go to my grave knowing the proper techniques for creating perfect apple cider, and, as an added bonus, I got to lounge in the sun eating fat, juicy peaches on a crisp fall afternoon.

At day's end, I realized I was close to the town I'd started from that morning. Remembering the theater marquee with the name of a movie I'd wanted to see, I decided to get a room downtown.

My hotel was across the street from a community center where a number of formally dressed high school kids were gathering. I was wearing the only long pants I carried on the ride and a nice sweater, so I decided to wander over, blend in as best I could, and see what all the excitement was about.

As I turned back to lock my hotel door, a familiar face caught my eye. Ranada was sitting on a bench in the moonlight. There was a small park that separated the hotel from the community center. It's a pleasant coincidence to run into the one person that you've already met in a community.

She was wearing a prom dress.

"I can't go in there," she told me. "Lots of those people are still my friends, but I've been away from school for six months. I thought I could go through with it, but watching the girls I used to hang out with arriving in limos with their dates is just too much. One girl even pulled up in a horse-drawn carriage."

Ranada sat back in defeat, allowing her wrist corsage to fall to the ground. She summoned the strength not to cry. Instead, she asked why I was still in town, and when I told her about my day in the orchard, Ranada lit up.

"I haven't been out there in years. We went on a class outing once, but to hear you tell it, the orchard is a blast. I guess anything can be great depending on how you look at it."

"You haven't tasted their peaches, lately, have you?" I added.

Ranada's laughter gave me a foolish idea.

"Look, if it's okay with you, maybe I could play the role of your date tonight. I was planning to stick my head in there and see what all the fuss was about, anyway. Let's pretend I'm, say, your college boyfriend from . . ."

"Princeton," she chimed in, warming up to the idea. "Everyone in there thinks Princeton is the limit."

So we hatched our plan in the shadows of the park. I went back to the hotel and managed to borrow a navy blue blazer from the hotel staff, and the next thing I knew we were wandering from table to table, Ranada introducing me to people she'd known since elementary school.

We settled into a table near the stage and were soon crowded by individuals wanting to talk with Ranada. In a single evening, she had become the prodigal daughter, a woman of mystery with a stranger from out of town by her side.

I played my part with competence. To explain the fact that some people might have seen me ride into town on a bicycle, I improvised a story about taking part in an experiential studies semester at Princeton, touring the country in an effort to broaden my horizons. This added information elevated Ranada's status to exotic and worldly.

We danced and socialized; I even posed with Ranada for a prom picture. As the evening wore on, I listened to my date paint a future for herself that included travel, adventure, and a career track incorporating her desire to work with children.

What I got from that evening was a second chance to attend the prom without all the baggage of it being at my own high school, a little bonus along the road of life. Ranada, on the other hand, came face to face with the realization that she could mold her future into anything she was willing to go after with all her heart and soul.

Near the end of the night, Ranada announced that I would be

joining the Peace Corps soon. With an appreciative smile, she indicated to me that she was gently retiring her Princeton boyfriend to a far corner of the globe. Our little scheme had given her the boost to walk through the world alone again.

I met a lot of incredible people during my cycling adventures, but kept in touch with only a handful. Sometimes life just moves too fast to hold on to everyone. But I did try to check in with Ranada a few years later.

It gave me great pleasure to hear her older sister say that Ranada had quit her job at the factory, loaded up that Jeep, and headed out. Word had it she was giving ski lessons to children on the Colorado slopes.

I remember the dance ending that evening with a final send-off of childhood: that group participation number, the hokey pokey.

The floor filled up with people, Ranada and myself included, putting our whole selves in and taking our whole selves out, and shaking ourselves about.

Maybe that *is* what it's all about.

Trying Not to Miss the Boat

HAVE YOU EVER FELT AS IF YOU WERE MOVING THROUGH LIFE IN SLOW motion? The guy who hits the snooze button long after he should be out the door? I'm talking about a hapless loser who never grasps the fact that life is not a dress rehearsal. Ever felt like you were about to miss the boat?

So have I.

The first day of September is an exceptional time to find yourself cycling along the coast of Maine. Cool mornings give way to bright, crisp afternoons. The air always carries a hint of salt as the ocean spray rockets off the smooth, dark stones and fishing boats prowl the channels.

The lighthouses that dot the edges of those narrow points look even better than in the National Geographic calendars of my childhood. Fortunately, reality doesn't have to pale in comparison to society's ability to market it on postcards.

"Where you off to?" a fisherman in his twenties asked politely. His forearms were as thick as trolley cables. His face was peeling slightly from windburn.

"Working my way north, beyond Bangor. See a bit of the state, then as much of New England as I can before the weather turns ugly. That's when I'll head south and pedal till I make it to Florida."

He nodded, appreciative but not envious or overly excited. Days spent in a boat on the Atlantic were probably adventure enough.

"You planning on a trip out to Acadia National Park?" he asked.

The park, located on an island a boat ride from Bar Harbor, was actually the easternmost goal of my ride.

I nodded, thinking that he was going to tell me about a rather famous hike to the island's mountaintop. How it's the first spot the rising sun hits on the continental United States when it breaks the horizon.

He smiled, not unkindly. "Better get a move on then. The last ferry leaves tomorrow evening at 5:30 sharp. And don't be surprised if the weather gets ugly before you make it south. Maine's like that."

I had the ferry schedule in my bag and knew he was wrong, but decided I wouldn't call him on it. Not clear on fisherman's etiquette, my guess was that disputing the departure times of vessels was like trying to argue a close call with a seasoned umpire. The weather he could be right about, but I would just have to take my chances.

It wasn't until the next morning while I ate an affordable but hearty breakfast—eggs Benedict with lobster instead of ham—at a cozy little seaside diner that I even bothered to pull out the ferry schedule again.

I was busy mopping up the last of my eggs with a thick slab of toast, feeling fat and happy, when a frown settled on my face.

The weather, I observed, was perfect, but as my eyes went from the pristine view to the schedule, I noticed that the year on the left-hand corner of the brochure was wrong. The information appeared accurate—for last season. The Bangor Chamber of Commerce had slipped one by me. A big one.

Word to the wise: Never try to ride fast and hard immediately following a hearty breakfast.

Even using the most optimistic map measurements, I was more than a hundred miles from the dock; no big deal if broken into two fifty-mile rides, but I had less than twelve hours to get there.

I really did have my heart set on seeing the sunrise from that lofty perch, so I chose to ride like nobody's business. Less than three weeks into my first long-distance solo bicycle trip, and I was already falling behind the schedule I'd set for myself.

This was the sort of thing that I'd said I was making my journey to get away from, or at least come to terms with. In the months building up to my first ride, I was always repeating that quote: "The problem with the rat race is that even if you win the race, you're still a rat."

About 3 that afternoon, with my legs feeling like two heavy bags of dirt, drenched in sweat, and oblivious to anything but keeping my own rhythm steady, I certainly resembled a rat on a treadmill.

The scenery was better than is afforded most rodents, but I was riding with my head down so much of the time I barely noticed.

In my battered state, I didn't register the cyclist on my left for a few seconds, but his smile was so clear and radiant it pulled me from my trance. The time was a little after 5 P.M.

"Where you headed?"

Still on the fly, I hosed my mouth with some water before answering. "Bar Harbor," I managed to croak.

He glanced at my loaded bicycle then eyed his watch.

"Trying for the ferry, are you?" He shook his head. "I'd say it's a long shot."

I smiled for the first time that day, happy to have some company.

My travels to that point had been filled with many well-wishers, surprisingly warm hospitality, and great conversations. But that was before I had a boat to catch. In retrospect, I probably lost out on meeting some real fine characters that day.

But I was late, late for a very important date.

Quickly wiping sweat from my face to get a better look at the rider beside me while always keeping my legs pumping the pedals, I began to realize why Lewis Carroll decided to call his manic character the Mad Hatter.

The cyclist, Nathan Branch, a family man who rode his bike a couple of afternoons a week before dinner, was for some reason sympathetic to my plight. It didn't seem to matter how crazy I must have appeared.

"Maybe if you draft me the rest of the way, you'll make it," he suggested, and without another word he grabbed the lead spot, leaving his back tire less than a foot ahead of my front wheel. Slowly at first, then with growing momentum as the waning sun made everything appear bathed in an ethereal light, we tore up the wooded back roads of Maine together, hooting and howling as we went.

A perfect stranger had joined my cause. It was an adrenaline rush in my exhausted state to keep my balance and timing. And for a few glorious minutes I forgot about the boat and the stress of pushing myself to conform to a schedule. I pedaled simply to feel my heart in my chest and the cooling coastal air rush through my lungs. I rode to celebrate youth, speed, and abandon.

We pushed over hills and barreled by pastures. When we shot beyond the final rise, the ocean, a slate blue by this point in the day, opened up before us. The ferry was already a small dot on the horizon.

I coasted past Nathan to the beginning of the dock, dumped my bike as it came to a stop, and allowed myself to collapse on the damp wood. Nathan sprawled out beside me.

After several minutes of panting, Nathan said, "Sorry you missed your boat."

I began to make some sounds. It was hard to tell if I was laughing or crying. Nathan helped me up and took a good look at me.

"You okay?"

And as my heart began to dip below a couple of hundred beats per minute, I realized I was fine, better than fine; I'd just experienced the sort of moments of clarity I would probably spend much of my future trying to rekindle. I broke into a chuckle

"To hell with the boat. I suppose the sun will rise just fine without me."

It was Nathan's turn to laugh.

We got to know each other a little better on the cruise back to his home. I spent a comfortable evening enjoying good food and the company of his wonderful family. We stayed up late talking. The last thing Nathan said that night was, "That was more fun today than I've had on a bike since I was a kid."

I made it to the mountaintop later in the week. Nathan hooked me up with a friend of his, a commercial fisherman who took me right to the island the following day. The final ferry of the year would head back to the mainland the next afternoon. I wasn't too worried I'd miss that one.

At dawn, I hiked to the spot where my face would be the first in America to feel the sun pour over it. I felt powerful, exalted almost, when I realized I was the only person on the summit that morning. Like I would own the day for a moment. But it was not to be.

Clouds rolled over the ocean and the sky lightened slowly, in a placid display of the day's arrival. I stood up there for a long time, somehow pleased that I didn't need to see the sun first, or at all, to know that it had come up again.

It's invigorating to be reminded that life is so much more than what you want and who you think you are. Each day starts with the promise of what all of us might become in the time that remains.

THIS STORY IS DEDICATED TO THE VICTIMS OF THE CRASH OF SWISSAIR FLIGHT 111, THEIR FAMILY MEMBERS, AND THEIR FRIENDS.

Mistaken Identity: I Pedaled a Thousand Miles Just to Slip This Skin

"YOU KNOW WHO YOU LOOK LIKE?"

I was trying to keep my loaded bicycle balanced while searching through my bags for a driver's license. The campground attendant required some form of identification before I could set up my tent in what amounted to a patch of gravel in the desert.

The ID routine seemed rather ludicrous. What was I possibly going to steal while riding a bicycle? The damn thing was already too heavy on some of the more daunting uphill climbs, so I certainly wasn't interested in acquiring any more possessions. I'd just pedaled across Monument Valley, then plunged down and crawled back out of the Grand Canyon. My bones ached and skin burned, but my spirits were rather high.

At least the campground had a pool, laundry facilities, and rest rooms with showers. There was no shade to be found anywhere, but you can't have it all.

"Kiefer Sutherland is who I look like, right?" I said to the girl behind the desk, before handing over my ID.

She nodded vigorously and gave me a larger-than-expected smile.

I indicated that she should lean in, I had something important to tell her.

"That's because I am," I whispered.

At the time, Kiefer Sutherland, actor and the son of master thespian Donald Sutherland, was on the front of every tabloid and teen magazine in the country. He'd stood up another actor, Julia Roberts, at the altar, and was said to be in seclusion. Though I'd been cycling the less traveled roads of the West, I was aware of this guy's actions. That's how high his profile was at the time.

To this day, I can't explain why I led the young person behind the counter to believe I was the celebrity. Maybe it had something to do with people mistaking me for him a lot during that ride. When I say a lot, I mean at least a few times a day.

His face was ubiquitous because of the marriage scandal, and when people saw me ride up, many of them matched my mug with his picture and called it good. My defense could be they wore me down over time. My rationale: What could it hurt to have a little fun with the whole thing?

The girl let out a squeal, clapped her hands and began looking me over with more care.

"You're a lot bigger in person. Are you working out for your next film or something?" she asked.

I grinned; this was going to be more enjoyable than I thought.

"I'm sort of taking a break from the world at the moment." I pointed over to my bike. "I wrapped a movie recently and when the whole relationship with Julia fell apart, I decided I needed a real challenge."

The girl's eyes grew wider with each lie that escaped my lips. I nearly lost it a few times, wanting to laugh at the garbage I was flinging about in that cramped little office.

"That's why my driver's license says Joe somebody. I needed a cover, a fake identity so the paparazzi wouldn't hound me to the ends of the Earth," I said. I squinted out the window of the office and decided this little oasis in the desert did indeed qualify as the ends of the Earth.

She patted my arm, asked sheepishly for an autograph, told me how sorry she was about my current love-life problems, and swore up and down that she'd keep my identity a secret. No harm done! In fact, it had been kind of exhilarating, the act of pretending to be a big shot on the run. I forgot about the exchange almost immediately. The pool's cool water beckoned.

A group of half a dozen people stood over my lounge chair. The sun was in my eyes so I couldn't see their faces very well.

"It really is him," one of them announced.

Uh-oh.

Pens and tabloid covers were thrust at me. The click of a camera sounded as people began asking me to sign things to their sister, mother, cousin, or brother.

I leaned forward, shaking my head calmly.

"You don't understand; I was kidding around earlier with the front desk clerk. I'm not really who you think I am. . . ."

But it was no use. Everyone seemed to already know about my cover story. I had cried wolf and there was no convincing them otherwise. But I gave it my best shot, showing them multiple pieces of ID and journals with my "fake" name on them, and reasoning that I'd been on the road for weeks. The real Kiefer Sutherland was all over the television. How could I be in two places at once? I learned that day that people would rather have a little excitement in their lives than the truth.

Also, it doesn't take much to impress us. When I determined that these individuals weren't going away without my signature, I went to work. To this day, I wonder how Mr. Sutherland really signs his name. He'd be happy to know that in northern Arizona he prefers to go by the abbreviated autograph, Kiefer.

Things got progressively worse. In a few short hours, word had gotten to the town five miles down the highway. Cars crowded the parking lot of the campground, everyone hoping to get a glimpse of the celebrity. I tried reading a book, in a lawn chair by my tent, but they circled like buzzards.

The parents of the girl behind the counter came over to my tent site around dinnertime.

"We want to apologize for all the inconvenience our daughter has caused you," her mother said. "Our daughter had no right telling people you were here"

I tried to explain that it was no big deal, that this whole thing was just a case of my own foolishness and mistaken identity.

"We'd like to make it up to you by doing your laundry, and we've prepared a nice dinner in the lodge, if you'd do us the honor," she said.

Honor? Laundry?

This situation was completely out of control. I thought about the Disney cartoon classic *The Sorcerer's Apprentice,* and cursed myself for ever putting this little prank into play.

I declined the invitation to dinner, but because I am a weak man on occasion, I posed for a few pictures with the family and left my laundry at the front desk. What laws was I breaking? It had to be a crime to impersonate a public figure. I was already receiving the punishment, though. As I rode my bike into town for a bite to eat, and maybe a beer at the bar, a caravan of cars trailed me.

Everyone thought they knew who I was. Being a celebrity is exhausting work. My dinner got cold as I fought off well-meaning fans and signed more slips of paper.

Finally, in the recesses of a dark bar, I thought I'd found a quiet moment to contemplate the error of my ways.

With beer in hand, I glanced tentatively around the place. No one seemed to give me a second look.

Ah . . . sanctuary.

"I don't think you had any sense, leaving a girl like that at the altar."

It was an old cowboy talking to me from the end of the bar. "She starred in *Pretty Woman.* You must have rocks in your head."

The next morning I rolled down the road at first light, free from the prison that comes from being a celebrity. I pedaled hard, promising never again to pretend to be anyone . . . but myself.

Complications

I MET MY FIRST IN-THE-FLESH PRIVATE INVESTIGATOR BY ACCIDENT. AT least I thought it was by accident, but would come to find out later that Sherri had been keeping tabs on me most of the day; she was that good.

Actually, she got the drop on me while shopping for party supplies in a convenience store at the intersection right before an exit for Lake Winnipesaukee. We would have bumped into each other if a car full of Labor Day weekend revelers hadn't stopped me in the parking lot, first. They hooted and whistled from the seats of a sporty convertible, literally marveling at my gear and bicycle. I never thought of myself as an actual attraction until that morning.

"Where the hell are you coming from?" asked one of the young urbanites up from Boston for the long weekend. He was hiding a beer in a Trinity College coolie.

"A galaxy far, far away," I joked. "No, actually I looped the state of Maine, and now I'm checking out New Hampshire. Beautiful." I leaned back in the saddle. The sleeping bag and miscellaneous gear almost formed a padded backrest.

"Eventually, I'll roll up to my doorstep in Florida. That's the plan, anyway, but I'm flexible."

They were quite friendly. Maybe it was the holiday spirit talking, or it could have been the fact that they had power jobs in the city; advertising consultants, junior commodities traders, law firm partnership pledges—jobs that would lead to early retirement if they didn't mind ulcers—and they saw in me those exotic daydreams of telling family, tradition, and the guy who signed their checks to take a flying leap.

Still on my bike, I leaned against their car while one of them ducked into the store for ice. A beer and some chips were relayed over to me.

"I'm a journalist," I declared. This was true, but maybe I announced it to give my endeavor an air of legitimacy in the eyes of a carload of prep-school-educated future leaders of industry. I had few published credits to my name at that point.

The group wanted to hear more about my adventures. "Why don't you toss your bike in the back and come to our party?" the driver, a brunette who practiced international copyright law, encouraged.

A blowout was just want I needed, but plans to meet a friend at a cabin on the lake couldn't be changed. There was no way to get in touch with her.

"Well, here's the address. You can bring your friend. It's in Wolfeboro, on the other side of the lake."

Now that might work. The cabin was only eighteen miles away. We could be at the party by lunch. I could almost smell the barbecue and hear the ski boat.

At some point during this exchange, my detective slipped past unnoticed. Because Sherri is an avid cyclist, she almost came back and introduced herself right then, but as she put it later, "I've got nothing against them personally, but I break out in hives around the combination of yuppies, beer, and sports cars. It feels too much like grown-ups pretending they're back in high school for the weekend."

Sherri was great at sizing up a situation in one scathing sentence.

The next time she saw me I had my head down, sucking air as I pedaled to the top of another in a series of hills that surrounded the lake. When a touring cyclist has one expectation in mind regarding the terrain, in this case flat, meandering roads along a peaceful lake, and reality turns out to be something else—a continuous series of short, steep climbs—it's a psychological hammer blow, not to mention a great way to induce leg cramps. Inhaling that beer at the store didn't help my performance. Again, Sherri almost stopped but there wasn't enough room to safely pull over.

It took more time and effort to get to the cabin than I would have liked. A note on the door informed me that I would be spending Labor Day alone, and upon further inspection there wasn't even a way into the cabin. Damn.

Halfway through the unpacking process, I changed my mind and set off in search of that party. The map indicated it was another twenty miles, but I did some creative addition and whittled that distance, at least in my mind, to under fifteen. It's fascinating what bikers will tell themselves to keep pedaling. Maybe all the hills were behind me. And maybe a bag of money would show up on the side of the road, and peace would erupt in the Middle East. I rubbed out a few cramps and concentrated on how I wanted my burger grilled.

Not far from Wolfeboro a scorching hill forced me off the bike. I felt shame. A hill hadn't beaten me since Bangor, Maine. Pushing my alloyed albatross slowly beside me was bad enough, but then the horn honking from vacationers and half-lit partygoers filled the afternoon breeze. Yeah, I know, I'm a loser and you people are having a wonderful time.

Sherri saw me then as well, but she knew all about hitting the wall and the bleak state of mind one has spiraled into by the time it actually comes down to dragging a loaded touring bike up a rise. I can't say the pain of pushing is any worse than pedaling; it's just different. Out of respect, she drove on.

I arrived at the party well after the top of the festive arc had been reached. People were on the mellow downside of the day. The volleyball games were over, the jet skis out of gas, and a few withered hot dogs huddled on a paper plate like refugees after a bomb blast.

My friends from the convertible greeted me with pleasant, hazy smiles and called over the remaining clusters of people to make introductions. The appearance of a cycling writer perked things up for a while. People tossed out questions and someone dolled up a hot dog with a bunch of fixings for me. I gazed across the lake and realized I'd cycled around the better part of it that day.

When I emerged from a soothing shower, the core group wanted to know if I'd be up for a little barhopping in town. I felt whipped, but

I hadn't pedaled this far just to crawl into a guest room bed.

"Be right there," I called from the basement laundry room. But I wasn't going anywhere unless I found a pair of shoes. I carried khakis and a decent shirt for just such occasions, but my Topsiders had been mortally wounded during an unfortunate camping incident that culminated in a wrestling match with a deep, sucking bog. At the time, I felt fortunate to have extricated myself from that mud hole with both of my shoes, but studying what were now blocks of crusted earth dried to the consistency of cement, I thought maybe it would have been best for everyone had I donated them to the bog. Those shoes were adding at least five pounds to my load. A couple of days soaking in a bucket of strong chemicals might have some effect on them, but beating the shoes forcefully against a wall in the basement certain wasn't accomplishing anything. Fearing I might actually chip the brick, I went to plan B.

"What's that clicking?" someone asked.

I thought I could slip into the booth without detection. I'd walked stealthily on the heels of my clip bike shoes from the house to the car, and almost made it through the bar when my toes began to cramp. In addition to looking ridiculous for nightclubbing, those shoes made a helluva racket with each step.

The group did seem riveted by my account of the battle with the bog, but the live band upstaged the climax a little. When it came time to hit the dance floor, I found myself sitting alone in the booth. The bed in the guest room was beginning to look like the better choice. Feeling foolish, I clicked over to the bathroom, then decided what the hell, and clicked to the bar for another drink.

"You ride your bike here tonight?" I heard the voice of a woman ask. I should have stayed in the booth. My worst fears were about to be realized. The question originated from a good-looking blonde with a glint in her eyes, a self-assured creature whose idea of fun was probably, with one well-placed put-down, crushing the local guys who cruised the bars for a good time.

My kingdom for a quiet pair of shoes.

"Actually, I spend so much time on that damn bike, I had these permanently welded to my feet. A bit extreme, maybe?" I joked, bracing myself for the crack that would round out the day's other embarrassments nicely.

"Yeah, well, I wish I had that problem." She took a sip of her beer. "I haven't been on my bike for a week."

What was this, a comrade? I clicked proudly onto the stool beside her. Sherri said the hill into Wolfeboro catches a lot of riders off guard.

"Oh, you saw that display of failing muscles and diminished lung capacity?"

We talked straight through the band's second set. When I learned that Sherri was a private investigator I had to mete out my questions so as not to sound too much like a overly excited schoolgirl.

Truth was I never missed an episode of *Magnum P. I.*, and I even went through a fashion-impaired semester in college when Hawaiian shirts dominated my wardrobe.

"Tell you what," she said after I hit her with yet another job-related question. "You meet me for a bike ride tomorrow, give you a chance to redeem yourself after that hill, and I'll take you with me to an assignment I have to check on."

I could almost hear the theme song to my own personal detective series cranking out in the background. Thank God for loud bike shoes. She handed me a business card. I clicked out the door, head held high.

I told my new friends the plan over breakfast.

"That address is on the other side of the lake," one of them pointed out. It was going to be a long trek just to get to the starting line. I wanted to give this detective a decent riding partner, not some leg-cramping heap on two wheels.

"We're going skiing today. Why don't we toss your bike in the boat and drop you there?"

It's humbling to watch the distance it took me all day to cover on a bicycle sliced down to a ten-minute boat ride. I wasn't complaining, but it felt a bit like cheating, as if I were one of those impostors who joins the Boston Marathon during the last mile.

My Labor Day friends watched me assemble my bicycle on shore. The guy with the Trinity College beer coolie held out the last pannier.

"You know, we've got all the trappings of society in our professions, but you, man, you're practicing without a net."

I shrugged.

"Well, you've got some guts—I'll give you that much." He paused. "It would scare me too much to do . . ." He spread his arms in front of my bike, "this."

I smiled. "If it's any consolation, your jobs scare the hell out of me, too."

It took Sherri no time at all to get her bike on the road. We pedaled along a relatively flat trail near the lake. It was clear to me that only the locals knew how to avoid the harsher climbs.

We talked components and training schedules, Presta versus Schrader valves and the almost mystical realm of flat-tire avoidance. Sherri loved cycling for what I considered all the right reasons. The freedom and speed, the balance and symmetry, and the understated grace of using your own power to magnify your abilities and rush along silently just a few inches above the earth. Surely the bicycle is definitive proof of a higher power.

But most of all Sherri embraced the way pedaling a bicycle on a quiet afternoon transports its rider back in time. You see an old man coasting along on a bicycle and that puckish little boy always shines through.

"If I could sock away enough money, I'd like to tour across Canada," Sherri mused. "I've never really been on anything longer than a weekend ride."

I pointed out that this was a sin against man and nature which should be atoned for with a summer of cruising the northern provinces.

"It will happen—if I can ever get people to pay their bills on time." The edge in her voice led me to believe Sherri really could handle the seedier aspects of investigative work.

"So just who are your customers?" I asked.

"Well, they certainly aren't tycoons and dignitaries. I do a lot of divorce proceedings investigations, insurance fraud, and missing persons. Sometimes I handle security systems and there's always the odd-ball case that goes nowhere."

Sherri had trained at the police academy in hopes of working her way into a detective position. It took three years to get promoted off the street.

"Bastards gave me a desk and a tutorial on the inner workings of the coffee machine. I gave my notice."

Sherri took us away from the lake. The hills appeared like old nemeses, but I felt strong. Having a competent partner to draft off and pull along helped, like I'd brought along reinforcements for the rematch. When we eased up for a break, I asked Sherri if she'd ever shot anyone. It was a stupid question and I regretted it moments after it rolled off my lips.

"No, but this job killed a really close friendship," she said.

I waited.

"A guy hires me to follow his wife. Rule number one, if you think your one-and-only is cheating, you already know the answer. Once in a while it's irrational jealousy, but—"

Sherri stretched out.

"I do a lot of the cases that fall into the sad, country music ballad category. I didn't know this guy and I didn't know his wife when I got her in a Kodak moment with her new man, but unfortunately, I knew exactly who her lover was. It stopped me cold, seeing the guy I'd had dinner with the night before."

"He was your boyfriend," I said, shaking my head.

Sherri chuckled. "No, he was my best friend's fiancé. Couldn't even wait for them to get married before he's out cheating on her. It's nothing I haven't seen too many times to count, but this was my best friend. I lost a lot of sleep trying to decided what to do. In the end, I confronted him instead of her."

Sherri wasn't short on courage, but when I thought about it, giving him a chance to right things was the honorable move.

"He punched me in the face. Coldcocked me right there behind the video store. I almost passed out holding a copy of *Ghostbusters*."

"Jesus," I whispered.

"Then he went home and told Sarah I tried to jump his bones and that's why he had to hit me. I remembered the pictures, but then realized that I'd given everything, the negatives, all of it, to the client. Sarah stopped speaking to me. The real horror is: Not only is she married to an adulterer, but it's a good bet he'll lay fists on her one of these days."

I asked Sherri if she was working on any other ways to unmask the guy.

"Yeah, come back in a few months, maybe I'll have a different answer to your 'Have you ever shot someone?' question."

We laughed, but I wasn't so sure.

Maybe to counter her depressing story, Sherri described the time she was hired to stake out a sporting goods store, deduce how so much money and product was leaving the premises without detection. The staff, who had been together for years, took polygraphs. Sherri did a thorough inspection of the building and even shadowed the employees because she doesn't think polygraphs are worth a damn in most cases. Nothing. Even when the money was locked in the safe, someone skimmed a portion. She went so far as to check into the owner's background just to see if he was pulling something desperate and using Sherri to cover himself with the insurance company. He was clean.

"I spend the better part of a month parked outside, eating doughnuts from the shop next store, and wondering how many miles I would have to ride to take off the extra weight. And still, money kept disappearing. I even pulled all-nighters inside the place and, believe me, a damp storefront full of archery gear, animal heads, and baseball gloves is not the choice location for a slumber party. The place didn't stock a single bicycle."

We groaned.

"It would have remained a mystery—if I didn't have a weak spot for those old-fashioned doughnuts. You know, the ones that dip so nicely in coffee. I stumble into the shop around 4 A.M. hoping to salvage an old cup of java with some doughnuts, except I can't find the clerk anywhere. I keep calling out, but it is the middle of the night so maybe I'll just leave my money on the counter. I poke my head into the kitchen for extra creamer, and that's when I see it."

Sherri raised her eyebrows.

"What!" I asked impatiently.

She stood up, brushed herself off and reached for her bike, taking plenty of time about it.

"A little trapdoor behind the doughnut conveyor belt. I followed it to an opening in back of the archery range. There was a false wall there but you couldn't tell because of the hay bales."

"Oh, that's so Nancy Drew!"

"Yeah, well, I don't think that's what he said when I put a gun to his head. Nailed that doughnut maker red-handed with a stack of cash and what I'm told were some rather valuable baseball cards."

"It's those moments that got you into the business?" I asked cheerfully.

"Job discrimination made me a P.I. It's not about fast cars, exotic locales and having loads of free time, but for a few seconds there, when doughnut man looked into my eyes, I suppose I was having fun."

We crushed a few more hills before riding up to a civic group cleaning their adopted stretch of highway.

"Let's pitch in for a couple of minutes," Sherri suggested.

This woman was winning my heart. As we picked up trash I asked Sherri how she kept from loathing humanity, what with the people she came in contact with on a daily basis.

"I call it the ten-to-one rule. There's ten people out here picking up trash for every one I catch robbing his neighbor. Besides, if there were more scumbags walking around, wouldn't I be rich by now?"

I offered an uncertain grin.

"Let me have my delusions."

We didn't want to turn back but it was getting late and Sherri still had to take care of that investigative work. Pulling into the driveway of a middle-class vacation home tucked in the woods, my adrenaline started pumping. Surveillance, wiretapping maybe? All I needed was one of my Hawaiian shirts and a pair of Ray-bans.

We went around the side of the house. Sherri opened a little box and started pushing buttons. This was promising.

"Joe, would you get the hose?"

Hose? "What is this assignment?" I asked.

"People I met through a friend of a friend asked me to make sure their alarm system was hooked up properly for the off season. For a few extra dollars I agreed to water the plants."

That was my big debut as a P.I.'s sidekick. No chases, or running down license plates, just me standing in a yard watering a total stranger's rosebushes for the last time before winter. Sherri was quite amused by her deception. I sprayed some water in her direction.

We went inside for a final check of the alarm system. Sherri grabbed a couple of Cokes, then directed me to a deck overlooking the lake. Standing against the railing in the complete silence that is a vacation spot after the party ends for another year, I realized Sherri was leaning in. At least I thought she was. You don't want to get your signals crossed with a woman who carries a gun. I started to go for the kiss, but pulled up short, opting to destroy the mood with the standard question.

"You want me to kiss you?"

She smiled. "You'd make a helluva detective."

We set down our Cokes. She added, "But only a kiss—we don't want to complicate things too much. . . ."

"No, we wouldn't," I said just before our lips met. It was one of those kisses you remember for a very long time; soft and lingering. Sometimes a few moments of tenderness is enough to erase miles of loneliness and uncertainty.

When we got to the convenience store exit, I told Sherri I needed to head south, case closed. There had been some talk about a pullout couch at her place for the night, but we knew that wasn't realistic, if we really did want to keep things from getting . . . complicated.

"I'm gonna send you a postcard from Canada next summer," Sherri said with conviction. "No matter how many side jobs it takes."

I watched her pedal away, growing smaller and smaller until, when my detective reached the bottom of the hill, she had become that winsome little girl with a youthful heart, a glint in her eyes, and a powerful time machine under her feet, one that no matter how old she got, would never let her down.

When The Going Gets Tough, Metal Cowboys Head for Aruba

IT BEGAN WITH A HARMLESS POSTCARD.

"My teaching contract ends in June. If you're going to experience life on an island paradise, you'd better get moving!"

It was my friend Toni Riha, waving the good times in my face again, daring me to accept the challenge of sand, sun, and slothfulness on the last island in the Caribbean chain. I'd been told that Aruba combined the arid beauty of the desert with beachfront property and a steady sea breeze year-round.

Toni and I had met at the end of a bicycling adventure years earlier, and remained close. Toni's quest for adventure mirrored my own. Her choices led her around the globe, landing this strong, fearless woman a job teaching physical education at an international school near the tip of the island, far from the madding crowds of tourists splashing about the resort areas.

The postcard fell through my mail slot on the coldest day of that winter. Desert Storm had just begun, I kept avoiding a novel that needed editing, and an island setting had a certain Hemingway ring to it.

When the going gets tough, any Metal Cowboy worth his salt heads for . . . Aruba? With a few thousand dollars tucked away at the bottom of one of my bike panniers, meager prospects for gainful employment on the horizon, and the snow building up outside my window, I beat a fast path to the airport.

Toni sounded genuinely thrilled about my decision. Her only request was that I purchase a half-dozen regulation-size beach volley-balls.

"Certain things are hard to come by on the island," she said by way of explanation. "We play a lot of volleyball down here." Any doubts I had about expatriating for a spell evaporated.

As it happened, my island sojourn almost ended in a fiery plane crash miles from the equator.

"Folks, we've hit a tropical disturbance that wasn't on the radar. We're going to try to dodge the worst of it."

The twenty minutes of my life that followed are best forgotten.

Needless to say, the "worst of it" must have caught us. We lost hundreds of feet of altitude at a time. Strangers only moments earlier were now tightly holding hands.

When the captain briskly announced an "unscheduled landing" on the small island of Curaçao, I closed my eyes and thought about my family, friends—all those words unwritten—and silently pleaded for more time. Whimpering could be heard around me. The lights went out for a few seconds. God, this is it.

Cheers and applause filled the cabin when the plane, still whole, finally came to a halt. We were greeted by two chubby black men who wheeled a rusty ladder contraption to the door at the front of the plane. Several angry Americans en route to St. Croix wanted to speak to the president of the island—now!

The smiling men nodded repeatedly and put them in a separate room. The airline paid for the rest of us to stay at the island's one hotel, and Heinekens were on the house.

The angry Americans arrived hours later. I had my doubts they'd wangled a sit-down with the president. For them, beer was priced at four dollars a bottle, and all the rooms were full so . . . "Sorry, you'll have to sleep on cots in the lobby." Laid-back island justice.

A picture of how things worked in the land of mañana began to take shape. The pace felt comfortable. From the moment I touched down in Aruba until I broke free of her lazy latitudes months later, my life read like a chapter out of one of Hunter S. Thompson's journals —hazy and surreal. We all have a lost weekend somewhere in our past, don't we? Aruba was mine.

My days began around 10 A.M., after a pair of parakeets gathered in the bush outside my bedroom window—a natural alarm clock. A swim in crystal blue water usually cleared my head. I'd play dominoes with jolly, aging characters at a beachside canteen for a couple of hours.

If you accidentally jostled the table, spilling the dominoes and thus prematurely ending the game, or at the very least forcing everyone to cover their hands, you were calmly walked to the edge of the dock and tossed in, regardless of what you might be wearing. Island justice.

Volleyball games picked up about midafternoon, and, because there were two beer bottling factories on the island, Amstel Light and Heineken flowed like water. Locals passed them out as if they were sodas.

I lived in a bungalow not fifty yards from the water's edge. The volcanic rock that made up most of the island was dotted with iguanas. A decrepit leathery lizard about three or four feet long lived in the towering aloe bush in our backyard. Toni liked to toss it leftover sandwiches and fried Cheerios from her hammock.

In Aruba, everything was fried! Maybe it shortened the locals' life spans, but the sunsets were otherworldly and the pace of things gave people more time to enjoy each moment. The longer I was there, the more this trade-off seemed agreeable to me.

On many afternoons, after Toni got off work, we'd grab our bikes and face into the ever-present headwind. She would smile and howl all the way up and over the first long incline. I'd follow with less enthusiasm. Toni's life, liberty, and pursuit of happiness were wrapped up in exercise. Her family tree was riddled with heart disease, but Toni planned to wipe out years of evolution by force of will and perpetual motion. Not so easy to bring down a moving target.

Over time, Toni had carved her body into something of freakish beauty. Muscles shimmered and twitched when she walked. I'd never seen so much power locked beneath tight strips of tanned skin. There was a pull-up bar in the bungalow doorway. The first time she challenged me, I gave Toni a generous handicap. But from then on, it was an even playing field, and I still went down in flames on a regular basis.

Sometimes those bike rides took us halfway around the island. Aruba is only sixty miles long and twenty miles across at its widest point. We'd explore places that caught our attention along the road. I remember standing inside the opening of a cave at dusk. A rustling sound engulfed the cavern. In the half light I watched bats, their numbers too great to count, dart around me for the entrance. I panicked for a moment before realizing they weren't going to hit me. The experience was riveting. I twirled around like a child as a cloud of wings whistled past.

Another time, Toni climbed down to a natural arch of rock formed by millions of years of harsh waves pounding the north shore. The tide came pouring in. The waves smashed closer and closer as she tightroped out just a few more steps. The rocks below would cut her to ribbons if she slipped.

Toni liked to take chances. She lived for them.

The photograph I snapped of her out there on the edge, one big wave away from eternity, showed a fearlessness I don't even pretend to possess.

"Made a great picture!" was Toni's only defense for such behavior.

Pressed harder, she added: "I'm two years older than my mom when her heart quit. Got to make things count—'cause I went over the edge a while ago."

In the fading light, we'd ride the wind home like a pair of hawks.

Nightfall was when my days really took off: parties on the beach, intense and playfully antagonistc talks with intellectuals who taught at the international school, saltwater fishing with long poles by moonlight at the breakwater.

One evening I stopped for a quick drink at the Paddock, a bar frequented by Dutch marines, only to find myself recruited for the Arubian national rugby team. My life was becoming a series of random zigs and zags accompanied by a reggae soundtrack.

The most surreal moment of my equatorial experiences came a few weeks later when I ran onto the field of a South American stadium to the roar of thousands of Venezuelan rugby fans. My face was flashed onto a Jumbotron screen by ESPN 2, instantly satellited around the globe. Bizarre.

At the victory party, I observed one of my teammates, clearly in pain, try to pop his shoulder back into place while the rest of the group cheered him on with a drinking song. I hung up my cleats that night, while I could still walk away.

It wasn't long before carnival season arrived on the island. We're talking complete madness comparable to Mardi Gras—night and day for a month.

Memories are patchy from that point on. Somewhere amid all the parties, snorkeling, windsurfing, volleyball, and lounging, Toni announced that she was planning to sell off most of her possessions before heading back to the States.

"I've been thinking about staying on for a while," I told my friend, believing my words sounded reasonable.

Plenty of island compadres had offered me shelter. I could have lived there indefinitely and let ten years of my life drift away in the tropical breezes. I could become one of the characters I wanted to write about. The novel I'd planned to edit remained at the bottom of my suitcase.

"You're getting on a plane at the end of the week, is what you're going to do," Toni said. There was a harshness in her voice. "You've lived it up right when you weren't pining away for that girl you met in Utah, but it's time to get on with your life."

Toni was right, of course, but it was so damn hard to walk away from that level of comfort; a baby fighting to stay in the womb. She took me for one more bike ride. Turning into a nasty headwind, Toni offered this advice:

"Go get your girl, write some sentences you can be proud of, find your edge, and step right the hell over it every once in a while."

A week later, Toni and I parted with a long hug in the airport. She was headed for Death Valley to compete in the "Bad Bart," a grueling footrace that began at sea level and ended on top of a mountain. People regularly died on the way to the finish line. God love her, Toni's plan was to win the thing.

I actually took my friend's advice, and got engaged to the woman from Utah a year later. I've even managed to write a few coherent lines of prose along the way, and when I find myself performing without a net on occasion, Toni comes to mind.

No man's an island. Nor should he live on one forever. But take it from me, it sure doesn't hurt to visit now and then.

The Brothers Who Dreamed of Buying Back the Rodeo

FOR SOME OF US, DREAMS DIE HARD.

One morning in 1985, I awoke to the dream of riding a bicycle as far as my strength, desire, and restlessness would take me. That one aimless but powerful notion carried me farther than I ever imagined. An example of the creative forces of the universe looking out for its most wayward fools, I suppose.

More than a few fellow dreamers bent my ear along the road, but the pair that stands near the top of that outrageous and sometimes dubious heap would have to be Red and Tillerman; two brothers mismanaging a hotel along a small spit of highway in Wyoming, with dreams of buying back the rodeo.

I ended up on their doorstep near dusk one rainy day because, well, because I had not properly trained for the bicycle tour I'd chosen to undertake. Even a young, healthy body will take its revenge on the dumb sod who decides to force it to pedal a loaded touring bike up and down the Rocky Mountains without any prior notice.

The agony of muscles on the verge of collapse couldn't have come at a worse moment. I'd been so high on life until that point. I'd recently abandoned a job that wasn't right for me and was enjoying the big skies of the West when my legs decided to lock up and my lungs to burn like a welder's torch.

Joining forces with a group of strong riders headed for Jackson Hole earlier that day hadn't helped matters. I'd kept a pace I wasn't ready for and when the signs of muscle freeze kicked in, I dropped away from this pack of interesting and lively athletes with no more than an unceremonious wave.

The rest of the afternoon was spent solo, nursing my legs forward.

I talked to them nicely with each pedal stroke. Then I tried mind over matter for a while and maybe even attained a higher state of consciousness for a few miles, but the pain pulled me back down and increased its level of punishment for my arrogance in trying to escape.

I ended up lying by the side of the road, performing what is known in the business as "The Cockroach." This is where the only relief from severe muscle cramping is to stretch out on your back with legs pulled close to the chest. Often the offended appendages will spasm involuntarily, causing you to resemble a roach in its death throes. There's about as much dignity in it.

The sky opened up at that moment and a biting rain began to pelt my body. "Like a million tiny fingers massaging the pain away," I heard the imaginary voice from an infomercial announce. Yeah, right. I began to laugh/cry at my misfortune and wondered if I would find the strength to stand up before hypothermia set in. Between my laughter and a few coughing fits, I thought I detected voices.

"Look at the poor bastard in all that spandex. I think his horse has thrown him."

Moments later a couple of young, robust cowboys were standing over me. If they'd wanted to strip my bike of its valuables I was in no position to stop them.

"Red," the one on the right announced. "Tillerman," the other guy said, extending a callused hand in my direction.

I placed them in their midtwenties, with features straight out of a Marlboro commercial. Red and Tillerman. I remember thinking their names, said in combination, sounded like the moniker for a brewing company with a long and distinguished tradition.

"I'll be okay in a minute, guys," I said, trying to right myself. "I was just taking a short break."

"You always take breaks by dropping your ride in a ditch and lying in the dirt with your legs pointed to the sky?" Tillerman asked.

I gave him a winning smile and willed my muscles to relax, but had to hold on to the side of their horse trailer to keep my balance.

"Guess I just ran out of steam."

Red was already loading my bike and gear in with the horses, and I didn't protest. Within minutes I felt a connection with these earnest young men.

They loved the story about my encounter in Idaho with the old blind rancher.

"If you were on the rodeo circuit, today your horse would have gotten the better of you," Red hooted.

I quickly learned that Red and Tillerman were brothers and actual rodeo competitors of decent caliber.

"Our parents owned a rodeo when we were growing up," Red said with no small amount of pride. "They sold it about ten years ago and bought a nice-size ranch out here, and this hotel."

I followed Red's finger past the parking lot of a weather-worn hotel with what can only be described as a campy, 1950s rustic cabin charm.

"Then they went and died on us in a boating accident a few years ago," Tillerman added softly. "We never were water people."

A moment of silence passed between us in the cab of their truck.

"Anyway," Red continued. "They were thinking about our future when they bought this place and the ranch, but. . . ."

And over the course of the evening, a rather merry time spent in the den of their hotel being regaled with fascinating stories about the rodeo, and perusing photo albums of an obviously close family having the time of their lives earning a few bucks at something they loved, the dreams behind that little word *but* grew until I understood it to encompass their entire world.

". . . but we want to buy back the rodeo that our parents had for their whole lives and carry on the tradition," Red explained.

"Our plan is to sell the ranch to one of these film stars. We hear this Turner character is buying up half the West. Then, when we have the rodeo in place, we'll sell this hotel and take the rodeo onto the open road." Tillerman smiled wide enough to reveal a lip of tobacco when he spoke.

I discovered that the brothers had never spent significant time away from each other and the easy bonds of true friendship that happen between some siblings were strong.

"Our gimmick will be a celebrity rodeo, you know, good riders that look like celebrities. That or we'll get them to wear masks and make up so they look like stars. People will pay to come see someone who looks like Clint Eastwood or Liz Taylor rope cattle and bust broncos."

I smiled at the absurdity of their dream. This being America, though, I also didn't question the fact that something like that might sell.

"Gonna be a good old time once we get some momentum built up." Tillerman had a faraway look, happily lost somewhere out there on the circuit.

Looking around their trophy room filled with roping and riding awards, and pictures of the brothers in their teens working the circuit as clowns, they always had real smiles on their faces, exuberant moments caught on film. I said a silent prayer that they would stay as full of life throughout their days, regardless of where their dreams took them.

At different points in the evening, when I found myself alone briefly with Red or Tillerman, each confided in me that he was really following this rodeo dream so as not to let the other brother down.

There might have been some small truth in that, but you could see the personal desire in their eyes, a certain spark that caught when they talked about their plans.

"The only trouble we're having is in selling this hotel," Tillerman said. "It was where our parents stayed on their honeymoon, but the traffic doesn't pass by here since the interstate came along."

"Maybe you should hold on to the place," I suggested. "Never know when you're gonna want to come home."

The brothers waved their cowboy hats, hollering out "Metal Cowboy"—the name they had adopted for me, and hooting and whistling goodbye the next morning as my bike carried me to greener pastures.

I'd keep my eye out for Red and Tillerman's Celebrity Rodeo Extravaganza if I were you. Like I said, dreams die hard.

Half the Battle Is Getting to the Starting Line

WHEN PEOPLE ASK ME WHAT THE HARDEST PART OF BICYCLING AROUND the globe was, I never hesitate with my answer.

"Getting to the locations where I planned to start my adventures," I tell them with the intensity and conviction of a war veteran.

Forget the harsh weather, aching legs, grueling pedals up the sides of mountains, lonely hours of desolate blacktop, and occasional jaunts with inadequate supplies of water.

"Did you ever see that film *Trains, Planes and Automobiles*, starring Steve Martin and John Candy?" I add with a grin. "Well, the mishaps and mayhem that befell them only scratch the surface of my odysseys involving trains, planes, cars, boats, and buses. But mostly buses."

I actually wrote for a humor publication a satiric article about my trials and tribulations aboard the United States' only interstate bus service. It was titled "The Way of the Hound: How to Survive Domestic Bus Travel Using Zen Principles."

As a young man in search of adventure, I had a financial situation that was usually tenuous, often frightening, and downright bleak after an exceptionally long ride.

Of course, happiness rarely eluded me, but when you follow your dreams, it's hard not to find a certain amount of peace and satisfaction. But the old saying about choosing between time and money held true during most of my travels.

The thing was, I didn't want to wait until I was so old I'd have to hobble around the world. And joining the military to see far-flung lands was out of the question. I understand the need for defense, and commend those who have fought for our nation, but realistically, I couldn't see myself in that corporation for more than about fifteen seconds. Hell, I had enough trouble with the nine-to-five grind. The idea of having to take orders around the clock, wear muted colors, and possibly shoot people when all was said and done sent me in another direction.

But every choice has its price. The cost of my freedom—the opportunity to pedal wherever my legs and imagination were willing to take me—was often having to travel in less than first-class style.

It's a good thing I was young and strong and could endure many hours without sleep, and really, really wanted to see the world, because the bus rides, red-eye flights, overcrowded train compartments, and boats packed so tightly we resembled refugees in search of asylum nearly did me in.

My article about bus travel included subheadings like "So You Say You've Got $59 and a Brave Heart?"; "Hey, Your Seat Doesn't Go Back Either?"; "Routes, Schedules, Connections, and Other Myths"; "Making New Friends and How to Avoid Them Once the Bus Comes to a Complete Stop"; "Nightfall"; "Luggage, Now You See It, Now You Don't"; and "How to Spot Concealed Weapons and Potential Ax Murderers."

The reason I boarded the bus again and again, long after any sensible life form would have abandoned the prospect because it resembled Dante's Inferno in too many respects, was, frankly, that it offered me a way to go anywhere in the country for fifty-nine dollars.

Problem was, that's all it offered—a ride. Safety, comfort, schedules, air quality: those things were for wimps and people with more than sixty dollars to spend.

The average passenger on any given bus ride fell into one of several distinct categories. I've listed them in their order of abundance on any route.

1) A person recently released from prison.

2) A teenage runaway from a tragic home.

3) A young person, usually a budding musician, actor, model, or

writer, planning to become an overnight success as soon as he or she reached the LA bus terminal.

4) A tourist from Europe or Australia previously unaware of the vast and important differences between his or her mass transit system and ours.

5) A single parent with a half-dozen small children in tow. The only portion of the bus ride deal they recall is "children under twelve ride free!"

6) A seasonal migrant worker.

7) A retired couple on a limited income trying to see a country that has changed drastically since they envisioned this golden-years adventure decades earlier. (Warning: These people are extremely bitter.)

8) A recently fired salesman or postal worker. (Warning: These folks, also bitter, are armed and dangerous.)

9) A dreamer, wanderer, or other malcontent.

10) Me.

There are too many horrific moments to capture all of them in print, but a highlight included crossing through Alabama and having the pleasure of nearly being lynched at a small restaurant during a food break.

For some reason, the people running the place hadn't heard the Civil War was over, and I was in the company of friends with dark skin. It was a terrifying moment and would have been rather educational if I'd not been actually sprinting for a bus as rocks and other projectiles were launched at it.

Another time, I woke the driver up moments before we drove off an overpass. The fact that the front of the bus was scraping the guardrail and throwing sparks in every direction was my signal to scream bloody murder. At the next station, I was joined—okay, *I started a mutiny*, which produced a new driver. The other driver swore revenge. To this day, I think I see him in the occasional large crowd.

In the dead of an Iowa winter, I was forced to ride atop a crate of live chickens en route to some slaughterhouse. Standing outside a locked bus station with my core temperature dropping rapidly, I took my chances on the crates. Every few miles, I felt small pecks to my bottom.

Plenty of outright lunatics tried to sell me on get-rich schemes as the miles of highway rolled under us. I've been lied to by some of the most talented sociopaths in the business. Con men abounded, usually occupying the back of the bus, and more than a few strange propositions were fielded as I tried to get comfortable in seats designed, I believe, as sinister medical experiments.

Customs officials have searched my bags, small fires have been doused in bus bathrooms from Florida to Montana, and I actually learned to sleep with a can of Mace poised to go off at the first sign of danger.

Regarding the pain and agony of having to listen to other passengers' theories and philosophies: As the sun set across some breathtaking canyon lands in Arizona one evening, a pair of geniuses argued, in monosyllables, the existence of God while the rest of us tried to enjoy the miracle of light playing off rock.

When their debate reached a fever pitch after a solid half hour, a large man with dreadlocks that hung to his waist calmly set down the book he was reading and straddled the aisle. With the light silhouetting him from behind, the man resembled something from another world.

"Listen to me, and listen good," he bellowed in a voice with the depth and pitch of Darth Vader's. "I believe I speak for God and all that is creative in the universe when I say you people better end this conversation while you're ahead."

I was impressed, the bus filled with applause, someone said, "Amen," and we had a bit of peace the rest of the evening.

There was the occasional moment of tenderness between people, the touching goodbyes at stations, and some fun times that might have made traveling on the bus worth it, but I would be lying if I said good memories outweighed the bad times and long hours of misery.

The very last bus I rode broke down in the desert. As we huddled in some shade and one of the budding musicians broke out his guitar, launching into a very bad medley of Beatles tunes, I realized my bike was stored in the hull. Reliable transportation was only a few feet away. Canada was my destination on that particular journey, but I calculated that I could get to an airport faster than the bus was going to make it. The other passengers shook their heads as I pedaled away. Realizing a chapter had closed in my life, I rode with an energy I hadn't felt in a very long time.

Some of my plane rides were as bad as the bus, but never as long. I've been on trains that derailed, boats that have run aground, and aircraft that almost fell from the sky, but I never boarded another bus.

So the next time you rent the movie *Trains, Planes and Automobiles*, think of it as more of a documentary than a piece of fiction. And if you're a traveler, give a prayer of thanks when you actually get to where your adventure is supposed to begin.

For those brave, masochistic or financially strapped explorers waiting in the wings, I think they still offer that fifty-nine-dollar deal. Good luck and watch your back. And maybe, just maybe, I'll see you at the starting line.

Yo Ho Ho and a Bottle of Rum

On the last day of junior high school, Clark Mercer asked me if I wanted to sail to a spot of land near the Florida Keys known as the Dry Tortugas. We'd just finished spraying shaving cream on a horde of cheerleaders in training and were hiding out behind a sports shed waiting for the coast to clear. Our plan called for a quick dash to the bicycles and a clean getaway. The gauntlet was crawling with angry girls seeking revenge.

"It'll . . . be . . . a blast," Clark said between deep gulps of air. He was in the worst shape of any of my friends. At fourteen his build was that of a forty-year-old insurance salesman who'd logged too many hours behind the wheel. A shocking mop of dusty colored curls helped Clark resemble Einstein before fame and respect excused his appearance.

"Three weeks—just you, me, my dad, and open water. It's a family tradition. We've gone every year 'cept last summer. . . ." His voice trailed off as he studied the can of shaving cream in his hand.

Last summer his mother was getting ready to die. That's really how Clark and I became friends. All my cool pals made cracks about him on mornings when we'd ride our bikes into the lockup area. Big Red, Georgie Porgie. Acquaintances since elementary school, we grew closer when his mother got sick and couldn't drive him to class anymore. She'd asked my mom if Clark could bike with me to school—for safety. I protested at first, but my mom thought it a wonderful idea.

"We don't even have to talk," Clark said the first morning I met him at the corner. "I'm just doing this 'cause of my mom."

We bonded over the plight of overprotective parents, and, because we were fourteen, the misfortune of having any type of supervision, boundaries, or rules.

"So you wanna come to sea?" Clark wasn't breathing as hard anymore. I hopped to my feet, hit him with a steady stream of shaving cream, then broke into a sprint.

"I'll have to ask my folks!" I hollered, trying to get my bike unlocked before he paddled up with his can of cream.

" 'Course," he yelled after me, looking pleased that I'd agreed.

"Yo ho ho and a bottle of rum!" I sang once I was out of firing range. Three weeks of the pirate's life on the high seas had definite appeal.

We met early at our usual corner a few mornings later. I'd been instructed to pack light: one extra swimsuit and T-shirt, a cap, sunscreen, and something to read. I chose *Lord of the Flies* and a trash novel that had been wedged under our washing machine to keep it from rattling.

Looking at Clark in his deck shoes, tank top, and swim trunks, something was different. He seemed more self-assured, comfortable in his skin for the first time.

"Follow me," he said with confidence.

We rode our bikes to a spot behind the dockmaster's building. Someone's older brother whom I vaguely recognized, a guy from high school, an athlete for Godsakes, who wouldn't have given me more than a nod on the street was chatting with Clark like they'd served in a war together. He opened a backpack and displayed his wares; bottle rockets, smoke bombs, firecrackers, and Roman candles.

"I told you not to bring any of the loud stuff," Clark scolded him. "We'll take the rockets and the candles, but I was expecting some heavy duty product the way you were talking."

The guy asked us to wait while he went to his car, leaving Clark holding a backpack full of explosives. A gold mine we could have taken off with right then. I began looking for the hidden camera, this scene representing something outside the boundaries of the normal teenager hierarchy. And what had gotten into Clark, the Georgie Porgie of the schoolyard? I decided to chalk it up to the summer break. No more teachers, no more books. It was the hazy, lax season.

When the guy returned he was sporting a bona fide rocket: Two booster packets and a line fuse so long you just knew this thing was trouble.

"Three colors spill out from a petal burst, with a sparkle finale," the older kid boasted.

Clark bought the young entrepreneur out, purchasing an even half-dozen petal bursts. When we determined there wasn't enough room to smuggle all the contraband on board in my pack, we jettisoned everything but the sunscreen and the trash novel. I remember giving my copy of *Lord of the Flies* one more glance before tossing it into the dumpster. Honors English class was months away. I could be sailing the world with the merchant marines by then, or shipwrecked on a Carribean island with great reggae music and a couple of those cheerleaders in training.

Clark pulled up short as we pedaled toward the slip where his father was preparing the boat for departure. It was a thirty-four-foot Morgan, an actual yacht, with two masts and a small dinghy in tow.

What I knew that day about sailing wouldn't have filled a thimble, but the craft sure looked impressive, like it could almost sail itself.

"Dad's been a little off his game," Clark whispered. "You know, with everything that's happened this year. Don't take it personal if he's gruff."

How bad could it be? As a teenager I was required to take everything personally, but Clark was forgetting that I had a father of my own back at the house.

"Damn it Clark, I wanted to be through the channel an hour ago!" Herman Mercer bellowed, a can of cheap American beer in one hand and a bow line in the other.

He could have been Archie Bunker's twin brother except that the wardrobe was straight out of Gilligan's Island, right down to the white canvas boat shoes and skipper's cap.

"No time to stow those bicycles back at the club." He took a long pull on his beer for inspiration. "Lash 'em down inside the dinghy, then untie the stern lines."

Mr. Mercer made no acknowledgment of my presence until I crossed the threshold onto his vessel.

"Welcome aboard, Kurmaskie," he grunted. "Call me Herman, or Captain if you like. Now, let's see if we can make a sailor out of you!"

Given the fact that Herman, in his glory days, had won the SORSY, a brutal sailboat race covering the length of the Atlantic seaboard, his proposal was intimidating.

"This is some ship," I said, trying to make conversation.

"First lesson, this is a sailboat, son, a yacht to be exact, not a sloop, a schooner, or a pram. Ships have a bowsprit and three masts, each with a lower, top, and topgallant sail." He looked at me as though deciding whether to toss me back on land or use me for bait.

"Put your gear below deck and watch that boom," He tapped a long, swinging metal pole the mainsail attached to. "I've seen it crush a skull and knock another man's teeth into the ocean."

Herman grinned like a banshee.

I clutched the pack of smuggled fireworks to my chest, ducked into the cabin, and steeled myself for a three week pleasure cruise.

Confronting me in the forward storage cabin was a veritable brewery. Cases of canned beer lined the crawl spaces. I started to wonder just what I was getting into.

"Kurmaskie, bring me up another beer."

I felt the ship, I mean yacht, begin to move through the water.

"Aye aye, Captain!"

The great winch-handle debacle of 1979 took place late in the afternoon on our first day at sea. As we rounded Eggmont Key to begin a straight run down the Gulf Coast, Herman spotted a snag in the mainsail. It was near the top, some twenty-five feet above us. A line had tangled some of the nylon while we'd been engaged in a rather placid conversation about my family name.

"That's Polish isn't it?" he asked.

"Lithuanian," I clarified.

That's when he spotted the snag. After a number of unsuccessful attempts to free the line from the deck, Herman set down his beer.

"Clark, rig a pulley chair with a life jacket and have Kurmaskie winch you up there."

They might as well have been speaking Latin.

Clark quickly demonstrated what needed to be done on my end. As I cranked the winch, he rose in the makeshift chair until he neared the top of the mast. Though slowing, we were still sailing along at a decent clip. Clark appeared perfectly comfortable on his precarious perch. If my cool pals could see this kid now.

"Lower me a few feet." For some reason the winch was stuck.

"It won't budge," I yelled into the wind.

I couldn't hear Clark's reply, but Herman did.

"It's locked," the old sailor said. "Turn it clockwise first then back it off—but don't. . . ." I missed the rest of his instructions, what with the boom coming right at me and the wind carrying his words away.

After ducking, I tried repeatedly to free the winch.

"Clockwise, Kurmaskie . . . clockwise," Herman bellowed.

With Clark dangling thirty feet over the water, I was closing in on panic. The last thing I heard before I discovered a little black knob on the handle of the winch was Herman screaming: "Mickey Mouse, you Polack . . . Mickey Mouse!"

I would learn later that he was refering to the hands on the Mickey Mouse clock over the door of the galley. A cryptic message that seemed perfect reasonable to him at the time.

I flicked the black knob and the winch began spinning out of control. Clark plummeted to earth, Herman threw the boat into a sharp right turn, and I dove for the winch handle, which was now airborne and headed for the water. It bounced three times along the deck as I scrambled after it.

The winch handle and Clark hit the water at the same instant. I watched the expensive tool sink like a stone only inches from my fingertips. Clark, who'd missed the deck by a foot or two, was now being dragged alongside the vessel like a tarpon hooked on a line, his head barely out of the water, and the guy had the audacity to be smiling. I heard the sail drop behind me, nearly bringing the boat to a standstill.

"Pull him out of the water, Kurmaskie."

We sat on the deck licking our wounds in silence.

"At least the sail's not snagged anymore," Clark said.

Herman announced that he was going belowdecks for a while.

"Clark, you've got the helm. Don't let Kurmaskie near it, 'less we want to end up in Cuba."

Underway again, Clark whistled for me to join him.

"Got a little wild there," he said, like it was just another day at the office.

"Your dad hates me!"

"If he calls you names he doesn't hate you. When he stops talking to you all together you can start worrying."

A few hours later Herman emerged in a new shirt (the last clean item I'd see him wear that trip) carrying three cans of beer.

We toasted our safety and pledged a fresh start.

"Clark's mom was a quarter Polish," Herman announced as a way of apologizing for his earlier slur. "Now give me the rest of your beers, gentlemen. You're too young to be drinking a whole one yet."

He paused, surveying the horizon.

"Me and Clark are gonna teach you everything we know about sailing. By the way, the winch is coming out of your pay." He cracked a smile. "Come over here and let me show you how to tack."

"Aye aye, Captain."

The next few days passed without incident. We fell into a lazy routine, sailing the peaceful waters of the Gulf of Mexico. Dolphins would run the bow for miles, as I cultivated something between a tan and a burn and read my trash novel on the hammock near the front of the boat.

Herman had an affinity for show tunes and Broadway musicals. We listened to the soundtrack from *South Pacific* until I knew the words by heart. While the rest of the world was Staying Alive to the Bee Gees, we were Washing That Man Right Out of My Hair. When we tuned in the radio once, Herman went ballistic.

"It's all crap . . . 'less you can find a little Sinatra on there?"

Midway through the first week, with a good coat of salt on my skin and my hair quickly tangling its way toward dreadlocks, I felt like I was getting the hang of sailing. No more equipment had gone into the water and I understood how some things worked. Enough so that I put in my two cents when it came time to plot a course or determine wind speed and direction. Then I experienced my first squall line at sea. It was twilight on what felt like another evening in paradise.

"Better start tying things down?" Clark asked his dad.

Herman nodded.

"How do you know it's gonna blow?" I wondered.

"Winds out of the south after 4 P.M." Clark noted. "And you can smell the fresh water on the breeze."

By 8 P.M., under clear skies, I couldn't help giving them a hard time, but they didn't seem to care.

Clark and Herman were in a increasingly heated discussion about whether to bring down the sail and dig in or add the jib and outrun the storm.

"What storm!" I chuckled.

Clark asked me to find the stars on the western horizon. I couldn't. A wall of darkness was slowly chewing them up. As the first raindrops arrived, the two real sailors aboard were engaged in a screaming match.

"We can outrun it, Dad!"

"I'm ordering you to tie down that jib!"

"This ain't the navy, Dad. We could be anchored in a nice shoal by now."

They each had a hold of a section of the jib.

"The only person in this family ever listened to me was your mother."

Clark let go of the jib.

"She had to. . . . She was afraid of you!"

Herman tried to say something, but all he managed were stammering sounds. Clark stomped back to the wheel just as the first real sheet of rain arrived. The boat keeled drastically with the swelling waves and I couldn't tell if Herman was still on board.

"You might want to head below, Joe," Clark ordered. "It's going to get nasty for a while."

I'd love to say that I bounded though the rain to help Herman lash the jib down, but in truth I crawled into a bunk and fought a bout of seasickness. The waves pounded and the wind howled. At one point in the night I thought the boat was going to capsize and we'd be lost at sea. I wrote off the dinghy and our bicycles, and cursed myself for ever wanting to be a pirate. Somehow, I drifted off and when I awoke the sun was shining and the smell of pancakes filled the cabin.

Clark was no longer the dumpy kid from school. Freed from the rules of the land he'd turned into Captain Ahab standing up to his dad and braving six-foot seas to hold the boat on course.

"Get some food in you so we can go spinnaker flying," he said.

There was no judgment in Clark's voice regarding the way I'd handled myself during the storm.

"Sorry about last night. Is your Dad talking to you?"

Clark tossed me a pancake, Frisbee-style.

"Stayed up most of the night together on deck. It was a wicked bit of weather. We're fine. Sailors have thick skins, you know."

I didn't know, but I was learning.

On a small dot of land dubbed Cabbage Key, Herman motored the dinghy to shore and dropped us and our bikes on the beach for an afternoon of exploring. We'd been down to swim trunks and tennis shoes for days. The plan was to meet at the island's one restaurant at sundown.

"What's he gonna do?" I asked.

"Fish and drink," Clark replied. "And probably think about Mom. This was one of their favorite places. They came here for Christmas once." As the trip progressed, Clark became more comfortable talking about her.

Cabbage Key was practically deserted. It was a lush Florida island, something right out of *Lord of the Flies,* though I couldn't make that comparison at the time, since my head was filled only with semi-lurid scenes from a trash novel. Nevertheless, I felt more like a pirate during those few hours than at any point since.

I nicknamed my bike the Jolly Roger, tied a bandanna around my head, and raced Clark up and down the beach. Our chains were so dry and encrusted from all the salt water that the bikes made a terrible racket. Still, we pedaled into the deep woods, jumping downed logs, trying to dodge large webs strung by king crown spiders and slashing our wheels through thick stands of palmetto bushes.

Clark mounted part of a large shell on the front of his handlebars, using the broken reflector post to hold it in place. And I fashioned a spear out of a piece of bamboo and wedged it across the frame. We thought to hunt for big game, but the noisy bikes warned what mammals lived on the island of our arrival.

A low spot inland was discovered and we spent much of the afternoon pedaling through it, splashing water and sandy mud in all directions, making crawfish and amphibious creatures scatter.

A soft rain began to fall as we pedaled our bikes along the packed sand en route to dinner. Straddling our bikes, we shared a ripe mango while the rain cleaned us of the sea.

"I was just starting to get to know her as a person," Clark said. "Not just as my mother. Now all the hoping in the world won't let me see her again."

We passed the mango back and forth a few times before Clark finished it off, then heaved the pit into the water.

"Last thing Mom said to me was, 'Take care of your dad for me.'"

We listened to the water lap the shore. I looked at Clark, this sad, strong kid whom no one at school knew a damn thing about.

I couldn't help it. I said, "Take care of him? That's a helluva tall order, don't you think?"

It took Clark a moment, but he found a way to smile. His grin spread until we both fell into laughter.

The restaurant was a building on stilts in a small lagoon. The room we ordered steaks in was covered, from floor to ceiling, with dollar bills shellacked in place and photos of fishermen displaying their enormous catches.

Before we left, Herman stood us in front of a picture of himself, his wife, and a huge tarpon. They looked radiant. I left father and son to ponder it while I waited on the deck listening to water lap against the roots of mangroves.

For one of our last evenings at sea, we'd anchored at Johnson Shoals. When the tide went out, Clark taught me how to dig for clams. Anywhere a little airhole pulsates, you dig. We brought a bucket back to the boat adding it to Herman's catch of Spanish mackerel.

"Three essentials for making any seafood dish taste perfect." Herman said, holding up a stick of butter, a couple of lemons, and a can of beer. He was correct. It's the recipe I still follow today.

After dinner, Clark told me to get the fireworks and meet him in the dinghy. Motoring a few hundred yards from the yacht, Clark cut the engine and readied the rockets and candles for launch.

"You know, if we hid these from your dad this whole time, isn't it defeating the purpose to shoot them off while he's sitting right there on the deck?"

Clark smiled in the glow of a lit match. "I wasn't hiding them because he'd get mad, it's 'cause I wanted to surprise him."

So we hosted our own Fourth of July fireworks display on a warm evening in late June. Between the whistling screeches of rockets shooting for the heavens, we could hear, now and then, Herman hooting and clapping from the deck.

"Well done," he said as we boarded, handing each of us a full can of beer. He gave Clark's shoulder an extra pat or two.

We sat drinking in comfortable silence, admiring the stars and mulling over a few of life's mysteries. Two kids looking forward and a world-weary sailor looking back.

I could see my family waiting for me on the beach across the jetty from the yacht club when we pulled into the slip. My people have always been big on reunions. Herman and Clark waved to me as I pedaled up the dock. For some reason it finally clicked into place. The boat was named the *Darla* after his wife. I'd always called her Mrs. Mercer, but now she was so much more to me than a face I barely remembered in the driver's seat of their station wagon. She'd been someone's child, sister, mother, lover, wife, and fishing partner. The realization that her absence gave me the chance to play pirate one lazy summer on the edge of my childhood will always taste bittersweet.

I wished that Clark's mom could have just one more ride across the waves. Seeing her name there on the back of the boat gave me hope that in a small way, maybe she always would.

Good Night, Samantha

A SOLO BICYCLING ADVENTURE OF ANY DISTANCE AND DURATION IS marked by ups and downs that have nothing to do with the difficulty of the terrain. My travels proved this beyond question—and then some.

Many of my days in the saddle brimmed to capacity with scenes of breathtaking beauty and encounters with characters so twisted, entertaining, or enlightening that I often wondered if I hadn't fallen into Alice's famed rabbit hole somewhere along the blacktop. My time on two wheels demonstrated that the world will always be a deeply mysterious place and immeasurable, not necessarily in geographic terms, but in wonder.

That said, for all the epiphanies the road served up, there were plenty of days when it was simply about survival. Memories of dedicating every ounce of strength to completing just one more pedal stroke haunt me in Technicolor. The recollection of cresting a gigantic hill in a steady downpour only to be faced with a pitifully short plateau, then (oh, the horror) an even more menacing incline, still sends shivers through me.

Lugging a fully loaded touring bicycle around the globe is no picnic. Gravity is a constant enemy, and it has many foot soldiers, not the least of which are wind, fierce weather, leg cramps, physical exhaustion, and traffic. These bad boys are always ready for a good fight.

But the real demons come from within—all those emotional challenges that hit you when the physical ones have worn you raw. Under the right conditions, a long-distance cyclist will beg the question, "Just why am I voluntarily participating in this agony?" If a rider has the strength to make such a query, it means he has plenty of gas left in the tank.

It's when that primordial portion of the cyclist's brain takes over and his only focus is to find the sweet comfort of shelter and the cradling arms of sleep that he has touched bottom. I was given the privilege of exploring such depths a few weeks into my first long-distance ride.

Dragging myself through a small hamlet in Maine, not far from the capital, I noticed I'd already logged triple digits in the miles department, the day was nearly over, and the rain had not let up since South Gorham.

The lights of a store tucked away at the base of a hill beckoned to what was left of me and I braked hard, throwing more water onto my already drenched body. A quick morsel of advice to potential globe-trotting cyclists: never skimp on rain gear. Just don't do it.

The couple who ran the store were friendly and warmhearted. In an endearing Maine accent, the man told me I reminded him of a tabby cat he'd fished out of the river once. As we made a bit of small talk, the woman brought me a towel. By that time of day, the shop was almost as empty as I felt. I inquired if there was a hotel or bed-and-breakfast in the area. Failing that, I'd be more than willing to pay someone to let me dry out myself and my gear in a barn or shed.

They educated me about the dimensions of their little community, then took a long moment and shared some eye contact with each other, before offering me the use of their guest room above the store. I figured the pause had been to size me up. Later, I would realize that it had more to do with the upstairs room, and the person who'd once occupied it.

While I drank in the soothing warmth of a pot of tea, the couple asked about my travels. As we talked, my eye caught the image of a clear pickle jar labeled SAMANTHA SMITH MEMORIAL STATUE FUND on the store counter. The name rang a bell, and I asked the couple about it.

Samantha Smith was an eleven-year-old girl who, in 1982, wrote a letter to the leader of the Soviet Union, Yuri Andropov, telling him she was worried about the possibility of nuclear war. A young girl eloquently pleaded for peace, and the leader of a superpower responded.

She made history when she was invited to the Soviet Union, beginning a journey for peace that took her on all manner of adventures around the globe. Her journey ended in August 1985 when she and her father were killed in a plane crash on their way back to Maine.

The couple sitting across from me that evening were Samantha's relatives. It had been a little more than a year since the girl's death. I tucked a few bills into the jar.

When I hauled my gear into the upstairs room, I knew immediately it had to have been Samantha's place when she visited. Exhausted beyond rational thought, I planned to fall right to sleep, but maybe the tea had been caffeinated. Whatever the case, I sat for a while on the edge of the bed, shaky and wired, soaking in the vibrant flavors of a young girl's room.

I once read a piece of fiction once about a civilization of people who had cheated death. They'd found the secrets of immortality; suffered no more pain and injury, nor the effects of age. Free to build utopia, they lost the desire to do more than reach a certain level of comfort. They put off their dreams until tomorrow, because tomorrow was an unlimited resource. Then, for no apparent reason, one member of this world began to age normally, bleed, and feel pain. Gradually, he became filled with passion, urgency, and the ability to see his dreams through. He also became the envy of the world.

Because his time was limited, it held value. The man created works of art, laughed with abandon, and went straight to the heart of things.

That night, I lay down in what might have been the bed of a girl who appeared to have lived fully in her short ride through life, who got to the heart of things. I slept soundly and well, surrounded by her memories.

The next morning I would travel into the rest of my own dreams, and over the years, when I've fallen short, or have felt like putting them off until tomorrow, I've taken strength and comfort in the fact that, though I never met Samantha, I brushed past her essence, and came away changed.

Before surrendering to sleep, I found a tape player on the bed-stand. Through the darkness I listened to the voices of a group of friends—girls having fun at a slumber party, maybe—reach into the night.

They were singing doo-wop tunes and harmonizing. On the final seconds of the tape, the girls pretended to be on stage at a rock concert. They made crowd noises and one voice called out, "Good night, America," as the tape ended.

I want to believe it was Samantha.

What I do know is that the arc of her life soared, and the things she believed in and worked for, peace and friendship between Russia and the United States, came to pass, if not in her lifetime.

Good night, Samantha.

Big Air

THE KIDS THESE DAYS WILL RISK EVERYTHING FOR A FEW MOMENTS OF "big air." And in what I like to consider my more adult moments, I scoff at such brazen risks of life and limb.

When ESPN 2 runs film clips featuring grinning teens hopping from helicopters to snowboard the near-vertical faces of mountains, I mumble something like, "Speed kills." And when I see other reckless souls intentionally paddling into waves the size of skyscrapers in search of prize money some magazine is offering to surf the biggest wave of the season, I cringe and yell, "The ocean doesn't care if you've got an endorsement contract!"

My wife only has to remind me how I spent the majority of my youth to quiet me down.

"At least I used my judgment when I risked my life. The saddle of a bicycle is a safe perch compared to where these kids put themselves today."

But my conviction falters as I watch young bodies defy gravity, laughing at the edge of the abyss. Have I gotten so settled that I won't allow for the privileges of youth? At least I'm not standing in the front yard wearing black dress socks, boxer shorts, and a V-neck T-shirt, snarling at the neighbor's kids yet.

The hint of a smile creeps across my face as I remember not-so-distant glory days. I did take a few chances now and then, so maybe it's just jealousy.

I watch a guy on television with a spiderlike build climb a rock face without ropes. Talk about not leaving yourself any margin for error. No, it's not always jealousy on my part; some of these people are certifiable.

Fortunately, I got to meet a number of these characters, or maybe it was their older brothers and sisters, during stops along my cycling adventures. Tagging along with a few of them gave me a bit of insight as to why they live for risk. What many of these folks lack in the caution department they compensate for with loads of enthusiasm, intensity, charm, and a certain zest for life. During the time I hung out with them, it was never boring.

In Perth, Australia, I remember being mesmerized by surfers tackling monster waves with casual abandon long after I'd put up my board. I thought I saw a large pistol with a holster strapped around the waist of one of the surfers. I wrote it off to the strong sun of the southern hemisphere playing tricks on me.

Later, sitting around a campfire with a group of the same surfers, I had to ask.

"You weren't seeing things, mate. That's just Trevin. He had a nasty run-in with a Great White a few years back. Now he packs a plastic-coated 9 mm in case another one tries to make him lunch. He got off several shots a couple of months ago, but it turned out to be a manta ray. He digs the rush of shark hunting in the big waves."

If I hadn't seen the weapon, I'd have thought these guys were trying to pull one over on the American. Instead, I conjured visions of Trevin sliding down the face of an enormous wave, snapping off shots as a Great White gave chase.

Maybe the Olympic Committee should consider including this activity as a sport during the 2000 Games in Australia. But then, Trevin might be the only competitor.

I don't know what was more disturbing: That Trevin packed heat when he surfed, or that none of his peers thought it out of the ordinary.

Everywhere I went, there were people willing to risk it all for a few moments of adrenaline. A kayaker in South America told me he intentionally went down large falls and over rapids *backward* to get that high that comes with uncertainty and imminent disaster.

In Yosemite, I spent the better part of a week with a group of thrill-seekers who enjoyed climbing mountains, then base jumping from the peaks. That's where you leap into space with a small parachute and hope for the best.

I bumped into two of the climbers at a summit gas station, the last building before an eight-thousand-foot winding descent takes you into Yosemite Valley. They were on bicycles and resembled sane individuals during our first conversation. They asked about my travels and got a kick out of the case of wine bungeed to the back rack of my bike.

"I don't have some rabid drinking problem," I explained. "I acquired this extra weight from a rich guy I met yesterday—pushed his overheating SUV off the road along an especially steep section of Priest's Grade." We were dodging motor homes and station wagons piloted by reckless tourists trying like hell to stay on a schedule that would allow them to see all the notable points of interest during their seven days away from the salt mines.

"I've been trying to flag down some help for nearly an hour," the rich guy told me. "But I never dreamed it would arrive by bicycle."

We spotted a loose tube to the water pump and all was fixed in a matter of minutes. He invited me for dinner at his vacation home. When I left the next morning it was with a case of rather expensive wine, hand-selected from his cellar. "I didn't have the heart to leave it. Besides, I like the occasional glass of wine."

One of the climbers got off his bicycle to look at the label on the wine. "It's got to add a lot of wind drag, but I wouldn't have left it either," he said.

We decided to ride as a group to decrease the chances of a vehicle trying to pass us on such a tight hill. It wasn't the cars I should have been worried about. As we sped down the hill, the front rider began pedaling to pick up more speed. I had to match his cadence to maintain the tight formation. If I slowed down, I ran the risk of the rider directly off the left side of my back wheel smashing into me. I yelled something about easing up, but my words were lost in the wind, or the front man just didn't care.

My little computer that measures speed showed us at 52 mph.

Trapped, I held on for dear life, thinking the next pebble in the road was going to do us in.

Then we shot through a long tunnel. Orange neon lights ripped by every second or two, my ears popped and my eyes teared up as they tried to adjust to the rapid changes. The lights blasted by so quickly that it felt as if they were leaving a phantom trail of color. When I came out the other side of the tunnel, we were still barreling down the road at more than 50 mph. I let go of a primal yell and held on.

That's when the front man slammed on his brakes. Somehow I managed to avoid him, pump my own brakes, and bring myself to a gravity-defying stop, all in the course of an instant or two. I held my breath as I waited for the rider behind me to knock us both off the cliff.

"What the hell were you thinking?" I asked, still a bit shaky.

"Look," is all he said.

And I did. Stretched out around and below us was something from an Ansel Adams photograph. Mountains, trees, and a waterfall spilling thousands of feet to the valley floor jumped out at me. The sun was setting behind the peaks and everything was bathed in a purple light. My near-death experience forgotten, we stood there a while in silence.

The rest of the week, I voluntarily camped and climbed with these lunatics. When conditions weren't right for climbing, we played no-shirt hacky sack, a game in which the goal was to leave on your opponent's bare skin as many red spots as possible from the hacky sack.

I played that game only once.

And I climbed up Half Dome only once, but I don't regret the experience, though it was one of the hardest things I've ever attempted in my life. I'm not built for rock climbing, but months of bicycling allowed me the stamina to reach the top—that, and grim determination. I had plenty of time during the climb to listen to members of this group of thrill seekers speculate why they traveled the world, existing as nomads in search of the next, and possibly the last, rush of their lives. It was one of the few times in my life I was too exhausted to speak very much.

So they carried the conversation as they hoisted themselves, and me at times, up the mountain with grace and skill.

There was talk about the possibility of perfection, of being seduced by the obsession and passion found only at the edge of the envelope; the personal struggle to conquer fatigue and master rage, fear, disappointment, weakness, and other emotional boundaries. A few of them said they started out doing it to shock their families, but grew addicted to thrill.

But a guy nicknamed Fez summed it up best. He had, by some miracle, hauled a small BMX bicycle up the mountain with him. He planned to ride it off the cliff, free-fall for a time before opening a parachute, and land safely on the ground. Not only was this against park regulations and several laws, it seemed a step beyond foolhardy.

"You only die once," Fez told me. "And while I'm here, I'm looking for big air and a clean ride. The rest is just waiting."

"Even if it's your last ride?" I asked.

He answered me with a smile, then pedaled into space.

I remember thinking at the time how distorted and misplaced this kid's energy was. But as he flew off the mountain, for a moment—just an instant—I wanted to switch places with him. I longed to navigate in the rarefied atmosphere between madness and epiphany.

Back at the campsite I ended up sharing that whole case of wine with those gonzo climbers getting ready for another assault on Half Dome. Everybody drank right from the bottles between games of killer hacky sack and stories of daring told around the campfire. That evening reminded me of a postbattle scene from Tolkien's *The Lord of the Rings*. Reckless warriors who just didn't think that much about tomorrow.

Over the years, I've found my own thrills in less drastic ways, but when I add it all up, I can't say that riding a bike around the world is that much different from pedaling off a mountain. So who am I to throw stones? I'm just a Metal Cowboy piecing together the puzzle of life in my own time and way. And taking my rides, grabbing my big air where I can find it.

But just for the record, the guy with the surfboard and the pistol . . . now he really was out of his mind.

The Angel of Cherry Hill, New Jersey

THE FUNNY THING ABOUT RIDING INTO ADVENTURE WITHOUT REGARD for the consequences is that often you get more than you bargained for. Sometimes the adventure swallows you whole and spits back only a pile of bones.

I was more lucky than careful, but never flinched at the cost of doing business in the land of adrenaline-charged abandon. I complained at times, but couldn't seem to back away. These rides were just something I had to do.

Each day sitting tall in the saddle of my bicycle was an experience that, when taken as a whole, has yet to be matched. The highs soared, but when things fell apart, there was no safety net.

Who you gonna call when the water runs out along a bone-dry red strip of Australian desert? Or the bolts of lightning are crashing so close that the sharp, metallic stench of ozone is everywhere, and you're the tallest thing for miles—pedaling a chunk of metal, no less? In that particular situation, I chose to lie down along the side of the road and scream, knowing that I was still the high point on the horizon.

Vehicles ran me off the blacktop, dogs gave chase, food in developing nations and Georgia poisoned me, and several nasty little confrontations—which could have gone either way—arose with my fellow man. And still I dusted the panniers off every year or so, flipped open the atlas, and set out again.

I wanted to explore, see things firsthand, and there's no denying the powerful urge to claim my time and place in this world. But an incident that occurred during my first ride, the trip from Maine to Florida, helped spur me forward and, I believe, provided the courage to roll farther than I ever considered possible.

Cherry Hill, New Jersey, looked like the end of the line for what was then a rather novice Metal Cowboy. Several paychecks from my former employer were supposed to rendezvous with me in Long Island, at my relatives' home. When the cash didn't arrive, I brushed it off. Seven hundred miles of cycling under my belt had produced a cockiness and high level of confidence, however misplaced.

I'd just make do. Also, I still had a few bills tucked inside the tent bag.

A week later and a couple of hundred miles farther south, the situation had become, at least in my mind, critical. I stood on the campus of a beautifully manicured Ivy League school holding a telephone receiver in my hand long after the line had gone dead. Payroll had screwed something up; checks couldn't be reissued until the following month.

Studying fresh-faced students walking with bounce and purpose to their classes, I found that my anger dissipated, only to be replaced by fear. I mounted my bicycle with twenty-nine dollars to my name, the confidence long gone.

On later cycling adventures, money never determined whether a ride would continue, but at that moment I allowed that I'd seen some great country, had enjoyed what I rationalized was a lifetime of experiences, and decided that this adventure needed to be wrapped up before it became too real for comfort.

Truth was, I'd never wanted for much growing up, or had my limits tested outside of a controlled setting. I was tired, and more than a little relieved by the notion of loading my bike into a Greyhound bound for Florida.

It was dusk on the following day; I'd made it to the Cherry Hill bus depot with twenty-five dollars left in the till, and things appeared to be going my way. I scavenged a box that would fit my disassembled bike and dove into the task of taking apart the trusty ride.

"What do you mean twenty-five dollars will only get me to

Virginia? It says right there fifty-nine dollars will take me to the other side of the country!" The clerk agreed with the logic of my argument, but could only issue a ticket that might get me as far as the Mason-Dixon line. I pointed at the taped-up box with all my gear secured inside, but no one was watching.

It's a cruel world out there, and the light was fading from the sky. I needed to put my bike back together and find somewhere to camp outside the downtown area.

I remember trying to boost my spirits with thoughts of people suffering atrocities in war-torn countries, but I couldn't shake the idea that I was still in a tight spot. It's a long way to Florida on a bike with twenty-five dollars in your pocket.

I stormed over to my box, starting to feel defiant as the desperation crept in. Then, I noticed a well-dressed man in his fifties watching me. He'd worked his way over from the other side of the station, close to the doors. Great; the way things were going, he was probably some sexual deviant on the prowl.

He asked me about my travels, the different pieces of bike equipment I was dealing with, and what my parents thought of this adventure. I answered his questions, but didn't put a lot of effort into it. My thoughts kept drifting to jobs I might have to perform along the road. Images of backbreaking work like mining coal or picking cotton kept coming to mind.

Asking my parents for help was not an option. They would have jumped at the chance to lend a hand, but I had something to prove. What it could be was not very clear at that moment, but I kept putting my bike together just the same.

The man followed me out into the parking lot. I'd discarded any fear of him. He had kind eyes, and I was nearly a foot taller and outweighed him by fifty pounds. He held out one of my panniers and began to speak in nearly a whisper.

"Watching you work on your bike in there reminded me of my son." The well-dressed man peered out at the highway. "His name was Steven and cars were his thing. He built my old Plymouth into an honest-to-goodness muscle car. Never talked about college and I never pushed it. If he wanted to work on cars the rest of his life, that was okay with me."

I was listening now.

"His friend said the car had stalled out at the top of the hill and Steven was pushing it off the road when the other car slammed into the back of the Plymouth."

The man explained his reason for being at the station was to pick up some relatives for Steven's funeral.

"Years ago, I brought Stevy down here to meet a family member coming in for the holidays. We threw snowballs at the buses as they pulled in and out of the lot," he said.

It was nearly dark by then. The man reached out to shake my hand, tears welling up in the corners of his eyes.

"I hated the music Stevy listened to and was always giving him grief about it." The man shook his head. "You probably enjoy the same god-awful stuff."

I laughed for the first time that evening. "Probably," I said.

"Look, I overheard your situation. Stevy would have loved what you're doing. He always wanted to drive cross-country."

I realized that he'd slipped a wad of money into my hand.

"I'd like to see you finish your ride safely. Maybe that will help."

I tried to give it back to him, but the man wouldn't hear of it.

"Think of it as a gift from my son."

A quick calculation showed that I now had enough money to get back on the bus, and part of me craved to do just that. But as I pedaled out of the city, the night air helped to clear my thoughts.

His money might get me as far as the Carolinas; after that, I'd have to take my chances, but the resources had become secondary in the bigger scheme of things. I was determined to finish the ride—coast right up to my parents' doorstep.

Steven gave me something intangible that evening. And though my taste in music changed over the course of my travels, I often imagined him riding shotgun, forever young, laughing and turning to another page in the atlas as I wheeled my bike onto the road for just one more adventure.

The Next Parade

WHAT IS IT ABOUT A PARADE THAT SENDS PEOPLE FLOCKING TO THE curbs of small towns and big cities like moths to the light?

Shut-ins will find someone to wheel them to the edge of the route, parents who are chronically late for everything leave hours ahead of time to secure prime parade real estate for their children, shop owners happily close their doors for a few hours, and young couples can be seen bouncing toddlers on their shoulders and tying balloons to the handles of strollers.

So what's the appeal? Why will people drop what they're doing to stand in the heat of a July afternoon or the numbing chill of a December evening to watch their fellow citizens, friends and strangers alike, drive, cartwheel, spin, lumber, and march down Main Street? Dressed in ornate, silly, and sublime costumes, they wave like royalty from floats that only the day before were ordinary flatbed trucks loaded with produce and parked unceremoniously behind the local grocery store.

And it seems no one is immune to the lure of a parade.

Even the jaded businessman can be observed, jacket tossed casually over his shoulder, tie loosened, hovering a few rows back in the crowd with a bag of popcorn in hand. He watches longingly as youngsters dive and scramble for cheap beaded necklaces, plastic gold coins, and hard candy. Despite his best efforts to act his age, the occasional smile betrays the businessman's memories of a simpler time.

Parades are so simple. You pick a date and announce it. Tell the

marching band where to march, the Shriners where to drive their
funny little cars, put the sheriff with his flashing lights out front and
the politicians somewhere in the middle to help break up the excitement of all those floats, and always, always save something special for
the finale.

Easy as pie.

At least that's what I thought until I bicycled into a small North
Carolina town preparing for its annual Halloween parade and hoedown.

"Where you coming from on that bike of yours?" a rotund gentleman in his late fifties asked from the only booth in the diner with a
RESERVED sign on its table. I was pedaling through the high country
along the Blue Ridge Parkway, taking in wrenchingly beautiful
scenery, and, at that moment, taking in another piece of apple pie
à la mode. You can never go wrong ordering pie from a small-town
diner. It's in the Constitution somewhere.

"Canada," I offered with a smile that presumed he'd want to
know more. For no particular reason I often gave vague answers to
initial questions about my travels. Maybe I enjoyed cultivating the
mysterious-stranger persona a little too much when I was on the road.

"You don't sound like a Canuck," he declared merrily and proceeded to bring his sizable girth, along with a rather large serving of turkey
and gravy, across the room.

"May I join you?" he asked.

I'm gonna refuse a man this big balancing a plate of food and
breathing heavy from the six-yard hike across the diner?

"Please!" I stood and we shook hands.

He came down with a solid thud across the booth.

"The name's Stewy Strickland. I'm the mayor of what I believe to
be one of the finest communities in all of the Carolinas."

You've got to figure when somebody's been given a name as colorful as Stewy Strickland eventually he's going to rise to most of life's
occasions.

Stewy did not disappoint me.

I shared that I was headed for Florida—a young writer pedaling
the blue highways of America in search of freedom, exercise, good

stories, and a few indelible images, moments of clarity and beauty to tuck away for that day when I would be well on the way to decaying, and need them the most.

"That's damn good," Stewy hooted, slapping the table "With a plan like that, son, you may never feel old enough to call upon those memories. Nevertheless, I hope our neck of the woods hasn't let you down?"

Miles of fiery red, orange, and yellow leaves, some dropping as I rode along, the dying embers of the fall along the parkway, sprang to mind.

Stewy's face turned serious, bringing me back from my daydream.

"Are you saving your receipts? You can charge this trip off your taxes, call it field research!" he said, a helpful spark in his eye. I liked this large public servant right away, but if there had been any doubt that Stewy really was a politician, it was dashed right then. I didn't have the heart to tell him I wouldn't make enough money that year, or for many more to come, to worry about tax shelters and write-offs.

Stewy gobbled up his lunch while I entertained him with a few choice stories from my roads-less-pedaled collection. When a break in the conversation arrived, Stewy finished the last swallow of his iced tea, wiped his mouth thoughtfully, then picked up my helmet, which had been sitting on the table between us. He was mulling something over.

"How'd you like to hang around our little hamlet for another day or two, courtesy of the mayor's office?" He gave me a wink reserved for southern gentlemen sharing whiskey and lies.

I flashed him a wry smile. "You sitting on a good story, Stewy?"

The mayor let go of a hearty laugh. "Hell, every town has its share of good stories . . . a few humdingers and others, well, not for public consumption, but what I'm talking about is our Halloween parade. It comes once a year whether I want it to or not, but it's something to put on the calendar."

"Not exactly Pulitzer material, Stewy," I remember thinking, but it was a cute town, my legs were beat, and I couldn't remember the last time I'd seen a parade without a remote in my hand. "Lead the way," I told him.

The way took us to Roger's house, one of Stewy's many relatives in town. There a family was in swing, assembling the coveted tobacco queen float. Mrs. Strickland, Stewy's sister, waved as we pulled Stewy's pickup truck into the drive. She was knee-deep in colored streamers and chicken wire. Debbie, who couldn't have been more than ten, was enthusiastically assisting her mom. Clifton, whom I placed on the verge of becoming a teenager, was meticulously decorating a go-cart with blinking lights, skeletons, and pumpkin cutouts. Every once in a while he'd break his concentration to shoot the staple gun into a nearby bush or tree. He did this as much to enjoy the little slices of metal fly though the air as to see if anyone would tell him to stop.

"Don't waste those staples, 'less you want to buy the next box!" Mrs. Strickland scolded, not even looking up to witness this latest staple-gun safety violation.

And off to the side, wearing headphones, short shorts, and a selection of makeup one could only politely describe as the darkest depths of winter, sat Donna.

I recognized the sullen look on her face, the familiar disenfranchised slouch: She had to be a high school senior counting the months until freedom. As her paintbrush labored across a small section of the float, I thought, "She's almost moving slow enough to find employment in the fast-food industry."

Stewy called the group away from their tasks and introduced me around. I can honestly say that at few times in my life have I ever felt more welcomed, comfortable and accepted at face value by a group of strangers. My arrival gave them an excuse to break for lunch.

Clifton got off a couple more shots with the staple gun.

"You'd better not be aiming for those birds, mister," Mrs. Strickland called out from the back porch.

The local fowl scattered for safety. I wheeled my bike into the garage.

Over tuna fish sandwiches and soup, I learned that the tobacco queen float was the second to last in the parade. The queen, who got to wave from her perch atop a throne while being fanned by tobacco-leaf-bearing slaves, was a much sought-after role chosen via secret ballot by the high school student body. It was the finale.

The arrival of the scarecrow float actually closed out the rolling celebration, but the tobacco queen held more zing. Like Santa's appearance at the end of Christmas parades, the scarecrow propped in his place along a fence line surrounded by an idyllic fall scene simply signaled the crowd to head for the community center and enjoy themselves at the hoedown.

"I'm going to be one of the ladies-in-waiting on the tobacco queen float," Debbie said.

Donna offered a pained expression filled with loathing and sarcasm. "And I'm gonna be one of the maids-a-barfing on the sidelines when that float rolls by."

Ah, sisterhood. There aren't many things as placid or touching.

"Mom, tell her to stop," Debbie complained. But it was not necessary. Donna had excused herself to wait in the driveway for her boyfriend, who was coming over to help finish the float. It was my guess that Donna's productivity level would drop off even farther with his arrival.

I spent that afternoon and evening getting to know the Strickland family a little better. It didn't feel like they were on good behavior because a guest was there. I liked that. They were all humility and calm, steady strength, as if they'd known who they were for years, and that knowledge allowed them to relax and just live.

"You think Donna will skip tomorrow's parade?" I asked Mrs. Strickland as she was bidding me a final good night in the hall.

"Oh lordly, Donna wouldn't miss it for the world. There's far more drama in scoffing from the sidelines. Right now she just wants everyone to look at her, so she can turn away like nothing matters. It's standard operating procedure. She'll be okay. Underneath all the makeup she knows right from wrong. Least she'd better; she's a Strickland. Tell me if you need an extra blanket."

It was controlled chaos the next afternoon behind the Methodist church downtown. Drivers were jockeying their floats for better positions than they'd been assigned. It was a sea of crepe paper, balloons, pumpkins, and costumes. The sounds of a marching band could be heard murdering something by Sousa. Maybe they were just getting warmed up.

And at the center of it all was Stewy, headquartered behind a table at the door of the church social hall. People rushed at him like bullets, but he stayed rooted in place, delegating and troubleshooting some of the more serious problems, laughing at the more outrageous requests, and making chitchat with entire voting blocks.

"The Lions refuse to follow the Rotarians because of that thing that happened at the softball tournament fund-raiser," a woman with a clipboard and a towering beehive hairdo announced to Stewy. "But the Save the Earth float refuses to wedge between them on account of the Lions and Rotarian floats are powered by diesel."

Stewy looked up to the heavens for a moment. "Put the recycling float behind the marching band. They shouldn't have a problem with pedestrians, and let Dell know that he can move the Lions' float back in the batting order as far from the Rotarians as he wants, but not ahead of them. If he doesn't like it tell him I might have to start taxing his Thursday night poker games," Stewy chuckled. "That should settle things. Hell, half the Rotarians play poker with him."

It was as though I were watching a top athlete or a seasoned concert pianist. Stewy worked his constituents like others work in oils or pastels.

Then what seemed like an insurmountable series of obstacles came at him. Pete, who ran the hardware store and was supposed to take repeated plunges on the dunking booth float, had been training for his cold-water entries by standing in a tub full of ice water over the past week. His wife was troubled to report that the hardware store owner was laid up in bed—chills, fever.

"Pete never does anything halfway, now, does he?" Stewy announced. "Good man, but a bit anal in that respect."

The dunking booth job was a harder slot to fill than one would think.

"Let me work on that," Stewy said.

And then the other shoe dropped. Beehive came over in a state of near panic.

"The scarecrow float isn't going to make it. They've been trying to get it started out by Green Valley Road, but it's got transmission problems."

She set her clipboard down. Nothing on there was going to make this dilemma disappear.

Stewy pushed back from the table. It was grave indeed if it got the rotund mayor out of his reclined position.

He took a long look at me, then asked Beehive if someone could at least shuttle the scarecrow costume here in time for the start.

"Done," she said, snatching up her clipboard and pulling a slip of paper and a pen from somewhere inside the cave that was her hair.

As the starting time approached, I observed a heated discussion taking place between Stewy and young Donna. The only part of the conversation I caught was when Donna's boyfriend came onto the scene.

"Cool, I've always wanted to do the dunking booth. It would be fun, babe."

And with that one statement from her boyfriend, Donna's face softened and you could actually see pleasant features peek out from under the cosmetics. Love, or in this case probably lust and a mutual affinity for alternative music, conquered all.

Moments before the parade set off along the route, Stewy walked up with a scarecrow outfit in hand. I felt a bit like that red-nosed reindeer character when he asked me if I would stuff my bike panniers with hay, hang corn wreathes from my handlebars and strap a pumpkin across the rack, and be their scarecrow. Performing as a brainless scarecrow blowing in the wind: Too many of my friends would agree this was a role I was born to play.

The costume was so bulky it made controlling my bike a chore at times, and real straw against my skin itched something fierce, to say nothing of the challenge to one's visibility while wearing a scarecrow head. In other words, I had a ball.

Waving when I could manage, I rode in circles as the parade inched up the road. Clifton honked his go-cart as he went by. There's something very immediate about briefly joining in a community's rituals. It's ghostly in some ways because the act is so transitory, but I also remember feeling never more alive and real as I took an active part in what was my first parade not viewed from the sidelines.

As the cheers washed over me and the sun set behind the hardwoods surrendering the last of their leaves, I caught sight of Donna heaving balls at the dunking booth. Powerless to hold back the enjoyment she was feeling during her last parade as a kid, Donna's failure to remain sullen and distant from her own life meant, to me, that she was going to be fine navigating the coming years—confusing years I was only just in the thick of.

Handing over the scarecrow costume, I realized I too was going to be all right in this world, as long as I remembered to stop every now and then, to let the good stories just under the surface happen—and to keep an eye out for the next parade.

A Petroglyph Is Worth a Thousand Words

THE ROAD CAN BE A LONELY PLACE FOR A SOLO BICYCLIST, BUT OFTEN, all I had to do was wander into a local diner for breakfast if I wanted a bit of company and excitement. The adage that colorful individuals tend to attract other interesting souls was proven again and again on my rides.

That's how I found Gene Reagan—no relation to the former leader of the free world, but a president in his own right. At the time of our meeting, Gene was in charge of the Wascha Basin Rockhounder's Society in Utah. Balding, and overweight in a Santa Claus way, with muttonchop sideburns and a Polident smile, Gene wore a baseball jacket covered with patches.

It was the jacket that brought me over to his table. Decorated in emblems for rockhound clubs and societies from Utah to Florida, the garment was striking for the number of elaborate pictographs and petroglyphs it displayed. Being new to the West at the time, I was captivated by the idea that these drawings, made by past civilizations, dotted the landscape I'd been riding through, but I had yet to see any of them up close and personal.

I had only to make one comment about Gene's jacket for him to pull me up a chair. A few minutes into our conversation, the jolly old man slapped his hands together, excited to be talking about a subject that clearly fascinated him. He lowered his voice and conspiratorially asked me if I wanted to throw my bike in the back of his car and set off for a remote spot in the desert to check out pictographs rarely seen by anyone but those in the know.

Aside from my interest in the subject matter, Gene was such a character that I would have accepted his offer regardless of what we were going in search of.

"Are you planning to finish that?" Gene scarfed up the last piece of toast on my plate, adding some butter and jelly for good measure.

We stopped for supplies on our way out of town. I bought us lunch and extra water. At that point in my ride, I had a healthy respect for the dangers of dehydration.

"Could you get us a box of those Little Debbie brownies? I do like those things," Gene said as he pumped gas into a small foreign car and tried to catch his breath. The walk from the car to the store and back caused Gene to break into a sweat and his face to turn red.

I'd expected that, as president of a rockhound society, Gene would be motoring around the rugged West in an oversize pickup truck with a couple of worn-out dogs in the bed. But his little car seemed to have the appropriate wear, tear, dust, and grime on it for the journey we were about to take.

Like his jacket, the car was plastered with rockhound paraphernalia: clever slogans, and gem-and-mineral show bumper stickers. Some of them might have been holding the car together. I didn't ponder the thought too long.

As for the Little Debbies, Gene seemed hell-bent on enjoying his declining health for as long as he could.

It had rained the night before. The sky appeared a deeper blue than usual, like it had just gotten a fresh coat of paint. A steady breeze kept things comfortable as we took short hikes into slot canyons and over to rock faces not far from the roadside.

While I received a thorough and animated education about cave drawings, pictographs, petroglyphs, and Native American cultures of the region, Gene sketched out the story of his life in an easy, singsong narrative.

It had been quite a life. Gene was a young geologist when World War II broke out. The military put him to work on a hush-hush detail called the Manhattan Project. For several years, he mapped the landscape in central New Mexico, taking core samples and filing reports. In his spare moments, Gene scoured the canyons and bluffs for drawings in the rock. He kept a separate file for this research.

After the war, Gene married one of the nurses at Los Alamos, raised a family, and traveled the world studying rocks. But working on the bomb had a profound impact on his life.

"I could never shake what I'd had a hand in doing. Yes, we ended the war, but on the other hand, look what we dropped on the world. Life gets so complicated when you choose to kill in the name of life. Maybe that's why I like rocks . . . no hidden agendas."

When Gene's wife died and his children became voices on the phone a couple of times a year, the aging rockhound sold his big house in Phoenix and bought a fifth-wheel.

"I base myself out of Utah 'cause there's more drawings here than I could find in a lifetime, but I travel to conferences and shows much of the year."

He smiled at me as we got out of the car to see what he kept saying was his best-kept secret.

"My life's a little quiet these days," he said. "I can't tell you what a treat it is to share this stuff with you today."

He pointed at a mound of rocks jutting out of the desert floor.

There must have been hundreds of drawings on the east-facing rocks of the small mountain.

Gene explained that the Indians worked on their art in the mornings, when the best light was at their backs and it was still cool.

Picking our way through the rocks, I could hear Gene wheezing and puffing. I asked him if we needed to rest.

"Hell, I got some nitroglycerin pills in my shirt pocket. Pop them in my mouth if I fall over and hope for the best."

He paused, chuckling between breaths.

"If I don't get up, leave me for the birds, or throw some rocks over me and call it good. I'll have dropped doing what I enjoy most!"

I didn't want to think too hard about the legal ramifications of covering a decorated War World II veteran with rocks and driving away in his car, but I appreciated Gene's utter disregard for his own mortality. This was one old man who hadn't forgotten that he was still alive, that there would be plenty of time to rest when he was dead.

We sat at the top of the mound, eating lunch. An incredible pictograph of a bear claw was only yards away. A small stream was running at the base of the mound. A place had been built up with rocks to capture fish. Gene explained how the Indians waited for the fish to swim in, then blocked their escape with rocks.

"There's a drawing about it over there," he said.

We sat in silence, taking in the subtle beauty of the area.

"The great state of Utah has plans to level this stretch of rock," he said. "There's some precious resources down there they have to get their hands on."

Gene looked sad.

"Hey, I spent my life digging up the land, so I don't have much right to throw stones, but I've looked at the numbers. They could leave this spot alone. It's a monument to another time. I plan to fight for it."

I thought of the words of Edward Abbey, who said that modern man is killing the last best thing by taming the West.

I hope Gene won his fight for that pile of rocks, or convinced someone else to take it on as a crusade. Those slabs and boulders hold the stories of people whose voices only echo because of lines carved in stone.

Way Down Upon the Suwannee River

THE SIGN ATOP AN APPARENTLY ABANDONED TRAILER TUCKED BACK IN the northern Florida woods indicated we'd arrived at our destination: WELCOME TO SUWANNEE COUNTRY TOURS: BICYCLE AND CANOE ADVENTURES.

Vines grew over the building in Sleeping Beauty fashion. There were rusted parts of old vehicles returning to earth, and a complete quiet that indicated one of two things: a peaceful, Thoreau-like solitude, or unadulterated evil lurking close by. The friend I'd convinced to drive me deep into these woods that Saturday morning settled on the latter.

"Man, we can leave right now. Just give me the word," he whispered as I unloaded my gear and bicycle from the rack of his Jeep.

Only the half-finished husk of a painstakingly carved wooden canoe on sawhorses gave me a glimmer of hope.

"Don't do that, Bro," he pleaded. "We can't make a quick exit with all your stuff on the ground. Maybe this job offer was some sort of prank. I'll take you wherever you want to go."

A kind gesture, but I had convinced myself there was nowhere else I wanted to be.

After a two-thousand-mile solo bicycle adventure from Maine to Florida, my perspective had shifted. I was basically the same guy on the outside, but how I planned to spend my time and what I wanted from my days—those things had been altered forever.

"I'll be all right. Why don't you head out?"

"And leave you here with some walleyed, banjo-playing freak wielding a sling blade?"

My friend must have grown up too close to a drive-in.

"Hi, you must be Joe. I'm David Pearce, walleyed, banjo-playing freak, at your service!"

I admit to being startled. David, though not fitting my friend's description, had a unique look of his own, not to mention he seemed to materialize out of thin air.

At just over five feet tall, rail thin, with a disconcerting waddle to his walk and sporting thick black hair and a beard the likes of which had not been seen since Woodstock, David gave the appearance of an unbalanced leprechaun on acid. He turned out to be a brilliant individual—clever, resourceful, and a pleasure to work for.

My friend took one look at him, started up his Jeep, and got out of there as quickly as possible. So began my tenure with Suwannee Country Tours, a personalized adventure company that offered the lucky few a glimpse of the "other" Florida. Nancy Kessel, a friendly woman and competent bike mechanic with a dry sense of humor, rounded out the staff. The three of us helped people discover some of the less traveled back roads and waterways of the Sunshine State.

Some nights we were up until 3 A.M. making salads and picnic lunches, or loading an extra canoe onto a trailer and fixing a broken chain. But always there was a sense of fun, a feeling that we were getting away with something because people paid us to go pedaling and paddling with them.

Along the way, there were forts and historic old homes, one-room churches and sprawling plantations. Bird-watchers loved our tours, and the occasional alligator could be spotted lounging on the banks of a slow-moving river.

The accommodations ranged from small inns to bed-and-breakfasts and state park campgrounds. On certain routes, we'd house our customers at a buffalo ranch, a summer camp, and a log cabin hunting lodge once owned by Teddy Roosevelt.

But what made those three seasons so memorable were the people. They arrived in pairs, families, large groups, and sometimes alone.

Each customer was there for a different reason and it was my job to figure out what that was, and work with it.

We provided meals, lodging, van support, equipment repairs, and maps. But the thing most of our customers really craved was an adventure. For some, this meant riding farther than they thought possible or pedaling up to a roadside waterfall. For others, their joy was found in talking with an old-timer standing by his tractor in a field of cotton or peanuts. And for still others, it included wandering along the shore collecting clams for a bonfire dinner on the beach. Something always caught their eye and left them changed for the better by the end of the week.

Bonds were forged, and when people loaded their vehicles or got in the van for that final drive to the airport, a sadness would fill the air. Many of our favorite customers returned each season.

"I reckon that river's the color of a tall, cool glass of iced tea," said Ben, a southern lawyer taking his third ride with us through the backwoods in so many years. The river we were cycling beside was indeed filled with tannic acid, one of the ingredients in tea. It gives it that brown color. Legend had it that pools along the river's edge were used by the Indians as healing baths.

"Every time I come here I'm quite tempted to scoop out a glassful and drink it."

Other members on the tour made faces.

Ben just laughed. "I'm gonna do it." He stooped down near the bank and got his water bottle open. A hushed amazement fell over the group. From my angle it looked like Ben was squirting water into his mouth, but actually he was shooting it down his right cheek.

"Stop, you fool," a pediatrician on a Cannondale chided. "Who gave you a law degree? That stuff will make you ill."

Ben turned to show us his deception, then hosed down the group, no exceptions, with cold river water. He was overpowered at some point and tossed into the river, where he remained, floating on his back until the tour was brought to a halt on account of unscheduled fun. No one stayed out of the water. We made it to camp later than usual, but in much higher spirits.

Some of my favorite customers were the ones who weren't sure they could make it for a full week on two wheels. Not the hardcore whiners destined to pack up their gear in the middle of the night on day two and leave a brief message attached to the windshield of the van. Something about biting off more than they could chew, or that bicycling was not their cup of tea, after all. I'm talking about the folks who surprised us and themselves over the course of a few hundred miles.

For years Leslie had managed the desk of a nice resort in southern Florida. She was always watching fit people launch out on adventures, while she stood in the same place. Now, in middle age, she'd retired and wanted her turn. She'd done a day ride along the beach with a cycling club. But diving into a week of solid riding, more than three hundred miles, was chancy.

One afternoon after lunch Leslie hit her first wall. That week's group wasn't going very fast but she couldn't keep them in sight. I hung back with her. We talked through the final twenty miles. I got to hear about the family, not hers but Leslie's sister's.

"I didn't have any children of my own. Too busy working. That's why I have to do something special with the rest of my life. I . . . I want to be someone my nieces and nephews can look up to."

I'd be damned if Leslie wasn't going to make the entire week.

It was no picnic, though. Well, actually it was seven days of nothing but picnics, and seaside restaurants, wooded campgrounds, and cute bed and breakfasts. But for Leslie it was a battle. Her seat gave her such pain we bought bags of party ice for her to sit on during the evening fish fries and square dancing. I kept her water bottles filled with Gatorade, her bike tuned to perfection, and encouraged her when it looked like she was going to throw in the towel. Through bee stings, flat tires, a good-size downpour, and Leslie's lactose intolerance, she managed to keep rolling.

When she coasted into town for the final stop, an ice cream cone and group photo in front of the company headquarters, Leslie was smiling.

The mayor of White Springs, Florida, who ran the gas station and ice cream stand, always posed with the riders for the group picture. I still have the shot of Leslie, cone in one hand, helmet in the other, hugging this overweight stranger and beaming for the camera.

"I actually think I could keep doing this," were her parting words.

Of course, there was the occasional client we were relieved to get rid of. On an especially grueling canoe trip, one in which it rained the majority of the time, a woman who needed everything "just so" turned to me in exhaustion and disgust.

"Can't you do something about this constant drizzle?"

I wanted to laugh but refrained. There seemed to be no humor waiting behind her stare. Thinking I needed to say something sarcastic or even downright mean to whip this sourpuss into shape for the long miles ahead, I opened my mouth.

Fortunately, another participant stepped in to save the day.

"I love the rain. Out here it feels like we're in that movie, *Gorillas in the Mist.*"

My disgruntled customer didn't say anything for a while, the rain pelting her hat. "Didn't the woman in that movie die horribly?" she queried, chuckling wickedly for the first time in days.

Other moments of absurd behavior or ridiculous requests included the time the German cyclist who fueled himself on coffee and Power Bars demanded we pull the van over on a desolate stretch of road so he could brew up some java using the hot water from the radiator, a pie pan, and a makeshift funnel.

Fritz was actually a riot when he was properly caffeinated. I remember cruising along with him one morning, discussing the concept of baseball as a national pastime, when Fritz took off like he had bees in his bike shorts.

"Sprint!" he kept yelling until I caught up to him. It was a nice straight road with trees one either side and no traffic. And Fritz so desperately wanted someone to play with him. We rode side by side for a few glorious minutes, I'd better his front wheel by a yard or two, then he'd return the favor, pulling ahead. Finally, we called it quits, stretching out in the tall grass while we waited for the rest of the group.

"It always works," Fritz said in a relaxed voice. "You ride fast enough, the world stops for a few seconds."

I'm all for stopping the world now and then.

"It . . . revives me, somehow," he added.

That it does Fritz, that it does.

And I'll never forget the couple who argued so much about how to paddle a canoe that they kept managing to turn themselves backward. A small set of rapids became a bit more challenging on that trip.

Hands down, though, my favorite tours were with the teenage boys' groups from boarding schools, sent to ride away some of their spit and vinegar in the wilds of northern Florida. Like servants released from indenture, those kids had the time of the lives. Flat tires abounded, water balloon fights broke out midride, and camp each night felt like a festival of music, laughter, and controlled chaos.

Word of how much fun Suwannee Country Tours adventures were made its way into *Outside* magazine.

It wasn't long before the people at the *Today* show came calling.

A film crew followed us around one week. They captured hours of great footage, which was condensed into less than a minute of air-time. It didn't matter, though, because the film crew understood, by week's end, exactly what all the fuss was about. Over Key lime pie, the producer announced that he hadn't enjoyed himself so much in all his years of television.

Then a "personality" showed up. His limo pulled through the entrance of a beautiful state park just minutes before the live remote. He hopped out of the car in a pair of cycling shorts and donned a helmet. The interview was so staged, I actually felt sorry for this media big shot. What good is all that fame and fortune if you don't even get to enjoy a ride in the woods or a float down a river?

Suwannee Country Tours was sold years ago. It kept changing hands and shape until the company I knew and have so many fond memories of no longer exists.

The last time I drove through northern Florida, I stopped by the old trailer, really abandoned this time. The half-built canoe remained on its sawhorses, a silent reminder that all work and no play—well, you know the rest.

Before I walked away, I decided to flip around the handmade sign on the front door one more time.

GONE RIDING. SEE YOU ON THE ROAD!

Storm Warnings

FEAR WAS THE REASON I TOOK MY FIRST SOLO, LONG-DISTANCE bicycling adventure. I'd like to wax poetic about a burning need to swallow up new vistas, sing the body electric, and claim my place in the world—all ideals that I embraced once I was actually cycling about the globe—but the real reason I quit a job with a retirement plan and left my schoolbooks unopened on those university steps to bicycle from Maine to Florida was fear.

After only twenty years of life, I awoke to a terrifying possibility: There might be a real chance I could grow brittle and hollow . . . old before my time. If I didn't do something like ride away, then I might live bored and not know any better. And what was I doing with a retirement plan at that age, anyway?

Maybe it was too many viewings of *The Wizard of Oz* during my youth. I hadn't been taken in by the "never look farther than my own backyard" ending. It sounded like a public service announcement for the Future Dullards of America Council.

If Dorothy hadn't put one foot in front of the other, we'd all have missed out on so much. Attagirl, Dorothy. I spent the better part of my childhood waiting for that ruby-slippered wonder girl's next road trip. But then the drugs and booze took away her alter ego, Judy Garland, and I went and grew up, anyway. All grown up with nowhere to hide from my nagging fears, so I loaded my panniers and hit the open road.

I was seven hundred miles into my Maine-to-Florida adventure before I was pummeled by my first real storm. Not a fistful of rain like the showers that had already soaked me a few times, but a massive display of hail, lightning, and wind that hammered me in a small state park near the Pennsylvania border.

I had been riding through beautiful farm country, an afternoon's drive from the Big Apple, just hours before the storm broke. My tent was raised under striking blue skies, while three men drank and joked at a picnic bench about twenty yards away.

In the East, the woods grow rather dense, so I was concealed by a thicket. The men did not know that I was there, or did not care. They drank and talked about their boyfriends and jobs. About a half hour into their conversation, one of the men got sick in the bushes. I found this odd because they weren't a group of fraternity brothers pounding brews, one right after the next. I sat with a book in my lap only a few yards away and watched him heave until it was just empty contractions and pain.

"We'd better go back," one of the guys at the picnic table said to the other. Neither of the men came to help their friend bent over in the weeds.

He looked up and met my stare. His eyes were bloodshot and the skin across his cheekbones was pulled as tight as the cover on a drum. He had the look of a deer I'd hit with a truck in the Everglades the summer before. The deer had worked its way into the brush, blood clouding up the corner of its eyes, dying . . . proud.

"I'm tired of always having to go back!"

This statement came from one of the men at the table. His voice rose a little with anger and booze. "I want to live a little and if Steve's not ready for this kind of trip anymore, then . . ." His voice dropped a few notches. "Then, what I mean is, do we always have to stop our lives for him?"

The other guy said something too quietly for me to hear, while the sick man found the strength to sit up to his knees.

"I'm okay," he said, trying to make his voice sound stronger than he must have felt. Again, he looked at me, then continued to speak. "To hell with this disease . . . eh?"

He gave me a little nod before struggling out of the bush. I nodded back, but he had already turned around.

"Let me just stretch out on the table for a minute, will ya?" he said.

It sounded like the other two men made some room, moving coolers and whatnot. No one spoke for a while. I thought the sick man had fallen asleep, but then I heard his voice.

"I don't mean to be a burden, I really don't."

When he cried, the man hardly made any sound at all. I heard the other guys opening more beer.

"I'm glad we came, I am," he announced abruptly. "My dad used to bring us here, on the way back from hunting in Pennsylvania. I never thought it was much of a park, but now, well, it's damn near everything." There was a long pause, "I don't think I'll be back here again."

"Stop it," the guy who earlier had been complaining said. "Let's just not do that. You're good. You're real good. You look fine."

No one said anything for a time. Finally, the sick man added, "It's good we came. I appreciate that you guys aren't afraid to hang out with me . . . not many of you left."

One of his friends choked up a little. "My sister's got these ruby slippers she don't wear much anymore—really. If I had the nerve, if I thought they'd help, I'd go get 'em for us and click my heels. Return us all to that wonderland we knew before."

The man who was slowly withering away chuckled, and spoke with more strength in his voice than he'd shown all day. "But life doesn't have a rewind button, so I guess . . . we just go on."

Later that night, after they had packed up and headed back to the city, I watched the front of the storm come in and wondered just who I would have been in that situation—one of his friends who made excuses for why they couldn't hang out with him anymore, or one who joined this shadow of a man for an afternoon beer in the park, one last time. I didn't have a quick answer.

In 1985, AIDS was still a mysterious plague that left most of its victims to die alone. Too often, it still does.

I now had a face and a voice to place with the disease, and AIDS never looked the same to me. I crawled deeper into the lush undergrowth of the park, and waited for the storm to hit.

There's a Little Greg LeMond in Every Touring Cyclist

IN MY FAVORITE DREAM, I'M ALWAYS GREG LEMOND, TOUR DE FRANCE winner and scrappy American underdog who owned the strength to neglect pain and ride like the wind; a man who battled back from gunshot wounds to reclaim the yellow jersey in the most grueling bicycle race ever conceived; a twisted, driven individual who never let up; a fanatic.

My dream always starts on the bike in the middle of a breakaway. There's no distinguishing where I end and the bike begins. My feet are the pedals, my hands the bars, and the rhythmic up-and-down motion of my thighs could be the steel rods driving a locomotive, they're that solid and steady.

Hey, it's my dream!

Color and sound are exaggerated as I bear down and take the lead. I can hear harsh cursing from several riders as I distance myself from the pack. This doesn't bother me, primarily because most of the insults are hurled in French, a language I know only from restaurant menus and Saturday-morning cartoons featuring Pepe Le Pew.

But they can say anything they want because I'm not going to be caught. I feel light and fast. I've broken the bounds of gravity, discovered limitless reserves of energy, and for a moment I'm free of everything as I blur across the finish line and triumphantly into the history books.

God, I love that dream.

But in the cold light of day, I'm a touring cyclist, nothing more, nothing less. There was a time, in my second year of high school, before I really hit the weights, when I thought I could have gone that way. Tall and lean, I loved to ride fast.

But bike racers, truly gifted racers, must possess more than a need for speed. They have something coursing through their veins and wired into their hard drives that allows them not just to ride through pain, but to pedal harder and faster as the agony builds. A world-class racer once described it as falling in love with that which hurts you most. Bad love, plain and simple. An Ike and Tina Turner sort of love. You crave the pain and serve it with everything you've got until it eats you up and spits you out. It changes you.

Maybe somewhere in there you're the first to cross a finish line or two, but that's more of a a footnote in this all-consuming relationship. Look into the eyes of topflight riders right after a race sometime. Like monks chasing nirvana.

At seventeen, I wanted to believe I had it in me; I thought I could join the chase. But that was just the testosterone talking. I went so far as to enter the Clearwater Jazz Triathlon in a put-up-or-shut-up challenge to myself. What I learned that day was that all the testosterone, Power Bars, equipment, positive thinking, and training in the world do not mean squat when it's time to meet the gods of the race.

My career as a touring cyclist began shortly thereafter.

For the record, riding a bicycle around the globe was no consolation prize. In fact, I dare say that, for me, it turned out to be the road to enlightenment. Not that touring a loaded bike is a pain-free experience, either, but it's a different mind-set; tenacity and patience are what the touring cyclist taps, not a constant, blinding pain.

But every now and then, after I awaken from my Greg LeMond dream, I race my bike down the back roads and contemplate a different destiny. As I pedal out the door with speed as my goal, I try to forget the time I hooked up with the U.S. Olympic cycling team and members of a French squad training for some winter time trials in Florida.

It was a few weeks after the completion of a long bike tour. I promised myself that this time I was going to maintain the top form I always found myself in at the end of a trip. How? By going for daily training rides. Maybe thirty miles round-trip, enough to feel solid the next time I wanted to ride, say, across China.

A few miles into it, with my blood beginning to flow, I fell into a paceline with a group of racers, serious athletes with expensive gear, but not the sort of flashy equipment a techno-geek straps on to a middle-of-the-road bike. These guys were riding rigs that cost more than my first car.

The strange and exhilarating thing was that I'd caught up with them, and was managing to hold my own as we whizzed along the wooded road. One of the racers, decked out in a red, white, and blue jersey with what appeared to be the official U.S. Olympic training team logo, began talking with me. What a thrill to be fit enough to talk back while holding a high rate of speed.

"You want to pull for a few minutes?" he asked.

It was almost like my dream. I hopped out in front, a few of the riders were whispering in French, and I felt light and fast as a bullet.

My laugh was almost a cackle as my speedometer verified that I was pulling the group at 26 . . . 26.5 . . . 27.2 miles per hour.

At that moment, I realized I could have been a contender. Wait, maybe it wasn't too late! I could enter a few local races, work my way up the ranks, then turn pro. I could get my name in the magazines. I could . . . see that the group was passing me like I was standing still.

I'd been used as a human pace car for these guys! Try as I might, they grew smaller and smaller on the horizon as I fought to hold my speed. Without the draft from their bikes, I sputtered back to Earth. I broke my cadence, slowed the bike to a crawl, then came to a complete stop and found a nice spot in the tall weeds to collapse and gather some strength, acknowledging, between shallow breaths and a deep burning in my chest, that I would never be a member of their club. The price was too high.

When I recovered enough to get back on the bike, the sun had edged close to the horizon, the wind was kicking up in my face, and I still had miles to go, a humble touring cyclist once again.

But for some reason, I was smiling, remembering the precious moments when I carried the pack. I knew I could always be light and fast, I could always be Greg LeMond—in my favorite dream.

The Man Who Couldn't Shoot Straight

THEY SAY ALL TRAVEL IS A VANISHING ACT. YOU MOVE THROUGH landscapes and other people's lives much like a ghost; touching some things and being touched by others. And on a few occasions you just sit back and take it all in, maybe even learn something.

I pedaled out of a campground to find an older man in a dapper-looking uniform leaning peacefully against his car, a police station wagon out of the late 1950s—a classic ride. It was just after first light. I was too cold to take off my Gore-Tex gloves, but sweating inside them, just the same.

He looked comfortable, like he'd leaned back against that same part of the chrome many mornings during his career. A pair of crisp, white gloves were laid out across the wagon's shiny hood.

As I flew by on my bicycle, the gentleman gave me the briefest hint of a wave. It was not the last time I would see this man. After the sun rose high enough, he started that vintage vehicle up, idled it a while, then drove into the small upstate Washington town he called home. He guided the wagon over spray-washed cobblestones, the town's wide streets greeting his wheels. The classic old ride pulled into a parking spot at a corner diner where I happened to be enjoying a thick stack of flapjacks. Sometimes people will do the damnedest things and you'll be in the right place and time to act as a witness.

The man got out of his car gracefully and proceeded to perform an amazing and rather bizarre feat. He jaywalked calmly through the intersection to a bright yellow utility box on the corner pole of the four-way stoplight. He removed a key from his pocket and went to work on the guts of the government-owned equipment. Then out came those starched-to-perfect-whiteness gloves.

The traffic light was no longer in operation. Cars were hesitating as they approached one another, slowing and working through the disarmed traffic light; an occasional horn started blowing. It was clear that a bottleneck was in the making, and an accident could not be far behind.

He was holding a small piece of silver in one gloved hand when he entered the stream of traffic. He didn't flinch, or appear to worry that one of the drivers running late for work might take him out in a devastating moment of screeching brakes and snapping bones. Then it began; the man started directing traffic like nobody's business—with style, poise, and skill.

The gentleman turned out to be Jake, and for thirty-five years he was one of those traffic cops in New York City, back when gloves and whistles got the job done. According to his friends at the diner, a sturdy, weather-worn group of retirees sipping coffee and trading stories they'd all told a hundred times, Jake had been one of the best traffic cops who'd ever worn the uniform, but progress put him off the streets and out to pasture. On the surface, that was fine by Jake. The table of retirees were happy to share a bit of Jake's story, and I was happy to hear it.

Jake had unfinished business back in his hometown, business that Jake felt would probably remain undone, but he knew he had to try, anyway.

Years earlier, before Jake moved east to chase his dreams, he'd married his high school sweetheart, Nancy. She had gotten pregnant, but since he had always loved her, Jake felt certain he would have asked her anyway.

When Nancy miscarried, Jake suggested that she come to New York. Maybe he was too excited about the idea, or maybe Nancy just wasn't ready, but she wanted to stay put. They tried to find happiness in that small western town, but the following summer Jake quietly pushed through their divorce and headed for the Big Apple.

Jake built a fine career—bright lights, big city—but when it was over he knew it hadn't been enough.

"Damn," one of the old guys at the table whispered.

But when Jake finally came home, Nancy was still there; neither of them had remarried. Though the pair became a couple, Nancy would not accept Jake's proposals of marriage. That was a bond he'd broken years earlier and Nancy wasn't willing or able to find the connections to reattach it. Jake said he was happy just to spend time in her company.

One morning in the spring, five years into their new relationship, Jake found himself running a great number of errands and looking after Nancy on account of her headaches.

She'd paint in the mornings when the light was best, and Jake figured it was because of the strain on her eyes that she was getting the migraines, but when he came back after breakfast with the boys one morning, Nancy was lying awfully still in the middle of her flowers. Doctors explained to Jake that the headaches were just a warning of something about to break loose inside her head.

"Nancy didn't completely leave him that morning, but most of her did. Now, Jake takes care of a body that keeps holding on—breathing and such. He makes sure her flowers bloom each spring, but the loneliness, or maybe the regret, began to make him a little touched," explained one of the retirees. "We saw the change in him."

One morning, Jake drove into his normal parking spot at the diner, but instead of coming inside for a short stack, he walked into the street and took out his standard-issue, State of New York firearm.

Jake crouched down in what must have been a stance he'd learned at the academy, and took aim at the stoplight. Three or four rounds went off before he hit the actual traffic light casing. Jake had been a traffic cop for thirty-odd years and never once had he had any cause to fire his weapon.

Bullets went everywhere but their mark. Finally, Jake stood up and extended the gun in a sort of awkward fashion at a certain angle above his head, and managed to knock loose the yellow and green lights before running out of ammo.

It was pretty early in the morning, so there wasn't much traffic on the street, but when cars finally edged up to the intersection, Jake was there, in his gloves and whistle, to usher them through to safety.

When Jake was done, he looked and acted better than he had in months. The only problem came when the active-duty police force found out that it was vandalism and not some kind of electrical malfunction that had put the light out of commission.

That afternoon, Jake walked down to the station and turned himself in. No explanation for his actions, just a look of satisfaction on his face. The cops didn't know what to do. Here was one of their own, a well-known, well-liked guy, shooting up the town.

They let Jake go home with a warning not to do it again. Of course, that didn't stop him from doing it again, and not long after they had the light repaired. This time he was brought before the judge and fined.

Some of Jake's breakfast buddies went before the city council and explained what they thought were the reasons for Jake's actions. Jake was doing the only thing left that would ease his mind. It was hard on him to look into Nancy's eyes each day and remember he'd left her alone all those years, to see what might have been.

The council kicked around several ideas, then offered Jake the key to the utility box and permitted him, as long as he cleared it with the local authorities beforehand, to turn off the lights from time to time and direct traffic. This way, Jake wouldn't have to keep shooting out the lights, the city would save the cost of repairs, and, most importantly, Jake would have a few moments of his old world back. Such a small thing, really.

So, Jake directs away his worries, and maybe a few of his regrets. The man's whistle, shiny black shoes, and those white gloves produce a concert of movement. Jake found a way of letting go of the things that make him feel lost while he's still living. He dances in traffic and his friends say he talks lovingly about the time he had with Nancy, the brief but glorious days in her garden when her smile was still bright.

"He just likes to slow things down from time to time, taking life back into his own hands—if only for a little while," the oldest retiree announced, finishing his last swallow of coffee before heading out the door. He added, "It's kinda beautiful when you stop and think about it."

As I rode through the intersection, Jake waved me past with a smile that still rattles my heart. I vanished like the good traveler I'd become, but Jake stayed with me over the years. What Jake did was part dance, part performance art, and all about believing that each of us has the ability to keep going.

The Spirit's Willing
But the Flesh Is Pedaling
on Borrowed Time

RESOLUTIONS CAN BE TRICKY ENTITIES. HOPE SPRINGS ETERNAL AND with it all those other feel-good, self-help platitudes, but when goals for improvement consistently falter somewhere around February, it's enough to make one resolve to stop making resolutions.

That's why I've always kept my January 1 list-for-a-better-me fairly short. One tradition, though, is that at the start of each new year, I try to take a challenging (but not too challenging) bike ride, regardless of where I might find myself, geographically or emotionally, then keep riding regularly throughout the year.

This time around, I was visiting my wife's relatives in California when all the New Year countdowns ended, and there was only the quiet morning, a rented bicycle, and the crisp, inviting mountains above Santa Cruz, California. The plan was for Phil and Doug, my brothers-in-law, to show me a decent ride through some beautiful single-track country near their backyards; something to get my heart going, but nothing that would put me in traction.

"No problem!" had been their mantra during the holidays. Sure, I'd sent Phil into the deepest wilds of the Gila during his last visit to New Mexico, but he couldn't still be harboring animosity about the rough terrain, loose rock, long distance, and desert heat. Hey, we were family.

Something to remember about paybacks: No one forgets where he's buried the hatchet. And the fact that Doug, who has completed triathlons, including the Ironman in Hawaii, said he'd like to tag along should have worried me, but I was full of New Year's cheer and positive thoughts.

When renting a bike that morning—key to keeping stride with my kin—the local bike shop owner tried to put me on a clunky Huffy suited for riding about the neighborhood, until I announced that I would need something lighter with real suspension. Phil chimed in that he was taking me on the So-Cal Demonstration Forest ride.

"Why didn't you say so?" the owner announced, flashing a wicked grin. "There are some killer views up there."

He escorted us to the back and set me up with a high-end hybrid bicycle. It gave the appearance that I knew what I was doing. And still, the hairs on the back of my neck hadn't begun to rise.

This was family. We were going for a pleasant morning ride—period.

My adrenaline ignited at the starting point, when, as we were slapping on gear and checking equipment, several carloads of guys straight out of a segment of *Extreme Sports* on ESPN began unloading expensive bikes and greeting Phil like an old friend.

"Joe, I'd like you to meet Dave. He was just signed by Schwinn's national mountain bike team. And Gus was ranked fifth in the country last year until a nasty spill put him out of commission for a while."

I studied the titanium brace holding parts of Gus's knee in place. What sort of a nut rides with something like that attached to his body? Gus smiled like it was no big deal. Uh oh.

I took a final look at myself in the window of the car. On the outside, I fit the part, but the rubber was about to meet the road and I was beginning to feel like an impostor.

I held my own for the first four miles. We were climbing at a steady clip, a pack of eight riders moving up the mountain. "This is going to be easy." I told myself, "as long as I stay with the pack." When we reached the first really steep grade, I stood on the pedals and lifted out of my saddle. The rest of the group made it look far too easy.

I was sucking down big gulps of air at our first break. I kept dropping off the pack until I found myself abandoned over a grueling series of climbs. Better to set my own pace than to dare my heart to explode as a member of an elite pack.

As I coaxed my rig forward, I was able to take in the view. Pockets of fog hovered over the valley below and the Gothic size of thick redwoods helped take my mind off my screaming muscles and swelling legs. At the top, the group was waiting for me.

"Expected you to be farther back," my brother-in-law announced, with a sly look in his eye. "How's this compare to New Mexico?"

And before I could answer, the pack moved on. I was privileged that day to enjoy some of the best downhill cycling in the country. Few riders know about those trails that resemble bobsled runs through dense old-growth forest. I held on for dear life and felt, for a few moments, that my youth, what was left of it, occupied center stage.

A pledge deeper than a resolution emerged from that morning ride. It is to stay in good-enough shape, maybe not to keep up with professional riders in their early twenties, but good enough shape to accompany my own children on a few cycling adventures as they grow up.

During my New Year's ride, I pondered that truism about people not knowing what they have until it begins to fade. I remembered there was this kid in my elementary school who craved the trappings of old age. Each semester he would try to flunk the hearing exam so they'd equip him with hearing aids, and he was always asking this sullen girl with a back brace if he could just try it on for a few minutes.

One year, he actually walked around school for a few days with an ornate cane, pretending he had a limp. The kid just wanted to stand out, but what he didn't realize was that his health and energy were the best accessories he was ever going to get.

I popped out at the base of the mountain trail, howling like a child on a roller coaster, ready to do it again. After I caught my breath and took stock of myself—battered and sore, but intact—I told Phil how much fun I'd had, then asked him where the cars were parked. He pointed somewhere far up the slope and laughed with a little too much enjoyment.

Like I said, resolutions can be tricky, and really, too much hard work, but for a Metal Cowboy with just a bit of rust under his saddle, this is one pledge I'm going to keep, if only so I don't miss out on some of those adventures waiting for me down the road, and to keep those smug smiles off my brothers-in-law's faces.

A Walk in the Park

MY BEST PALS IN THIS WORLD HAVE ALWAYS BEEN INTIMATELY LINKED to my cycling adventures. Albert Pantone was there from the beginning: the afternoon I stood over a couple of hundred pounds of camping gear, spare tires, tools, food—you name it—behind the director's house at a summer camp where I'd been working. The dog-eared chapter in the bike touring manual titled *Light Is Right! The Art of Packing for a Tour* lay open on the ground. Albert, who was trying to quit smoking for the umpteenth time in so many weeks, crushed out his butt and wandered off his deck to offer sage counsel. He was nearly ten years older than me.

Albert would hold up what he thought was a worthy candidate for expulsion from the gear list only to endure another of my passionate arguments as to why that can opener, complete works of Wallace Stegner, camera tripod, or third backup bathing suit was crucial to the success of the operation. After I pleaded my case for the inclusion of a bulky camping lantern, Albert cleared a space on the picnic table —shoving aside more useless gear—then picked up his garage sale banjo and began tuning it.

"You're a big guy. It's my guess you can muscle this load up the worst peaks the East Coast's gonna throw at you. The real concern should be that back wheel. You ever see one of those collapse on the downside of a monster hill—with the rider aboard?" Albert paused to tighten a string, giving me one raised eyebrow, just the way Belushi always did.

"Have you?" I fired back.

"Never," he shrugged. "But it can't be a pretty sight."

I mulled this over while Albert picked at the strings, finding something that actually sounded like a melody. He's the sort of guy who's always learning a new trick, tinkering with a craft project, or whipping up a tasty dish on the stove, a combination that suddenly came to him in a dream. If you and Albert Pantone are having a conversation, Albert's having a conversation *and* carving the face of an old man into an apple, teaching himself to play the harmonica, reading about Hindu knots, or gathering pinecones, rocks, and bark for some future project.

"Okay, time to start over. Albert, what would you take?"

He smiled. I'd made it too easy for him.

"A car, Joe. I'd take a car."

We managed to whittle my gear list down substantially. He allowed me to keep one item for every five he took away. This brutal exchange ratio straighten out my priorities in a hurry.

"So what's this quest about, Sir Quixote?" Albert asked when I had the bike completely loaded and upright for the first time. There were a few problems with weight distribution on earlier attempts. "Have you got a mission statement, a manifesto to accompany this expedition, or was it just next up on your list of things to do before you die?"

He was serious about the "to do" lists. We'd written them out together one evening after large quantities of chicken wings, battered mushrooms, and beer.

"I'm riding out there to . . . to look for America, my friend. I've seen the brochure, now it's time to experience it firsthand."

Ah, the privileges of youth. You'll walk through fire just to know you're flesh and blood, just to feel everything.

It's gratifying when a friendship is so comfortable that both people know when the other is being serious underneath all the banter. Albert produced a respectful nod, then a book of stamps from his back pocket.

"Well, when you find America, pal, send me a postcard."

And that's just what I did. Albert Pantone received cheesy tourist photos of forts and cultural points of interest. I dropped him cards of panoramic vistas, national monuments and those out of the way oddities, sidebars, attractions, and mom-and-pop freak shows for which our one-of-a-kind continent is so famous, and in a touching way, proud of.

After whatever message I hurriedly jotted down on the back of each card, I'd add the postscript; "America, Found—September 1985!"

It was another of those insider things, small details that the truest friendships are comprised of. Those same bonds wouldn't be as strong without a little conflict, a bit of adversity to overcome. With Albert, the trouble began when we went for extended walks in the woods.

I met my friend at the base of the Sierra Nevadas, near Fresno, California. We'd been talking for a while about our perennial camping trip. I'd been working and cycling in California all summer. When I called him up I assured Albert that I had plenty of friends willing to supply extra gear.

"Just come west, young man! Leave the rest up to me." Having spent two gorgeous summers in the California mountains, I thought I knew what to expect. But autumn is an entirely different animal above eight thousand feet.

The hike in was stunning. We'd gotten a late start after laughing together into the wee hours. It didn't help that I hadn't packed our gear. There was a sense of déjà vu watching Albert select certain camping essentials from the pile spread across the back porch. When he added these to his backpack of camera equipment, my nicotine-addicted friend was fairly loaded down.

Albert, among other things, is an accomplished photographer. His work crops up in magazines and graces the entrances to zoos and nature center exhibits. He was not going to part with any of the lenses or tripods.

"Let's just take this tarp, instead of the tent," I announced. "I've never been rained on in the Sierras."

As I predicted, the first evening at Twin Lakes was clear. Ten miles from the trailhead and almost nine thousand feet above sea level, the stars crowded the sky in such numbers that we hiked the short distance to the summit above the water without flashlights.

"Right now I feel like I could live forever!" I wasn't kidding. The chill in the air meant nothing to me. There are those rare moments when you feel so real that the universe could peel away and you'd just chuckle.

"Jewish people believe that to be remembered by loved ones down through the generations is to live forever," Albert said quietly. He was changing lenses for a moon shot. "Some Eastern religions say time is a construct of the human mind. Hey, no mind, no time!" He looked through his viewfinder. "But I don't want to live forever."

I asked him why not.

"I like knowing this is all we get. Makes it count for something, don't you think?"

He shrugged, then snapped the photograph: a sliver of moon painting a subtle glow over granite and water. I had it framed.

A lot of people talk about living fully, but Albert backs it up. He's always saying people are too concerned with not dying. For a guy who doesn't give a damn about immortality, he'll probably find it.

We stumbled onto a couple of crosses secured to the edge of the ridge by piles of rocks.

"Wonder who they were?" I said.

"Couple other guys who probably thought they'd live forever," Albert said with a nod.

It started as a drizzle the following afternoon. We were on the other side of the lake shooting some high-country wildflowers still in bloom when tiny rain droplets began to rustle the flower petals.

We ignored the weather for a while, but it didn't blow over. I kept flashing to the four-season tent I'd left on the porch. More distressing was the fact that I'd forgotten the tarp in the backseat of the car. It was getting too late in the afternoon to hike out. We used up more daylight scouting the surrounding area for a cave or rock overhang.

"Probably won't last, but let's try and construct a bit of shelter," Al said, hiding his camera in a waterproof bag. "Give us something to do."

There were few branches and no underbrush to build a tepee or lean-to, but wide strips of sequoia bark peeled painstakingly away from downed chunks of trees formed the walls of our temporary home. We used rocks to wedge three twisted walls in place, but the bark was not adequate for a roof—too many gaps and holes. Albert strung a line between two trees and stretched his poncho to the limit for a roof. We had to use the laces of his boots to tie down the backside. We shortened the walls just to get the poncho to fit, and still it resembled the head of a snare drum. I noticed very little room while arranging our sleeping bags. Too much like a coffin, but I kept this thought to myself. Proud of ourselves, we dubbed it the Sequoia Super Structure and let out a collective sigh of relief.

Obtaining shelter is such a core desire—very primitive. Albert squatted over a small flame and cooked our dinner of lentils and ham hocks between the rocks as the rain lightly fell. If a mastodon had wandered by it wouldn't have surprised me.

The drizzle turned into a downpour, forcing us and dinner into the Super Structure. It was a little after 4 P.M. We spent the first few hours in relative comfort. Old friends who don't see each other enough enjoy hanging out and talking, even if it means being bunched into the fetal position inside sleeping bags. A bottle of brandy was passed back and forth while we reminisced, argued trivia, and discussed the finer points of sitcom television.

"I don't know about the rest of the world, but it's plain to me that Mr. Ed was really a subversive commentary about the nature of hypocrisy in rural America," Albert pontificated.

A burst of laughter came from my sleeping bag.

"Ever heard the expression, Straight from the horse's mouth?" I was too cramped to see Albert's face, but I knew he was giving me that one raised eyebrow. Then he also began laughing.

That's when the lightning struck and thunder shook the ground straight down the valley. Gusts of cold wind arrived next. The Super Structure didn't feel as super after that.

When I poked my head outside what I saw was not so much a storm as a full-scale battle between the elements of earth and sky. Trees the height of tall buildings swayed mightily from gale-force winds. Whitecaps kicked up on the lakes and tree limbs crashed to the ground with alarming regularity. The rain was no longer splintered, but one solid, menacing entity.

"Still think you're gonna live forever?" Albert asked rhetorically, before rolling himself deeper inside the shelter.

We'd been cowering in the structure for eight hours straight when a small river of water trickled between our sleeping bags. Wordlessly, Albert passed over a small cooking pot and a hastily dug trench was put into service. Though we craved sleep, it was impossible to snatch more than fifteen or twenty minutes at a time. The poncho, once as tight as a drill sergeant's bed sheets, now filled so quickly with rainwater that it had to be drained by pushing from underneath, or else chance having the roof collapse on us.

In a stupor of sorts, I woke with a jolt, realizing that the poncho was so heavy with water it was actually resting on us. There must have been a couple of hundred pounds of H_2O hanging in the balance. Somehow I bench-pressed it, and the frigid water spilled in every direction. Still feeling dry, I fell back to sleep immediately.

The sound of complete silence was the only thing which could have brought me out of the coma I'd slipped into. Snow falling through the tall pines at dawn is a gift. I marveled as the landscape around us grew white. This turn of events was deadly serious, but I couldn't help basking in the false warmth of those delicate flakes.

Finally, I snapped into action.

"Albert, wake the hell up!" I was on my fourth try. If not for the raspy draw of his breathing I might have given my friend up for dead.

"Oh . . . that's nice." It sounded like he was commenting on a bridal gown. He rolled back over. There was none of the familiar sarcasm in his voice; there wasn't much of anything behind his words. I shook him harder.

"I . . . think we can ride out the storm another day. Let's get some . . . more . . . sleep," he mumbled.

It was harsh, but I tore the roof off of our shelter, then unzipped Albert's sleeping bag.

My stomach knotted up.

The bag I'd borrowed for my friend was not state-of-the-art. A cloth deal best used in temperatures above freezing. I wondered how long it had been absorbing water. Albert was wet from about the waist down.

"Come on, man," Albert complained. I didn't like the color of his lips.

"You're soaking!"

"I'm a little damp . . . that's all. Help me put the roof back on."

I'm not proud of what happened next. Someone arriving at that instant would have mistaken it for that scene from *Deliverance*. Two men in the deep woods, one standing over the other demanding that he take off his pants, all the while slapping and shaking him.

But the truth was I did this out of friendship and guilt. My sleeping bag was bone dry. He was going to put on my thermals, sit tight while I broke camp, then we were going down the mountain together before the snow buried the trail.

The weight of his waterlogged gear buckled Albert's legs. I took everything but the camera bag. We trudged through the snow in silence. It was Sunday morning. Thinking of my heavy load as an act of penance brought a grim smile to my lips.

Halfway to the trailhead, Albert began chatting about the flora and fauna, as if nothing had happened. We stopped at an outcropping of rocks, the valley unfolding for miles below us. Sunlight peaking over the horizon made me question whether any of it had happened.

Albert produced one dry cigarette. I guess it's good to have priorities.

"Well, now." He paused to inhale. "You may have saved my life back there, Joe."

I cracked a smile. He called for the rest of his gear.

"But don't think you can slap me around like that at the drop of a hat. Next time I'll be forced to kill you, and destroy the evidence."

When dear friends get together, the strength of their bond, that carefree movable feast that marks their shared time often works against them. Feeling secure and satisfied wrapped in the armor of true friendship, they push blindly forward—but the world's been known to push back, hard.

My roommate met us at the porch, holding the four-season tent like a smoking gun.

"How'd it go? I heard there was snow in the high country," he said, like this was some sort of news flash.

Albert dropped his gear. "It was a walk in the park!"

We'd made a pact never to tell anyone of my stupidity; as well, we vowed to go no farther than the local grocery store without a four-season tent in tow. To this day, when I ring Albert up from some far-flung country, the conversation begins with a tongue-in-cheek question about the location of my tent. It's nice to know someone cares.

"But it's still our pitiful little secret, right Joe? No one knows the details of that weekend?"

My lips are sealed, big guy. Who would I tell, anyway?

Heavy Loads

IF YOU MAKE ONE DEAR FRIEND A DECADE YOU'RE WAY AHEAD OF THE game. If Albert Pantone was the kindred spirit I discovered in the 1980s, then Matt Siegel, seven years my junior, and full of the same devil-may-care spirit of adventure I'd always claimed as my calling card, was his 1990s counterpart.

"Let me help you bring in some gear," Matt offered.

We were standing in the rain outside a house near Ruidoso, New Mexico, a place we would share for the rest of the fall. It was a forest service building, but one look at it and you prayed the government hadn't claimed to have spent a lot of tax dollars on renovations; it was essentially a cinder-block hull painted light pink with a government green roof. We lovingly referred to it as the Salmon Lodge—which, in my mind, imbued it with something of a Jack London quality.

The rain was coming down pretty hard at that moment. This didn't seem to bother Matt. I handed him a couple of panniers and a small dog my future mom-in-law had forced into my care. She'd pleaded that it was going to the gas chamber otherwise. I pulled the bike off the top rack, then tapped the roof of the car. The ride I'd bummed up the hill drove away.

"That's all of it?"

Matt looked skeptical.

"Well, you gotta keep it light when you're part of a witness protection program."

I winked. The little dog, eventually named Zion and given a nice home on a buffalo ranch in North Dakota, peed in Matt's hand.

"Whoa, doggy," Matt said, setting the mutt down. He was more amused than annoyed. The rain washed his hand clean, for the most part.

"Sorry 'bout that. I'm not really a pet owner. More of a parole officer for this one." I shook my head and then his hand in an act of solidarity.

"Hey, let's get out of the rain and talk," he said. "Looks like you've covered some ground on that bike. You know, I've thought of doing a bit of touring, someday." With that one statement our friendship was sealed.

As volunteers for the forest service, we received housing and a stipend to go hiking and mountain biking every day. Now this was a government program I could support. I'd had so much fun over the course of the previous spring that I'd returned for one more brief stint. My fiancée was stomping around the desert on an eight-week field study. I had to do something with myself. Matt, retreating from college for a semester, was also pining away for a woman. We made quite a team.

First thing we went in search of was a bicycle for Matt. The front office had put in the paperwork for a decent ride, but on short notice we were only able to wangle a metal structure with two wheels from the ranger's wife. Buried under some tennis racquets, it didn't look too horrible in the semidarkness of the garage. Certain equipment should not be passed off as a bicycle simply because, on the surface, it might resemble one. Matt has sprinter's legs; thick trunks for thighs with grapefruit-size calves. Even so, he had serious trouble cranking those pedals uphill. It was the sort of mechanical device that slowed down immediately unless constant force was applied. To make matters worse, regardless of how much lubricant we drenched on its moving parts, the structure squeaked and whined like a parakeet in its death throes. This thing could have been used as a form of torture during the Spanish Inquisitions. I believe it was on these first few rides, Matt groaning and pushing, occasionally lifting his head long enough to observe the ease with which I maneuvered my Raleigh touring bicycle, that he began to covet my rig.

Be careful what you wish for.

I suppose sharing every story I could remember from my two wheeled adventures might also have had something to do with it. Each night we'd take turns sitting on the one piece of furniture in the Salmon Lodge. We'd talk passionately and at length about the call of the wild, which, in my case, sounded a lot like the spinning of a free-wheel and the click of a shifter. Clearing trail, eating lunch at the summit of a ten-thousand-foot peak, or right before falling asleep on a camp-out, my bicycle adventure serial would continue. Matt peppered me with questions, good, thought-through queries about touring. Wheels were turning in his mind's eye, I could tell. It was just a matter of time before Matt set off on a cycling adventure. Every time he brought up bike touring, a look that I'm far too familiar with stared back at me.

We grew close that fall, which is not to say that we didn't hit a rough patch or two on our road to adopted brotherhood. Without the stresses of real employment—unless mapping out mountain bike trails by riding along fire roads in the national forest, clearing deadfall in the high country, and snapping photographs of natural resources while lounging atop a fire lookout tower is your idea of a real pressure-cooker environment—we had to create our own challenges.

Sometimes we pushed each other a little too far. When a couple of guys are evenly matched physically, and there are no wooly mammoths to hunt down, you turn on each other now and then.

Like modern-day Paul Bunyans we'd see who could clear more trail. When a good mountain bike was finally loaned to Matt, I changed the wheels on my own rig and performed a few other alterations, making it ready for serious off-roading. We pumped our way to the summits and barreled down loose single tracks well outside the boundaries of safe performance in our quest to outclass each other. Soon, everything was turning into a dare, a challenge, a competition. For the most part it was harmless fun.

But unlimited free time isn't always a good thing. One afternoon we hiked around a bend and were confronted by piles of twisted metal, steel rods, and rusting junk—in a wilderness area. We'd become rather territorial about our little playground at that point.

The rules forbid any mechanized equipment inside wilderness boundaries. This included our bicycles. So how dare someone drag all that equipment up there and just leave it? When we told the rangers about it, to our horror they informed us that the forest service was the offending party.

"That inventory was choppered in for a watershed reclamation project ten fiscal quarters ago," the ranger droned in his civil servant voice, akin to white noise from an air conditioner. "There was funding in the budget to remove it, but that was absorbed after . . ." blah, blah, blah. The bottom line: This junk was going to sit there until the end of time.

He tried to placate us by pointing out that metal does have a finite life span.

"So does the sun, if you wait around long enough," Matt added.

Something had to be done, and we were just the idle hands to tackle such a bureaucratic monstrosity. We decided to haul the entire eyesore down the mountain piece by piece if that's what it took. It was getting near the end of our tenure with the forest service, so if we wanted to cart all of it down the mountain we needed to get started. No matter how we looked at it, the only option was to drag it out of the wilderness strapped to our backs, then transfer it to the bikes.

Someone should have been keeping a better eye on us. But like most government programs, the oversight committee was back in Washington raising money for their reelection.

This quickly went from being a beautification project to a challenge of wills. It was the only way to talk ourselves into it. More than once we tried to get the other to back down.

"There's a lot of stuff up there," I would point out.

"Not that much," he'd counter.

"You think we should inform the feds about our little project?" he asked, knowing they would put the brakes on anything that had not been evaluated a dozen times by senatorial caucus.

"I'll be on the trail bright and early, with or without you," I said with conviction. My only chance was my friend's lifelong goal of avoiding sunrises.

"I'll bring some extra rope," was Matt's response.

This must have been how the arms race got started.

We stood at the base of the mountain, bleary-eyed and irritable. I was going to suggest a leisurely bike ride around the lake to help wake us up when Matt wordlessly shot out of the gate. I had to step up my pace three or four times just to close the gap. Now that he had a bike of equal caliber, and legs far superior, to mine, Matt liked to make me suffer. Hungry and tired with sweat rolling down my cheeks was not a pleasant way to start the day.

But by the time I'd fallen into a cadence with Matt's blistering tempo, the ride had become purifying. There's something spiritual about pushing yourself to the limit. One of these days I'll be little more than a memory, but for a few moments on a bright morning in New Mexico I made my presence known.

At some point during this epiphany, I actually caught my buddy and kicked up a little dirt as I passed. We pushed ourselves faster and faster along the switchbacks toward the top of the mountain, arriving at the wilderness boundary several hours ahead of schedule. The trash heap was only a few miles away by foot.

We basked in endorphins and the high-mountain air—the breakfast of champions and the gainfully unemployed!

Energized from all the riding and hiking, we were ready to make a thorough study of the pile. I think I remember whimpering. A crew of two dozen Sherpas working at the outer edges of their abilities and the blessing of their high altitude deities couldn't have brought this load down in one trip. Matt found a patch of grass in the sun and curled up with a book.

"What are you doing?" I asked, trying to hold on to the myth that our plan had any chance of succeeding. "We've got work to do."

Matt didn't say anything.

"Okay, so we're not going to get it all down the mountain today," I conceded.

My friend set the novel on his chest and sighed. We knew we were beat, or we should have. Anyone with eyes could see that.

I tried to relax. We never really wanted to carry all that metal on our backs, did we? And the thought of transferring it to the bikes gave me the willies. The accomplishment appealed to me, but not the actual labor. It was different from cycling across a desert, fighting a headwind for hours on end, or deciding which road to pick when you've cycled off the map. I knew how to approach those types of challenges. This pile was too unwieldy, cumbersome, foreign. If only it had pedals attached somewhere, or could be stuffed into a pannier.

We read in comfortable silence for most of the morning. Our reticence passed for an agreement to walk away from the pile.

Matt was surprised then when after lunch I went over to survey the heap one more time. I tugged here and pulled there. A few stray scraps spilled out, allowing the rest of the bulging mass to settle back in place. I managed to fill a wide steel tub with rods and hoist this cluttered package onto my shoulders. The pile appeared relatively unchanged. I stumbled over to my friend.

"Could you tie this down for me?"

Matt actually looked angry. "If we can't bring it all, I'm not bringing any of it."

I cleared my throat.

"We must never be afraid to go too far, for success lies just beyond!"

He picked up the copy of Proust I'd been devouring.

"You just cribbed that from some dead poet who never meant it to apply to trash removal on federal lands."

I had to lean against a tree while Matt finished tying the last knot. He gave the length of rope an exaggerated tug that almost put me on the ground.

"So, I'll see you at the truck?" I asked. Matt waved me off, returning to his place in the sun.

Balancing the load and walking slowly at first, I got a taste of what it might have been like to wear armor into battle. I flogged myself down the mountain; each step was a challenge, each stumble a reminder that I didn't need to be doing this, in fact, I was out of my mind for doing this. And still I trudged ahead.

At a certain point I decided there had to be some higher purpose for my undertaking, one I just wasn't privy to, yet. Like Mormons dragging their worldly posessions across the plains in handcarts, or Spanish missionaries who had given up their warring ways for a life closer to God—subsequently towing heavy armor behind themselves as a weighty reminder and an atonement for their sins.

I must have had my reasons. Was I trying to tax myself for all the hiking and biking the government paid me to enjoy? That couldn't be it. I've never lost sleep over my lack of a puritanical work ethic, and the feds weren't fretting about the twenty-two dollars a day going into my pocket. Maybe we like to break ourselves once in a while simply because we can. Show our bodies who's boss. Bleed just to know we're alive.

The only way to rest was to lean against a tree growing near the edge of the trail, but the weight still pushed heavily on my legs. I was so focused on the chore of keeping my balance and contemplating my reasons that I almost missed the man hiking up the path with a firearm strapped to his hip. He struck me as the sort of fellow accustomed to intimidating people, but when he sized me up there was fear in his eyes. He might have been packing heat, but I had a couple of hundred pounds of metal tied to my back.

Eventually, everything became inconsequental next to the goal of crossing the finish line. Men with guns, Matt's failure to join this foolishness, rationales, rest breaks, all peeled away, until there was only forward motion and sweet misery.

I managed, somehow, to stay on my feet when I spotted the pleasing sight of our bikes hidden in the bushes. My load hit the ground with a cartoon crash. After drinking all the water I could find, anywhere on Mother Earth seemed like a reasonable place to lie down and die. I don't know how long I stayed there.

"I'm . . . not sure . . . how we'll . . . get it onto the bikes."

I stared up at the hulking tower of scrap metal looming over Matt's back. He grinned through his obvious pain. Hot damn, one for all and all for one! It was no longer a competition, but a team. A team of fools.

I rolled to my feet just as his load smashed to the ground. It was an impressive sound. We beamed at each other through the deafening silence that followed, proud of our perverse accomplishments. Matt bathed himself in the water he didn't drink.

"You see the guy with the gun?" he asked.

I nodded.

"Good. For a minute I thought the strain of this stack was causing hallucinations."

Completely loaded, our bikes resembled jousting horses as painted by Salvador Dali. Crap hung off the back, over the handlebars, and out the sides, but it was all on there. We wore our backpacks, useless now, and when I snapped my helmet on I snickered at the futility of that safety device under these circumstances. Surely all that metal would slice me in half before my head ever hit the ground.

"This is so out of control," Matt announced with pride before we'd even started down the trail.

"We're golden," I assured him, then sent my bike over the mountain with a slight push of my heel. I say "my bike" because at that point I was simply along for the ride.

Braking only slowed things down slightly. Matt had been instructed to count to thirty, maybe forty, then follow. That way, when I did crash and burn he had a fighting chance of avoiding ground zero.

Maybe I had a fear of commitment and this was my attempt to avoid the altar. A death wish perhaps, or maybe it was that speedometer and the big hill from my childhood all over again. I can't say. At some point instinct took over and I was manuveuring on pure adrenaline. I could hear Matt hooting and screaming behind me. For a few minutes, barreling down that fire road one reflex away from disaster, we were a couple of lost boys fighting the mandate to grow up. Fighting, and, I daresay, winning.

Hey, we'd leave good-looking corpses.

Matt loaded the last piece of scrap metal into the truck before we staggered down to the lake. Afer all that, the rest of the pile was someone else's problem.

"I've gotta find something more productive to do with my life," Matt announced.

"You and me both," I added.

After a while Matt said, "I've been thinking." A lot of our best conversations started this way. "What if I went for a bike tour during the rest of this year off from school?"

He and the woman in his life had officially called it quits.

"You're gonna need the right gear," I said casually.

We sat studying Bonito Lake for a while. It was our job.

"Well, I'm gonna be busy getting married, soon. Why don't you borrow my stuff?"

Matt stood up. "What, like the bike?"

"No, like everything. The bike, panniers, camping gear, maps . . . everything."

"But then what will you have?" he asked, sincerely concerned that this favor was too big for any friendship.

My grin spread slowly. "I'll finally have someone who really understands what I'm talking about."

And that's how my bicycle made it to Australia and New Zealand twice. Actually, it's done more traveling abroad than I have. There's something unnatural about that. My bike's been to Tasmania, and parts of Indonesia. Places I've only seen on videotape.

I try not to be bitter.

"You're gonna dig New Zealand," I said. "Plenty of hills just like that one. The trick I learned to get through them was to always keep breathing."

And maybe it was the trick I was still trying to master that fall in the White Mountains of New Mexico. Pushing myself as hard as I could, just to feel the air in the depths of my lungs, trying to win some race that in the end is always a race against myself.

Matt's bike trip was a torch-passing of sorts as well as a chance to retrace my steps and discover a few new ones. Just as I'd mailed back little snapshots of America to Albert, my comrade Matt captured images and stories from Down Under that I'd missed the first time around.

The best friendships are like that, they let you live beyond yourself. They keep you breathing.

A Baja State of Mind

I'VE MET MORE THAN A FEW PEOPLE WHO SAY BAJA, MEXICO, IS ALL used up. Finished. Once a dusty little haven for the offbeat and laid back, it's overrun by movie stars and realtors now. While this might be true at the name-brand resorts, I found that for a man with a bicycle and a couple of pesos willing to venture beyond the tourist centers, the land of mañana opens up like a Georgia O'Keefe painting.

Denver was certainly there in the name of art. The rack of his mountain bike brimmed with camera equipment, and a worn burlap sack cluttered full of canvases and painting supplies poked out awkwardly, like a blister bulging on the surface of his more conventional gear.

I thought of van Gogh. Keeping pace a dozen yards off his rear wheel, I scrutinized the young man with more care. At least he had both ears intact. When he coasted to a stop along the dirt road, I actually contemplated riding by without stopping.

Denver wore black combat boots, baggy green shorts, and a tattered white T-shirt with the words NO DEPOSIT, NO RETURN stenciled across its front. He presented something of an intimidating exterior, or maybe I wasn't in the mood for a discussion about anarchy and the cultural contributions of the Sex Pistols. But the cameras and burlap bag held my attention. I squeezed the brake levers at the last moment. Denver was busy tossing a few scraps of food to a gathering pack of friendly, scroungy dogs. After traveling through a sizable stretch of Baja, I'm fairly confident its residents don't actually register or board any of their numerous canines. Maybe these animals are simply part of a massive, loosely organized, free-range petting zoo.

Denver turned out to be as mild-mannered as most of those mangy mutts.

"Last job I had was taking care of people inside a mental institution," he said casually. I tossed him an apple, he passed me a handful of chips. If Russia had been able to duplicate the communal system of food exchange so prevalent among cyclists, the Iron Curtain never would have parted.

"Job before that I worked for a raider on Wall Street. 'Cept for the bars on the windows, I didn't notice much of a difference."

We shared a conspiratorial laugh and watched the dogs pant in the noonday sun and sniff each other. Their subdued vigil for more scraps did not go unrewarded.

"Maybe the mental patients were more polite, I don't know," Denver added. Fair enough.

"So, you're a photographer *and* a painter," I noted, pointing at his gear. "Which would you say you enjoy more?"

His excitement level jumped a few notches. The dogs scurried away when Denver dug out a camera and a new canvas. I suspected I'd struck a nerve.

"Come on, let me show you something." He scrambled up a small rise. The beach was waiting on the other side. I'd established that his combat boots were more than a fashion statement.

The Sea of Cortez, vermilion and tranquil, stretched to the horizon. Denver focused his zoom on a cluster of brightly colored rowboats beached and over turned to keep them from filling with water at high tide.

"See, I could take a photograph of this scene, or I could paint it. Either way, I'm not going to show you what's actually there." He gave the camera in one hand and the canvas in the other emphatic little shakes. "By choosing what to leave in or out, the F-stops, speed, development techniques, I get to shape reality." He chuckled like a person who sticks a key into a lock and then is surprised when the door swings open. "How I position the canvas, the changing light, the act of mixing the colors, even the effects of this morning's coffee on my hand-eye coordination, will undermine the replication of that pure image over there onto this canvas."

He snapped a few frames of the fishing boats. "I'm gonna massage that one into something interesting."

We sat down in the rough sand. Denver was a bit manic at this point, which I don't necessarily find an unattractive state in my fellow man. If you can't get passionate about something, it's not much of a ride.

"The camera, the paintbrush, they're tools that allow me to twist and spin the world until it fits my mood, my desires, and fears. I guess I just like screwing around with reality." He stopped for a gulp of air. "I'm sorry, what was your original question?"

While I had him on pause, I decided to ask Denver something else. Something I'm always curious about when I meet another cyclist.

"Why'd you pick a bicycle to tool around Baja?"

He closed his eyes as though he were tasting something sweet.

"Bicycle touring? Done well, I like to think of it as . . . performance art." He eased back, pointed the camera at the sky and carefully depressed the button.

I decided to throw my lot in with Denver for a time. Hey, no deposit, no return. Besides, I hadn't screwed around with my reality in a long time. As we rode, I joked about my petting zoo theory. He grabbed on to the idea.

"I think that would make a great series. Do you mind?"

Yeah, Denver, that's going to wreck my longstanding plans for a one-man show at the Guggenheim next month.

"It's all yours," I said with a smile.

Denver made a decent riding partner. Not overly concerned with logging mile after mile just for the sake of meeting an arbitrarily set goal, we zigged here and zagged there.

His Spanish was much better than mine. A four-year-old with access to Hooked on Phonics, the Español edition, would speak more proficiently than me. But Denver was almost fluent. For instance, we learned that what appeared to be a group of locals leaning against a couple of trucks as if siesta had just been announced was actually a dejected party of construction workers whose truck had been stuck in the deep sand for more than an hour.

We were the extra muscle that put them over the top. "Gringo Power," one of them said with a laugh. They paid us in bottles of beer just this side of frozen. Denver took their picture.

"You ever paint from a photograph?" I asked, while we drank in the shadow of some trees.

"Occasionally. But most of the time I can work the image enough so it feels like painting in the darkroom. When I do break out a canvas, it's better to stay on location until the painting is done. Let the sand, twigs, and water, and whatever else sticks to the paint, stay right there."

I wasn't even sure if this guy had talent, or just talked a good game. As if Denver could read minds, he added, "Most of it turns to crap, but once in a while I get underneath there and find that *thing* I was looking for."

Now I really wanted to see his work.

The wandering dog pack series was coming along. He was more selective than I would have been. *All* the mutts had heaps of character to me. Like a casting director, Denver would audition an animal by capturing it in his camera sights, then following it for a few seconds. Most of them didn't make the cut. Only a click away from fame and notoriety, they'd wander off in search of their next meal, indifferent to their brush with stardom.

I noticed a trend. Denver was as concerned with the context in which we found the dogs as with the animal's actual features. When he spotted something he liked, a white poodle rolling in the mud outside a bar, a guard dog asleep on the job, or a mutt waiting next to bus stop sign, we'd pull over and stage a guerrilla-style photo shoot. He liked to encourage the animals with badly sung songs by the Clash.

The sign attached to the fence post dividing a junkyard from a small gas station should have been enough to send us on our way, but Denver's French must not have been as strong as his Spanish.

CHIEN LUNATIQUE! the sign warned. It had to be a joke; the animal in question was the size of a Nerf ball. Denver rattled off a few frames featuring the pint-size terror lounging inside a discarded box of Tide. Even the little yelp it emitted was laughable.

I saw the bigger dog before Denver. My travel companion was singing, appropriately enough, the lyrics to "Should I Stay or Should I Go?" when the rightful lunatique of the junkyard made its move. A tailless beast, slow from the heat, this animal still looked like it could do some damage. Denver kept shooting pictures as he back-pedaled through the gate. What we'll do for art.

Those combat boots kicked up a lot of dust as he made his getaway. I balanced his bike with one hand while he jumped on. The dog looked pissed, but a little relieved when we cycled beyond its territory.

"Be thankful it wasn't a goose," I told Denver. "They don't respect boundaries."

We stopped at a little roadside stand for Pepsi in the bottle and freshly made tamales.

"You think that dog looked a little like Jack Nicholson?" Denver asked.

"Well, that would explain his behavior toward the paparazzi!" I noted.

He laughed. "I can't wait to develop that picture."

The last time I saw Denver he was dancing in his big boots under the stars at a little community festival. It was after well after dark. We were resting against the still-warm stones of a building across from the square when Denver announced that he might like to stay in town for a few days. "I've spotted some things around here I think I want to paint."

A group of those ubiquitous dogs was nearby, so I asked for his camera and told Denver to let me take a picture of him huddled with them.

"You've got to have a photo of yourself with the dogs . . . for the artist statement when this opens in SoHo," I pointed out.

Not tired, and wanting to do a little night riding for a change, I suggested we say our goodbyes right there.

"Keep messing with reality," I said.

"And you keep writing those stories, the way *you* see them," he tossed back.

When I looked over my shoulder Denver had the camera pointed in my direction. I let the darkness swallow me, never sure whether I'd made his final cut, or even if there was enough underneath to give my friend anything to work with.

The road rolled almost silently under my wheels and the surf breaking on the sand nearby kept rhythm for me. While I pedaled along one phrase, like a mantra or a freshly minted set of operating instructions, kept sticking in my head.

No deposit, no return.

You give and take in this life, and you don't ask for anything back. And if you're a guy named Denver, maybe you try to shape it into something you really want to see.

The Tree Huggers versus the Tree Cutters, as Told by the Fence Sitter

*Far better to dare mighty things, to win glorious triumphs,
even though checkered by failure, than to take rank with those
poor spirits who neither enjoy much nor suffer much, because
they live in the gray twilight that knows not victory, nor defeat.*
—Theodore Roosevelt

WHEN YOU CYCLE FOR DAYS UNDER THE BIG TREES OF THE PACIFIC
Northwest it begins to feel like everything around you is breathing.
Moist, green, and fertile, the texture of the land, its vibrancy, seeps
into your pores, figuratively speaking. Of course, the right rain gear is
a must in this neck of the woods if you don't want seepage of a more
tangible nature.

I always made good time climbing the hills and coasting along the
secluded valleys of Washington, Oregon, and California's old-growth
forests. It was like taking hits of pure oxygen that all of those giant
redwoods, chestnuts, pines, and ferns were pumping out. Often, I
rode my strongest near the end of the day.

A park ranger tried to put his finger on it for me.

"It's like living inside a filter," he mused. "Quiet and wet, you sit
under the dense canopy and can almost watch the exchange taking

place, of bad air for good. I think it keeps the rest of the world from overheating . . . from smothering on itself."

True as the ranger's words rang, the deep woods can make a person feel a little claustrophobic after a while. I'd pause an extra moment or two at vista points above the tree line, then, like Jonah and the whale, the forest would swallow me up again. I found myself avoiding larger groups in the campgrounds, and before long, people in general. After stretching out for a time with a book against the trunk of a hulking tree, I checked myself, half seriously, for moss growth.

Before my hermitlike behavior really took hold, I spent a day with a pack of bikers—we're talking motorcycles now—at a campground in southern Oregon.

As the roar of engines assaulted me from every direction, I felt dwarfed and inconsequential leaning against my bicycle. I could have hooked my panniers back in place and pedaled away, such is the beauty of solo touring, but there was an undeniable energy in that campground. And no one was flashing me the evil eye; in fact, there was a festive, inclusive vibe in the air. Rowdy and loud, but there's nothing wrong with a party now and then.

Bikes kept arriving throughout the afternoon until they numbered well over a hundred. Space was getting tight. Randy, a logger from northern California set up shop next to me. He placed an oversize red cooler between our tents and gave a wave in my direction.

"Pretend it's your refrigerator, partner."

I stuck my mitt over his bike and we shook hands. He nodded in the direction of my ride.

"You're a little light in the horsepower department for this crowd."

I slapped my thighs. "That really depends on how strong these guys feel at any given moment."

Randy let out a laugh.

"More power to you. You know, this is just a warm-up ride for the Redwood Run a couple weeks from now. You wouldn't believe how many bikes show up at that thing. It's something else."

The noise level had tapered off, replaced by the general sounds of a big picnic. Or maybe I was adjusting to the powerful purr of engines. When packs of bikes hummed in unison along the tree-lined highway near the campground entrance, the pitch had a beehive quality to it. A line of parked bikes stretched from one end of the campground to the other.

"Can't imagine more bikes than this in one place," I said, helping myself to his beverage stash.

Randy quickly procured two lawn chairs from somewhere on his Harley and the next thing I knew we were lounging in the heart of my first biker rally.

We swapped stories. I learned that Randy had been "harvesting" lumber for nearly twenty-five years in northern California. Divorced, he had two children who spent part of each summer with him.

"Logging's always been a tough living," he stated, easing back in his chair. "It's gotten harder to make it pay since the corporate mergers, so I don't see my kids as much as I'd like, but they always get what they need. It's still a good job. Nobody over my shoulder, and I sure like the outdoors. The tree huggers are back in force, though. They haven't been this thick since the early 70s."

Sounded as if he was talking about mosquitoes.

"It's not like there's even a draft to dodge right now."

I decided to omit the part on my résumé where I helped organize cleanups on campus and raise funds for Bikes Not Bombs. Discretion being the better part of valor, I thought a biker rally was not the ideal place to flash my Sierra Club card and pass the helmet around for the next campaign.

Besides, Randy seemed like a stand-up guy. He wasn't the one shipping raw logs to Japan and signing the orders to clear-cut the big trees. He was paying alimony.

"I'm sure some of them think they're helping, but one of these days a tree hugger's gonna get hurt," he said, then caught me looking a bit too hard. "Not by me, mind you," he added. "But it's dangerous at a logging site, heavy machinery, and some of these kids climb up in the high branches."

If I was going to say something eloquent in defense of Mother Earth, that was the moment. Instead, I stayed quiet, nodded a couple times, and took another can out of his cooler.

It was quite an evening, though I was almost disappointed at the lack of the gunplay or public acts of debauchery rumored to take place at biker rallies. I met people who practiced law during the week and others who just rode the blacktop cashing their veteran's checks once a month. It was a cross section of America, from housewives and contractors to guys who hauled meat for living.

"Look me up when you get down near Scotia," Randy said after we exchanged addresses. From the tone in his voice, I knew he meant it.

"You time it right we can go check out the Redwood Run together. Might even be able to borrow you a bike with a bigger engine."

He gave me a Roman handshake, hand to upper forearm. I didn't know if that was a biker thing, a logger thing, or just a Randy thing, but I remember thinking at the time that it was a pretty cool gesture.

When I eventually made it to Randy's door, he was either working or sleeping. His bike was in the driveway and some lights were on in the double-wide, but no one answered the door after repeated knocks. I crammed a note between the slots on the porch railing and went in search of a campground. It was dark when I set up my tent so I couldn't tell who I was bunking near, but I was too tired to worry about it. As I drifted off, the distinct aroma of patchouli oil and burning sage was heavy in the air.

"Join us, friend, for some herbal tea," offered a soft-spoken man in loose-fitting clothing, earth tones, and lace-up moccasins. His beard was long and matted. I was still wiping the sleep out of my eyes when two women, gorgeous wood-nymph-like creatures with flowing skirts and no shoes on their feet, appeared at his left and right.

"Yeah, let me get my cup," I replied, though herbal tea was not my poison of choice in the morning.

"I'm Oak. This is Whisper and Cricket."

I watched the girls glide down to the river. I have a weakness for bare feet.

"Excuse me, did you say your name was Oak?"

I pride myself on my lucidity, even first thing in the morning, but those names weren't computing.

"Live Oak is my full Gaia name, but Oak is what my friends call me." He handed me a cup of tea. "I hope you'll call me Oak."

When the girls returned we sat in the damp morning air and discussed the beauty around us, my bike travels, and their mission to protect the forest from future harm.

"You guys are a fairly small regiment to be taking on the logging interests around here," I said with a smile.

I was more concerned with their live-and-let live dispositions than their actual numbers. No one was going to mistake this trio for tough ecoterrorists.

"We have . . . kindred organizations helping us champion our cause," Whisper whispered.

She pointed across the path to a collection of Subarus, an old International, and a retrofitted RV with camouflage netting draped off the back end as a makeshift tent area.

"Earth Firsters and some anarchists who are sensitive about being lumped into any one category," Oak noted.

As any self-respecting anarchist should be, I thought.

No one was stirring near the RV, but Oak said their group boasted a dozen members, and though he didn't agree with certain aspects of their lifestyle, especially the consuming of meat, everyone was free to make their own choices.

"They believe in the sanctity of these forests, and that makes us family," he added.

While the Earth First clan slept in, Oak and company explained the game plan. Work on a logging road was set to continue the following day. Progress had been halted due to some heavy-machinery failure. Oak couldn't contain his grin when he told me that part. Now I understood why the Earth First group was sleeping in.

"When they come to build the rest of the road we're going to be chained to the fence," Cricket announced. It was the first thing she'd said all morning.

My heart went out to these people. I understood their thinking if not their resistance to hygiene products, even the environmentally benign brands. As a species we *are* mucking up the place, and technology has its limits. A cure-all it's not. We're a clever lot, but will we ever become wise? This is a question for the ages, but, since the rise of global industries, one that's never been more pressing.

I said as much to Oak, Cricket, and Whisper. The gleam in their eyes let me know they thought I was on the team, and part of me wanted to be. I've always had a soft spot for martyrs, rebels, and the Earth.

What I didn't voice was that I found utterly repugnant the notion of chaining myself to a fence as a bulldozer bore down on me. Not only was it dangerous, but it was an act of futility. The trees might not fall that day, but it wasn't solving anything long term.

"It's helping to define the issues," a friend once lectured me.

The deeper truth: I was a bit of a coward, with a nasty habit of seeing things I agreed with on both sides of an issue. Call it the Jimmy Carter Syndrome, but I wanted peace in the valley, every valley. I drank my herbal tea, kept my mouth shut, and dreamed about caffeine.

The smart move would have been to pack my gear and head down the road, but I wanted to have dinner with Randy if I could, meet his kids, so I stayed put for another day. Also, when the Earth Firsters finally got up, they were quite entertaining. And Cricket and Whisper never did put on shoes.

When I woke the next morning, I still hadn't gotten in touch with my tree-cutting friend, but the heady atmosphere of a tribe, eclectic as it was, preparing for battle had an intoxicating draw.

I decided it couldn't hurt to ride out there and bear witness to the confrontation. I reasoned that I might learn something about where I really stood on the subject. Maybe, as a card-carrying member of the TV generation, I just hated to miss the show?

When I got there things were well underway. The protectors of the forest had arrived bright and early, getting the jump on the road builders. Most of them were in position, linked in various ways to the fence.

Oak and a few delegates from the Earth First crew were taking a conference with a guy in a hard hat, a forest service official, and a member of the law enforcement community.

"Even though you agree that these permits don't add up, you're still gonna tell me your hands are tied?" said one of the Earth Firsters to the forest service official. "The road will be built before it ever goes through the proper channels!" He was red in the face now.

Oak didn't say anything. He turned on his heels and came over to me. I didn't think he knew I was there.

"Can I borrow your bike lock?" he asked.

"I. . . ."

Handing it to him was not the smartest thing I've ever done.

He walked back to the first bulldozer and calmly locked himself, by the neck, to the blade arm of the big machine. It was an oversize U-lock but it wasn't looking very roomy around Oak's neck.

Things got ugly fast. A group of loggers in a truck parked behind the bulldozers cheered on the driver as he put the dozer into gear. Oak balanced along the top edge of the arm as best he could; the man's neck *was* locked in place. When the driver engaged the blade, moving it up in the air like an angry elephant's trunk, I gasped. There was no way to change this channel. Oak hung on.

The cop wasn't breaking any speed records in his efforts to stop the driver. A couple of Earth Firsters got in front of the dozer so it couldn't advance farther.

When the driver lowered Oak, I thought the young idealist was going to fall forward, snapping his neck like it was in a hangman's noose. That's when I realized the only key to that lock was in my front bag. I dug it out and ran into the mayhem.

More cops showed up. The loggers taunted the protesters as they were cut away from the fence line and loaded into a paddy wagon. When I got the lock unfastened, Oak's neck was bruised and red. An officer grabbed my arm. I snapped around.

"I'm not part of this," I said, realizing immediately how ridiculous that sounded, even to me. I continued my pleas after we arrived at the station. When that didn't seem to work, I got mad.

"My bike is still lying out there somewhere. If it gets stolen I'm holding you responsible," I hissed.

The deputy placed my lock on the counter. "Maybe you should have secured it with the proper equipment if you were so concerned about it."

I closed my eyes. Fingerprinting was next. That's when Randy came through the door. He knew the deputy by name. Said he had my bike in the truck and that there had to be some mistake.

"He was up at the biker rally with me in Ashland a few weeks ago."

Randy said he was with a second group of loggers, which arrived late. He recognized my bike as the cops were driving us down the road. "I've been out of town, but I got your messages," he said to me.

Looking from Randy to the group of stunned environmentalists, I felt like the only legitimate criminal in that building. The charges: first-degree fence sitting.

Oak, who had been standing beside me, stepped back.

"Are you some kind of narc?" one of the anarchists seated against a wall asked in a disgusted tone.

Oak looked down and shook his head. "I really thought you were one of us, Joe."

There was nothing else to say. The deputy let me go. Randy walked with me as far as his truck but he didn't offer to help me hoist my bike out.

"You got any sort of explanation for this?" Randy snapped. His eyes were angry little slits now.

"Not one you're going to believe."

I rode away fast and hard, friendless and more alone than I'd felt in years. So much for peace in the valley.

And now, farther down the line, I still take the middle ground on many issues, but I'm quick to let people know where I stand. It's better that way.

Randy's truck barreled past just as I cleared the city limits and the big trees began crowding the highway again.

Soon it was just me and the clean, moist breathing of an ancient forest. A quiet place to think . . . and try to exchange some of my bad air for good.

You Can't Go Home Again, But Pedaling By It Is Another Story

IN THE SPRING OF 1974, I WATCHED FROM THE BACK OF A YELLOW TAXI with Pennsylvania plates as my childhood home got smaller and smaller.

The excitement and preparations of moving to Florida had overwhelmed my eight-year-old hard drive for weeks, to the point that I hadn't really given much thought to my departure from the only world I'd ever known.

Of course, it was raining that morning. I reached out to wipe clean the fogging rear window so as to keep the white brick house at the bottom of the hill in sight that much longer.

My head crowded with random memories: games played in the front yard; the euphoric afternoon spent learning to ride on my sister's bicycle; trick-or-treating at dusk; snowball fights with my best friends; and the way I used to spin in aimless circles as I made up antiwar songs under the ancient elm tree in our neighbor's side yard.

Then we crested the hill and that world abruptly dropped out of view. A silent tear or two slipped down my face. I think it was the first time the concept of loss, of nonnegotiable endings, became tangible to me.

The rest of my family members were laughing and chattering as they faced forward. I felt they were betraying our childhood in some way, not respecting the moment. I wanted to be silent and reverent as I said goodbye to Jackson Street. My mother brushed her fingers through my hair as we zipped passed Dillworth Elementary School. I ignored her touch. Only when the neighborhoods became foreign to me did I turn around and embrace my future. But I vowed with the conviction of a religious zealot to return someday; to pick up where I'd left off.

I was too young to realize the truth of that statement, You can never go home again.

My brief return to Jackson Street came, fittingly enough, in the saddle of my bicycle sixteen years later. On my way west by train to begin a bicycle tour, I stopped in Pittsburgh to visit friends and pedal a little for my upcoming ride. I was harboring no illusions that Indian summer afternoon of reclaiming my bedroom from the strangers who now occupied our former home. Actually, I nearly passed on the idea of cycling down the hill and into the driveway, telling myself it was just so much brick and mortar to me now.

The whole world, with all its mysteries, was mine to explore. What could I get out of rolling through the old neighborhood but disappointment over how small everything had become to my adult eyes?

The neighbors who weren't dead and buried had probably moved away long ago. I'd stand around for a few minutes feeling melancholy, like a ghost from another era . . . and for what?

But curiosity is a strong and unpredictable force.

As the bike picked up speed on the descent, a wonderful transformation took place. Part of me became that little boy on his one-speed bike.

Baseball cards flapping against the spokes once created the illusion of power. I could almost hear them as I navigated the potholes, curbs, and sidewalks that were once second nature to me.

Of course, the scale was all wrong. Things *were* much smaller, but not everything had gone through the shrink cycle. The little saplings we'd planted in the front yard a few weeks before moving were now trees with thick, solid trunks.

I marveled at just how much had stayed the same. It was afternoon on a weekday so I decided to risk wandering into the side yard, maybe take a peek in a window or two, and stroll out back. That's when I heard the sound of a radio inside the screen porch of our old neighbors' house. It looked like the same decrepit model that coaxed forth classical music during my childhood.

The woman holding a paintbrush was familiar. She set the tool down, pulled off her bandanna, and smiled, and then it came to me.

"Peggy, I mean, Mrs. Ackerman?"

"Yes."

"I'm Joe Kurmaskie, little Joey!"

With that we were off and running. She took me inside and while we shared a couple of glasses of lemonade, I learned that her husband, an alcoholic whom I remember only grunting at us occasionally and sitting in the shadows of their porch, had died years ago.

"He wasn't the sort of person kids got to know," she said, "but he gave me my two boys and for that I'll always be grateful."

Grant, her son who used to baby-sit us, play all sorts of characters and perform magic shows for our entertainment, and drive us to the park in the convertible he bought a year before heading off to college, had become a human rights lawyer and was living in some corner of the world, championing a cause for justice.

This brought a smile. Grant was always a clear-minded person who burned bright.

"You remember Kurt . . . he owns a comic-book store in Los Angeles. He's been excited about this new show in development out there. Called it *The X-Files*. He says it's going to be huge and he's buying up collectibles for resale. He's always thinking about the next big thing."

She told me that a college professor with no family moved into our house some years back.

"It was never as lively after you kids moved away," she said softly.

Together we marched into my old backyard and somehow Peggy knew just when to keep quiet so the memories of that lifetime could rush back. I felt the happy voices of all those games of hide-and-go-seek and capture the flag wash over me.

As we came up to the ravine our parents were always cautioning us to avoid, I asked Peggy if she'd been lonely over the years since her boys left home.

A grin sprouted on her face.

"As a matter of fact, I've had a glorious time. It looked like I was going to grow old in this house with just a few visits a year from Kurt and Grant, but an unlikely thing happened. I met a man—a man who liked me over a bottle of liquor. He happened to be well off and took me around the world."

When we got back inside her home, I was shown pictures of Peggy on a camel with the pyramids of Egypt in the background.

"Howard passed last Christmas," she added as she brushed a hand across one of the pictures.

I began to offer my condolences, but she cut me off.

"Thanks, but Howard gave me such a second lease on life I can't really mourn when I think of him. It wasn't our style."

As I slowly rode my bicycle along the length of the street, turned around, and prepared to pedal away from my first home for what was probably the last time, I noticed an older black couple sitting on their porch.

"You wouldn't happen to be Alan Clark's parents?" I called out in a skeptical tone.

"In the flesh," the man responded with hearty enthusiasm. "And you're one of those towheaded little boys who used to ride Big Wheels with Alan, right?"

I nodded, straightening the panniers on my bike.

"I see you graduated to even larger wheels. I think Alan's got you beat in that department, but I bet he'd trade places with you in a second."

"Why's that?" I asked.

"He's driving a tank in this Desert Storm project heating up in Iraq."

His mother, who hadn't spoken a word, piped in with: "We're just praying he comes back in one piece. Joined the army for a bit of education money."

We visited for a while. From photos on the walls, I could see that the little kid doctors called "hyperactive" had turned into a sharp-looking man who kept in touch with his parents.

I walked alone through the wooded yard behind Alan's house. Still there was a not-so-terrifyingly tall ledge we once called the Wall of China. We dared one another to jump from it. Alan wouldn't do it, so we didn't let him carve his name in the tree next to the wall.

Kids can be ruthless.

I dug a penknife out of my pocket and added Alan's name beside our old initials and the jagged words: WE WERE HERE! '73.

This meager attempt to right a childhood slight was done with no clear reasons in mind. Alan probably didn't even remember the incident or those names on that tree. But as an adult, he'd taken probably the biggest jump of any of us, and I needed to recognize that in some way.

Hanging over my handlebars, I firmly shook Mr. Clark's hand.

"Tell Alan to take care over there, and let him know I stopped by."

Mr. Clark clasped my hand a moment longer.

"I'll show him the tree when he makes it home. That should cover it." He winked before taking his place beside his wife back on the porch.

Months later, when the casualty list from Desert Storm was displayed at a post office, a friend of mine wondered why I was so interested in searching the names.

Alan P. Clark wasn't on it.

Like me, he got to go home again—even if it was only for a visit.

A Friendly Game of Darts

"THAT'S A HELLUVA WAY TO TAKE A WALKABOUT," THE BARTENDER commented, inspecting my bicycle as I wheeled it into the bar for safekeeping. "If ya bush-bashed it all the way here on that thing, mate, then the first one's on the house."

I liked this place already, wherever it was on that map I'd lost days ago. Blame it on the heat, or the need for some lively companionship after mind-altering miles alone pedaling the far reaches of the outback. It could even have been the oversized bottles of Cooper's Crow Eater beer I'd imbibed through much of the afternoon, or the way I kept calling out the correct answers to a rerun of *Jeopardy* blaring from an ancient TV that hung at a precarious angle over the bar—but when my new friends suggested a small wager be placed on the next game of darts, I thought it a brilliant idea.

"Give it a burl,[1] mate?" asked Wes, a full-size Aussie with meaty forearms and hair bleached nearly white by the powerful sun of the southern hemisphere.

My "hotel" room hadn't set me back much; nothing more than four blank walls, a stained army cot, and a fan that made plenty of noise but failed to produce any noticeable change in wind speed. The beer was dirt cheap, and the munchies on the bar were quite stale, but free and plentiful, so I thought I was on something of a roll. How much damage could a friendly game of darts cause?

"We'll play for nickels and dimes then, right?"

That sounded a bit on the low side for a collection of larrikins[2] in the middle of nowhere who drank stout as if it were tap water and discussed acts of daring like mundane trips to the supermarket.

"What the hell, let's play for dollars," I announced with no small amount of bravado. Running the numbers in my head, I calculated that performing at my worst I might lose, say, twenty bucks.

Wes conferred with his mates, then gave me a nod.

The bar, lit like a cave, erupted with hoots and applause.

Someone called for a shout,[3] which brought on more applause. People who had been lurking in the shadows of the shadows pulled up chairs and settled in for the match. I guessed anything could be turned into an event when marking time along the red sand hills and salt bushes of the desolate Nullarbor Plain.

"Who ya gonna barrack[4] for?" I heard an old-timer ask a table of quarry workers.

"The Yank, of course. He's willing to wager those numbers, he's gotta be a ringer."

A bit of side betting began to take place.

If my beer-addled brain had been paying closer attention to what the quarry worker said, everything might have turned out different. But all I heard was that he was rooting for me. I had a fan base. It was only later that I would return to and examine the part about "wagering those numbers."

By virtue of having pedaled this far into the outback, I'd earned a certain celebrity status among the locals. They plied me for stories about the road and shook their heads now and then. It takes a lot to impress hearty folk, but I seemed to fit the bill.

Wes was taking the game too seriously, and his playing reflected this. Stiff and earnest, he kept missing the mark or tossing his darts so hard that a good score fell from the board just when he needed it.

I found myself up a few bucks going into the last set.

We took a break, I ordered another stubby,[5] and Wes stepped outside for some solar therapy. After his sunbake, my meaty competitor played like a new man. All of his darts stuck, he doubled and tripled nearly every round, and I was in danger not only of losing, but of taking, as the Aussies say, a real shellacking.

The crowd cheered me on, even the ones with money in Wes's corner. They love an underdog in the outback, it's like looking in a mirror. Still, I felt it slipping away.

"Looks like a no-hoper," the old-timer said with a certain amount of glee.

I took a long pull on my stubby. A note about Australian beer, specifically the stouts brewed in-country, not lightweight brands like Foster's, which they don't mind sharing with the rest of the world: Brew from Oz is fuel-injected stuff, but so tasty that it sneaks up on you. Holding my last dart, my last chance, and concentrating on the center of the board as all the noise from the crowd dissipated and it was just my heartbeat and steady breathing, I began to question my reflexes. Could I get on my bike at that moment and carve a straight line through the desert? Doubtful. And here I wanted this dart to find a home at dead center of a small board on the other side of the room?

Someone cleared his throat. I thought of the perfect jump shot as the dart left my hand, might even have stepped back, imitating a fall-away that grabs nothing but net. Swish.

But basketball is basketball, and darts, well, I learned that day that darts is not my game. It stuck to the board, but that's about all. I'd given it too much touch.

My smile was forced. There's something about losing, even at a friendly game of darts, that I'll never get comfortable with. You start palling around with failure, pretty soon he's sleeping on your couch and drinking right from the milk carton. That's no way to live.

People placed their hands on my shoulders, patted my back.

"Good game," one whispered. "She'll be right!" another said.

Wes shook my hand. "Ya gave it a fair crack of the whip," he said, indicating with a nod that he'd be with his mates at the bar when I was ready to settle up.

I reached into my sock and pulled out my contribution to Wes's drinking fund. The damage was nothing really, thirteen dollars and some wounded pride.

"Unlucky thirteen," I said as I handed Wes the cash.

He looked at me hard for a moment, which was a moment longer than I wanted, then the clouds parted and Wes broke into laughter. His push[6] joined the merriment with their own snorts and chuckles.

"That's a beaut, mate," Wes said.

I played along, laughing with the rest of them.

"Boys, I think this dag[7] is having us on."

Wes put that meaty arm across my shoulder and presented me to the group.

"He knows it's thirteen hundred dollars, but Joe here's a Yank with a genuine sense of humor, we don't get many of those."

Now, I had about a half second to choose my response. Inside, the bottom had just dropped out of my life. I discovered too late that dollar bets in that neck of the woods meant hundred-dollar bills and I was going to come up a little short of my tab. Maybe they were con men. No wonder the entire bar had stopped to watch our match. The alcohol helped mask my true feelings. Sober, I might have begun convulsing on the spot.

Cry foul?

A thousand miles of desert behind me, seated in a cave full of strangers, all of whom witnessed me lose the game fair and square, is no place to start arguing the fine print. Unless I wanted to hand over all my possessions and become Wes's indentured Sheila until my debt was paid, I had to win my money back, somehow. The first step was keeping my cool.

There's something rather calming about having no other options.

Making a run for it crossed my mind for about a nanosecond. Aside from the obstacles of a few acacia trees and knee-high scrub brush, a person could stand at any point on the horizon and track my progress for miles.

Somehow, I managed to convince Wes that I was good for it, or maybe he knew I wasn't going anywhere. There was the business of my bank wiring me some additional funds, I pointed out, but I was an established writer, awash in money, surely they'd heard of me? I even wangled Wes into buying my drinks the rest of the evening—since he did have a healthy chunk of my money now. I kept things light, acting casual and cavalier about my loss.

I broached the subject of a rematch at the high point of the evening, when the boasting reached its peak, the lies were at their thickest, and tongues began to noticeably slur. I'd been nursing beers and trying to sober up ever since the discovery that I was in the deep end of the ocean without as much as a flotation device.

"Now Wes, I'm gonna have to ask for a fair go[8] at winning my money back," I said, trying my damnedest to use the right lingo, create the impression I really was one of his mates.

This had been strategically timed to catch a lull in the conversations of everyone in the surrounding area. Wes would look like a real wowser[9] to his peer group if he didn't step up to the plate. Then again, with thirteen hundred smackers Wes could afford a new peer group.

"What'd ya have in mind, mate?" Wes asked through a sleepy grin. He picked a coin up off the bar. "Two-up[10]?"

I grabbed the coin and tossed it back on the bar.

"Let's make it more exciting than that." I stood, pretending to look Wes over.

"You're in pretty good nick,[11] my friend," I pointed out, like this was a surprise to me. Actually, Wes had a farm-boy build that was slowly going to seed, but anyone watching me at that moment would have though I'd stumbled upon an Olympic hopeful.

"What do you say to an off-road bike race? Give this station[12] a real spectator sport to come out and cheer on." Now I was heading for absolutely uncharted territory, thinking, "Maybe I should just slink into the darkness, take my chances."

Wes cracked a smile, but I didn't have him sold yet.

"Okay, I reckon I've got a slight edge on you in this area, so let's agree I'll race with all my gear aboard. Say, high noon, tomorrow." I threw in the high-noon part because it sounded right at the time. I wasn't thinking about the heat.

Wes squared his shoulders, like a boxer.

"Do you have a bike?" I asked

"I'll get one," he assured me.

We agreed to meet in the morning to map out the course. Maybe I could sell sponsorships in my team of one and raise a little scratch that way. The thought that I could lose even more cash tried to muscle its way into my brain, but I was in survival mode; nothing was going to come between my visualization of crossing that finish line ahead of Wes. I would be the victor of the first (but definitely not annual) Win Your Freedom Back Mountain Bike Race. Funded by I'm a Blooming Idiot Productions.

Despite the lively atmosphere in that bar, I detected the crushing weight of desperation teetering just above me; a gigantic black anvil —patient, inevitable. At least I'd bargained for one more dart. And this time it would have wheels on it.

I sat on a bench outside my "hotel" observing little insects entangle themselves in a spiderweb near the light. I took some perverse pleasure in watching this. So many bugs blundered into the web that the spider could have gone into the catering business. For some reason, I couldn't sleep. The old-timer, yet another person who had made money from my appearance in this little outpost, creaked to a halt and eased down on the other side of the bench.

"Don't sleep but a couple hours anymore," he explained.

We sat in silence.

After a while he said, "This damn body," holding his unsteady hands in front of himself as evidence. "It's turning wild and unfamiliar, mate. I had it domesticated for a while, but I see now it's going back to earth a bit at a time. One of these days it's going to cut me loose all together." He spat at the spiderweb. A few of the bugs were set free. The vagaries of fate.

The old-timer wandered off, and I spent the rest of the night flopping about on a cot, wondering what it would feel like to watch your dearest possession grow irretrievably wild, and not be able to do anything about it.

Just before dawn I gave up on sleep completely and went back outside wearing only my boxer shorts. The stars rained down by the millions. I spun around with my head tilted toward the heavens, slowly at first, then faster, like when I was a kid. It's amazing what you can create with your own two eyes, gravity, and motion. I held on to my celestial light show for as long as I could, then fell to the ground in a dizzy heap. When I gazed up again the silvery sheen of starshine was fading. For a few moments the horizon was bathed in a ghostly purple, its singular beauty a reminder to anyone who would take one instant of their time for granted.

Overwhelmed, I sat in the dirt producing sounds some might mistake for laughter and others would confuse with crying. Take your pick. In a land called Oz my adventures had finally spun me right off the map. I managed to crawl back to bed, falling into a deep, dream-less sleep.

The flies and cloying heat of my room woke me. It was after ten in the morning and I couldn't have felt worse if I hadn't slept at all. In the shade of an SU, I took in fluids and ate some fruit. I didn't want to be stuffed full of a heavy breakfast when there was a race to win.

The Tea and Sugar Train, as usual a day behind schedule, arrived that morning. The train always brought more people out of the wood-work. They came to buy supplies, get checked by the rural health worker on board, and socialize a little. There would to be a good-size crowd for the race after all. Jeff, the engineer I'd met in Port Augusta, wasn't going anywhere with that train until a winner was declared.

The mile-long course we mapped out was a lopsided circle. It crossed the railroad tracks twice and included plenty of thorny plants to be avoided, but no dips or climbs, this being flat desert.

Wes seemed rested and in good spirits.

"We thought maybe you'd try to shoot through on us last night, but you're dinki di.[13]"

I'd been in the country for weeks, and at times still had no idea what these people were talking about. Wes slapped my back. The heat was outrageous. I felt like puking. Not far from Adeleide I'd incorporated a modified pith helmet into the lining of my bike helmet in hopes that should a breeze happen to appear, I'd be ready for it.

"I'll just round up my bike, then," Wes said.

"You do that," I thought, expecting to see a rusted hunk of metal or a one-speed clunker fit for Pee-Wee Herman, but Wes came back from the train with a decent rig. Its tires were not as wide as mine, but by God, it was an adequate bike for the challenge. I swore under my breath.

"One of the fettlers[14] is a bikie, like you," Wes noted. He got on for a little test ride. "This is going to be heaps of fun, mate," he said, cir-cling me on his new bike.

I couldn't let this setback get me down. I still had months of con-tinuous riding under my belt, and the dark truth I'd buried in my heart until that moment was that win or lose I planned to keep right on going after I crossed that finish line. Sure, if I lost they'd probably come after me, maybe roll me for my possessions or worse, but I was not voluntarily handing over my assets (just under five hundred dollars and a plane ticket back to the States). I had to win.

Pressures of the moment aside, I couldn't help but appreciate the bedraggled collection of humanity lining the course: Aboriginal men dressed in golf shirts, women sporting neon halter tops long past their halter-top-wearing prime, children towing pieces of toys or sticks they had christened toys and used to draw lines in the dirt with as they ran along, and plenty of traditional outback blokes, hardy roughnecks in shorts, all baked a reddish brown. A few of them weren't wearing hats. I guess it wouldn't officially be the hot season for a couple more months.

The old-timer held a up a fading red bandanna. We gripped our handlebars and waited. The bandanna hung there forever. I remembered a Portuguese proverb, A good beginning is half the battle!, and tensed my leg muscles until I thought they might pop.

It was a clean start. The old-timer was in charge of his body for another day. Wes launched off the line first, only because I had a lot more weight to get rolling. It was not the sort of race that called for much strategy. My competition was going to make it a mile long sprint. I closed the gap and prepared to take the lead when disaster nearly struck. As we reached the dirt road before the first set of railroad tracks, I hit what is known as bull dust. This is a fine and often deceptively deep dust along outback roads. It rocked me forward, but I managed to avert a fall by pulling up hard on the handlebars. All that training as a middle-class child from the suburbs in search of popping the perfect wheelie saved the day. Ground had to be made up though, and in a hurry.

Wes was tapping reserves of strength rarely evidenced in people not descended from prisoners of penal colonies. His face was beet red and all systems were on overload. He resembled a boiling kettle about to scream and spill steam everywhere.

But I wasn't going to be able to close the gap. Another fifty yards was all I needed, but when Wes crossed the railroad tracks a few feet ahead of me, I knew it was less than twenty to the finish. I started screaming like a madman. Wes brought one hand up in a victory salute then went down hard. I was just clearing the tracks, bunny-hopping them in the only grab of big air during the race, when I witnessed the crash. Bull dust ended the short reign of the thirteen-hundred-dollar man.

I'd like to say I circled back, that I checked to see if Wes was conscious and ambulatory, and to bask in my win, no matter how it was earned, but the cheers of the crowd and the adrenaline in my veins pushed me forward. I followed the tracks beyond the last settlement and kept riding.

What if Wes claimed my howling at the end of the race caused his fall? What if he wanted to go best two out of three? I couldn't spend another minute with these fun-loving people. The price was too damn high. Never have I been so happy to see desolate miles of nothingness spreading out in all directions. I felt some quality time alone was in order.

Every few miles I'd look over my shoulder, expecting a caravan of retrofitted cars and trucks, buses, and motorcycles—a scene straight out of *Road Warrior*—to pop over the horizon.

Late in the day the Sugar Train chugged past, whistle blowing and engineer waving. I coasted to a stop, hoping for the first time on my trip across Oz that the train would keep going until it finally rolled out of sight. I heard the sound of brakes locking and the weight of heavy cars drawing to a halt.

I could always use more water. Grabbing one of the half-empty gallon jugs bungeed to the back rack, I walked to the community car and stepped up. My stomach lurched at the sight of Wes, road rashes and all, lounging in a chair near the pool table.

"Steady, mate," he said when I almost fell down the stairs. "Been enough tumbles for one day."

All eyes were on me.

So this was it. If Wes had taken the time to board a train, he could be coming after only one thing. Reflexively, I reached for the little pack around my waist that housed my money.

"I thought I won?" was my only defense, followed by a weary sigh.

"That ya did, mate. No worries. I was a little disappointed we didn't get to say our goodbyes is all."

I looked around, confused. "So . . . so you boarded a train?"

Everyone started laughing.

"I never told you what I do," Wes said. "Work for the railroad. We're all fettlers here . . . and I guess it's time I came clean with ya. For a bit of excitement we like to have a go at the tourists. It was never thirteen hundred dollars." He winked. "But look at all the fun we had. I missed it, but they said ya made quite a picture riding out of town—like a regular old bushranger.[15]"

Everyone must have been in on it. You know that feeling you get when you realize you've been walking around most of the day with your zipper down. Bingo.

I tried to be a good sport. Relief was the overriding emotion, but standing in that stuffy rail car, a bone-aching fatigue began to set in. I realized for the first time in many years that I might be getting tired of the road—or maybe just the ways of man.

I said a few hasty goodbyes and beat a path for the open road. Pedaling into the fading light, alone again as anywhere one can be on Earth, I began to wonder if the whole affair had really happened. The bottle of Crow Eater beer sweating in my front bag was confirmation enough.

What started as a chuckle grew into a fit of laughter.

I planned to avoid outback bars and dartboards for a while. But the road leading to the next adventure would always carry me forward, bull dust and all, until that fateful day when my body grows decadently, irretrievably wild, and sets itself free.

1 Burl—have a go, give it a try
2 Larrikin—an irreverent tough guy with likable qualities
3 Shout—buy a round of drinks, "it's your shout"
4 Barrack—cheer on a team at a sporting event
5 Stubby—small bottle of beer
6 Push—a gang or group of people
7 Dag—affectionate term meaning a dirty lump of wool at the back end of a sheep
8 Fair go—to be given an equal chance
9 Wowser—a spoilsport
10 Two-up—Australia's version of heads or tails
11 In good nick—in good physical condition
12 Station—settlement in the outback; also means a large farm
13 Dinki di—honest, true blue
14 Fettler—railway worker
15 Bushranger—Australia's equivalent of the outlaws of the American West

Big Plans on Little Buses

WHEN SOMETHING TAKES CONTROL OF YOUR LIFE, I MEAN SWALLOWS it whole, like a wave the size of the Sears Tower washing over a little man adrift in a small boat, well then, it becomes all you see. You sink below the surface, drinking in that addiction until it courses through every vein.

That's how it was with me and bicycle touring. After that first adventure, I spoke a whole new language; one that included brake calipers, drafting techniques, touring routes, thin red lines, century times, and tire pressures. Its punctuation marks were seat post heights, bottom brackets, and hub sets. I sweated bike grease, dreamed of road maps, bled gear lubricant, and jabbered on about the next trip with the zealousness of a fresh convert. One week the plan was to pedal across China and in the next breath I'd be headed for a circumnavigation of Nova Scotia, or on the next flight to Iceland, or maybe taking a look at the jungles of Paraguay. Nothing lay beyond the realm of possibility now that I had a successful tour under my belt.

From that moment on everyone needed a bicycle. My calling in the grand scheme of things was to direct them toward the open road as soon as possible . . . today . . . now!

This was huge, like happening upon a new continent.

I can imagine just how annoying I became during the early stages of my addiction, like a noisy drunk at a Quaker meeting. Friends feigned interest, a few even wandered the aisles of the bike shops and expo halls and sat by me while I pored over maps. I'd get giddy when I discovered a cartographer who had taken the time to detail the sec- ondary roads and scenic byways.

But like any subculture, it's called that because not everyone is interested. To the uninitiated, I was just another bike geek who had found a way to put off the real world a while longer. I was a monk chanting a dead language.

It was time to tone things down, just in case my peer group was planning some sort of intervention, setting a date to rip me from the clips of my pedals and rush me off to some twelve-step program.

"Hi, my name is Joe, and I haven't put on a helmet in seventeen days."

"Hi, Joe," would come the collective groan from a basement packed full of men and women munching on Power Bars and sipping Powerade.

So I took my urges, these almost improper desires to ride my days away, underground. It was in this quiet, determined place that they coalesced into a career, or at least a job where someone would actual- ly pay me to ride a bicycle.

On a weekend break from Suwannee Country Tours—the compa- ny that encouraged my "problem" by letting me lead people on bike and canoe trips along the back roads and riverways of Florida—I cycled the sixty miles to Camp Thunderbird to see a few old friends.

Before rolling onto camp property I made myself promise not to talk too often or loudly about my passion. Work (such as it was) should be left at the office. But an addiction is an addiction.

Camp Thunderbird provided recreational opportunities to the developmentally challenged, or at least that was the politically correct term they were using at the time to describe the people who came to camp. I'd guarded the pool and organized programs for a few summers, so the place felt like my second home and the staff and campers, old friends.

"Everybody grab an inner tube," I announced to my crew from the group home, who were standing outside a small bus awaiting further orders. I'd agreed to take them tubing during my visit. These were the same guys I'd been in charge of the previous summer so we weren't big on formalities. Long ago, I'd stopped thinking of them as poor, handicapped souls who needed my wisdom and strength to enjoy life. Mr. B, Bobby, Chuck, Pat, and Randy were just a bunch of guys, like anyone else. Of course they had their limitations—who doesn't? But if you treated them as if they needed help and pity from moment to moment, not one of the boys had any problem taking advantage of your misplaced emotions.

"Tw . . . tw . . . ttttttttt . . . two!" Chuck managed to squeeze that one syllable out of his puckered lips. Lean, with the tight face of a smoker, he reminded me of a manic party host, constantly darting about. Chuck held up a pair of inner tubes; proudest forty-two-year-old stuttering baseball cap collector on the planet at that moment. Today's ball cap, one of thousands in his armada, read: ASK ME ABOUT WAUSAU INSURANCE!

"Two," Pat confirmed with a slow, gentle nod. His cap was a standard engineer's blue-and-white stripes. Trains had been Pat's second religion since he was old enough to run his first miniature set around the Christmas tree.

Before the accident, Pat had been a foreman at a rail yard in Chicago: wife, two kids, a small brownstone in the city. Working on his day off, Pat had to take care of a few more things before he could zip home for a family dinner. He slid open the door of a rail car and a nearly lethal whiff of chemicals leaking from a poorly packaged shipment smacked him down. As Pat lost consciousness, those toxins went to work, chewing up various bits of his brain and nervous system indiscriminately.

When he awoke, it was a brave new world. A world in which his body didn't listen to most of the instructions he gave it. The hardest part of Pat's new life was that he did remember. I'd seen him pick up the stock page and study it the way a person might examine an old class picture, remembering the time it was taken but not the names of any of the children he stood beside. He was always telling me how good life was.

One evening at campfire I watched Pat humming the words to the songs. "Sometimes a verse will come back to me," Pat explained with a shrug. "Sometimes."

"All aboard!" Pat bellowed in a conductor's steady voice.

Everyone except Mr. B loaded onto the bus. Mr. B stretched an enormous black arm over my shoulder and left it there. A gentle giant who sounded like Jimmy Stewart when he spoke, Mr. B will tell you what he's thinking when he's good and damn ready, if he says anything at all. He's close to seven feet tall. The first time I met Mr. B, I mistook him for another counselor. The big man found someone's clipboard and greeted me at the door to the lodge. Maybe it was his calm, assuring smile or that looming presence of his, but I asked Mr. B which cabin group he was in charge of. It wasn't until he had me in a bear hug and two feet off the ground that I realized he was a camper.

The rest of the gang had their seat belts on already.

"Can we get . . . can we get us some coffee?" Mr. B asked. To obtain large quantities of coffee seemed to be Mr. B's vocation in life. He carried around a thermos and filled it as often as possible. A shame he wasn't born in the Pacific Northwest. As a southerner, Mr. B was surrounded by heaps of tea and lemonade, but precious little java.

"Holler if you see some," I told him. Fat chance, but it was enough to get Mr. B moving.

While we sat in the van waiting for another counselor to come back from chatting with the girl at the snack bar, a stupendous idea lodged itself in my brain. A big plan began to take shape and I was so focused on its symmetry, its possibilities, that I didn't even notice that Bobby, a boisterous man with Down's syndrome and a mischievous streak, had hidden Mr. B's backup thermos yet again. Mr. B paced the aisle, Bobby tried not to laugh, and I remained in my own little world.

"Everybody out of the bus," I shouted like the thing had caught fire.

"Bus, Bus, Magic Bus," Randy sang out. "The Who, *Who's Next*, recorded in Manchester, England, 1971. Artista Records."

Randy was an encyclopedia of music trivia. The man could not, to save his life, tie his own shoes, but he knew every song ever recorded. Randy would rock forward and back in a pair of black alligator-skin boots, cup his hands against his ears, then twist the lobes until the answer poured out of his mouth. He never missed. Randy was no slouch when it came to race car statistics either.

Mr. B brought my touring bicycle down from the rack, nice and easy, like it was a balsawood model. I started loading the frame with gear while the group looked on. Talking about my addiction with the passion of a traveling preacher at an old-fashioned tent revival, I breezed over the technical stuff and went right for the inspiration. I can't say they were worked into a sweat by my presentation.

"How many of you can ride a bike?" I asked after strapping the sleeping bag in place.

Everyone's hands went up enthusiastically, everyone except Pat, who was probably the only member of the group who really did know how to ride at one time. Maybe they *were* accomplished cyclists, but my guess was that if you asked these guys how many could manage a nuclear power plant you'd get the same number of raised hands. Optimists all of them.

I tried a different approach.

"What would you guys think if I said I wanted to teach you how to ride—so that we can go on a bike tour together next summer? Everyone up for that?"

Strange, no one raised a hand that time.

Mr. B sucked at the dregs of his morning coffee supply. Randy rocked forward and back a few times, and Chuck offered a tight, little smile.

It was Bobby, always the diplomat, who stepped up to the bike.

We managed to get him balanced on the seat, and I thought things were going fairly well during the first push around the parking lot. I held him up by the seat and he wasn't actually pedaling, but it was enough to fuel my daydream of the boys tooling along the back roads of northern Florida. This was going to be great. We'd make it a week the first summer, maybe turn it into a charity ride to raise money for the camp. Okay, Randy would probably have to ride a tricycle with enough space for his boom box and all those tapes, or possibly we'd set up a sidecar deal, which Mr. B could pull Randy in—but it was going to be fantastic. Mr. B's coffee addiction would have to be addressed, and I wasn't going to let Chuck bring more than a three-week supply of caps, but. . . .

In my excitement I must have let go of the seat. Bobby was pedaling now, but neglecting the handlebar portion of the task. For an instant he resembled a portly Tour de France stage winner (if there ever was such a thing), arms raised over his head and a satisfied smile wrapped around his face, before gravity and a palmetto bush found him.

"No more bike," Bobby kept saying. The scrape on his knee was superficial but to hear Bobby tell it, he'd cheated death that afternoon. I retrieved the rig from the bushes and wheeled it back to the group.

"Okay, who's next?"

Silence.

"Bicycle . . . bicycle . . . 'I Want to Ride My Bicycle,' " Randy sang. "Queen, *Night at the Opera,* Recorded in 1976 on EMI Records. Worldwide tour lasted through January 1978." With that bit of trivia dispensed, Randy went over and studied the wheels on the bus.

"N . . . N . . . No . . . th . . . th . . . th . . . thanks," Chuck squeezed out when I moved the bike in his direction.

Pat offered a fatherly smile and waved me off.

Scanning their faces, I recognized that look. It was the same vacant gaze I got from other friends who didn't know or care about the joys of cycling. So much for my big plans.

I drove the bus back to camp in silence. Pat started the group on a loosely adapted version of "One Hundred Bottles of Beer on the Wall," and by God if he wasn't singing all of the words. Everyone joined in and by the third or fourth verse each passenger was singing about a different number of bottles on the wall. When I pulled into the driveway, Bobby had nearly eight hundred bottles of beer up there.

As much as I believed that I treated these guys like "normal" folks, the fact that I thought I could just mold my group of handicapped friends into a touring club because, hell, they didn't have anything better to do with their time just proved that I still had my biases. Mr. B, Pat, Randy, Chuck, and Bobby were adults with their own interests. If they wanted to go biking they knew who to talk to. Until then, I'd keep my bright ideas to myself.

"You tell Mr. B he could ride your bike?" the other counselor asked. I looked up from the soda I was enjoying on the deck. "I didn't think so. He's down near the lodge."

When I turned the corner, Mr. B was atop my bike, pedaling leisurely in wide circles around Randy. The big man was chuckling quietly while Randy sang the words to "Bicycle Built for Two." I wasn't sure how long that frame would support Mr. B's girth, and I really didn't care. This, *this* was a dazzling sight.

Okay, now maybe that sidecar idea would fly. And Bobby, he'd forget all about that little spill, and. . . .

And that was the moment my need to get everyone hooked on cycling slipped away. Sometimes another person introduces you to your passion, but more often you find it by accident and keep it through determination and because of the sheer ecstasy it brings you. Remember staying up way past bedtime to make the perfect jump shot, play that piece of music without a missed note, or learn the steps of a dance so well that gliding across the floor was as easy as breathing?

I sat down in the gravel and simply enjoyed a couple of friends enjoying themselves on a Sunday afternoon. It just happened that one of them was on a bicycle.

"Daisy . . . Daisy. . . ."

In Transit

DAREDEVILS, FREE SPIRITS, SUICIDAL MISCREANTS, URBAN OUTLAWS, and adrenaline-charged warriors.

Bike messengers have heard all of these tired sound bites used to describe them, and somehow each one, no matter how catchy, falls short of reality. Like any label, there's some truth in there, but, as with hippies, hicks, teens, and debutantes, messengers are more than a demographic, more than a jingle or a punchy catchphrase. At their core most bike couriers have this in common: They love pedaling for a living, so much so that they'll endure the long hours, low pay, risk, and lack of career growth. Hey, it beats a desk job, and the dress code is hard to argue with.

"Look Ma, and you said no one would ever pay me to ride my bike."

Many take up the profession for a season or two, then move on, while a few stay with it for years. The long-timers have their own complicated and indescribable reasons for what they do. Or they've reached urban-legend status where justifications are no longer necessary. I had my reasons when I did it for a week in the Bay Area during a summer in the late 1980s—as a favor to a friend, to put some coin in my pocket between tours, and in no small part because, embarrassing as it sounds now, I'd seen Kevin Bacon in the movie *Quicksilver.*

Straddling my bike at the top of a hill just spitting distance from the TransAmerica Building, I discovered the first drawback of the job. I'm not a morning person, but I do possess the ability to get up early for short stretches of time. A week should have been a piece of cake. In this case, though, using the most charitable of mathematical equations, it was still the middle of the night.

"Let's go," my roommate P. J. said before dropping over the hill. "We'll get some coffee and hang out before we pick up our first tags."

Forget the java. The fog dampening my skin and the biting wind smacked me awake as we whizzed down the road. Not some happy-to-be-alive, breakfast-cereal-commercial awake, mind you. This state of consciousness was more akin to being shaken from a coma after pulling an all-night study session before finals. A wide-eyed, terrified state I imagine one might exhibit when zapped out of bed with, say, an electric cattle prod. I pedaled hard, hoping it would even me out somehow, that my soul would somehow ease back into my body through centrifugal motion.

"Save your legs," P. J. warned as I shot past him and up the next incline. "This is San Francisco . . . and remember—"

"I know, don't call it 'Frisco' or else the other messengers will beat me to within inches of my life and ship me back to the Midwest or wherever they think I came from."

"Nothing that drastic," P. J. said with a chuckle, "but we don't want you coming off as a tourist on your first run. These guys don't know you've just biked from Canada. It might surprise you how many people who can barely pedal to the corner pub wander in on a Huffy looking for work as a messenger. Like it's just coasting along the beach handing out towels or something. This job is beat the clock, man, plain and simple. You gotta come straight out of the gate and mean it."

Now I was awake and worried about my abilities.

P. J. shadowed me for the first day, to see if I really was up for the job, to introduce me around, and to offer up a few pointers. A much-deserved vacation in the High Sierras was on his menu. P. J.'s girl-friend had all their bags packed and loaded by the door. She didn't like what he did for a living, thought he was made of better stuff than his coworkers, and she wasn't too keen on the Bay Area for that matter. She was from back East and had never wrapped herself around the idea of so many people just hanging out smoking dope. It wouldn't have surprised me if she'd hit the interstate with P. J. sleeping in the passenger seat and just kept going.

P. J. was a cheerful person, a morning person. I needed this attitude like a ball peen hammer to the back of my head. We pulled up to a coffee shop downtown. Bicycles were parked against the windows. The brightly lit interior and the smell of greasy breakfast specials comforted me. P. J. smiled. I was one of them now.

With company names like Lightning Express, Lickety Split, Expresso, Flash, Velocity, and Silver Bullet, it's not hard to pick up on the theme of the messenger delivery game. It's all about speed. The more packages you can deliver, the more money the company makes. These aren't love letters being rushed across town at a breakneck pace. If the package is late, most customers won't pay. Speed kills, but what doesn't kill you pays the rent.

This particular business model runs into conflicts with the most basic of traffic laws, good sense, and self-preservation, but P. J. worked hard with me that first day—giving me a fighting chance to avoid becoming a statistic. Still strong from my Canada-to-California odyssey, I found the work hard but invigorating. At least with one of P. J.'s old sling bags worn across my shoulder I felt, on the surface, like I could pass for a courier. Yes, I'm the great pretender.

I got along with the other guys. There were some standout characters in that Bay Area bunch, wry talkers and intense dudes, athletes and dopers; and I'll say this much for the brotherhood: Their musical tastes, while all over the board, were cutting-edge. No one pressed the Barry Manilow selections on the jukebox. And they enjoyed their vices after work. You can't push it like that all day, then unwind without a bit of help.

The clawing tension you often feel just under the surface, that shimmering , desperate ambition that exudes from people jockeying for better positions within the corporate structure, was absent. You ride, you deliver, you get paid, you get up and do it again. Their unifying ambition was only to ride fast, again and again.

It might sound like another convenient label, but I most closely associated the job of bike messenger with the Pony Express. Young guys wait around on their steeds throughout the city, and when the call comes in they go for broke until the tag is in the hands of its new owner. Maybe I wasn't at the job long enough, but each run was a race, a game, a challenge, and by the time I hung up my messenger bag it was still fun and games. But I could tell even after a week that I wasn't cut out for the business in any long-term way.

As a kid, I graduated to my first bona fide ten-speed about the same time digital watches were all the rage. I think my parents paid some ridiculous amount of money for a timepiece that a few years later was being given out as a free gift for opening a checking account at the local bank. But that spring, with my digital programmed to stopwatch mode and my backpack on my shoulders, I'd lean forward in my desk during the last seconds of class, leg jittering with nervous energy, ready to break for the door at the first sound of the bell. Half of the fun was avoiding the hall monitors and weaving through the maelstrom of students. The meter started running the moment I left the desk. This meant I had to get the combination lock opened, the bike out of the rack and on the road as fast as possible. My reward was a huge ice cream sundae shaped like a caterpillar. M&Ms for eyes and a licorice smile. A few games of Pong rounded out my after-school revelry.

The entire semester my holy grail remained a four-minute finish. Like the mile for runners, I couldn't seem to eliminate those final ten seconds—without blindly sprinting through the stop sign at a busy intersection. As the semester wound down, I was desperate to blast through the narrow spaces between those fast-moving cars. It became a secret rite of passage. The fact that I never cracked the four-minute barrier was telling. For years I taxed my Type B+ personality trying to run with the Type As.

Each time I squeezed the brakes and relinquished those few seconds I had a sense of something impending, something that was headed in my direction and I didn't have to do anything but wait for it. Had no idea what it could be but I suspected, I hoped it was much bigger than a few ticks on a watch.

Eventually, the world opened up, but not until I stopped chasing that pack of future world leaders, litigators, and brain surgeons. That something arrived the day I tossed away the digital watch and began marking my time in terms of experiences. Maybe I'd just been waiting for the chance to stop racing for home.

I actually had to borrow a watch for my week of courier work. The clock constantly runs for the bike messenger. I got to know my way around the city in short order, and I kept riding by one construction site. There had been a big fuss over it in the papers. While digging to put in the deep pillars that would form the earthquake-proof foundations to some skyscraper, a gravesite had been discovered. The building company was falling behind schedule while all manner of professors poured out of their university offices to verify the findings. Politicians looked for an angle they could get behind for political gain, and news crews hung out on the fringes, hoping the story would grow. It had a circus atmosphere, and with each day, the excavated area expanded. There was talk that this had been a repository for Chinese workers during the railroad-building era—the low-pay, high-risk labor of their day. I was fascinated with the proceedings, so much so that I almost missed a run.

To make up time, I had to fly up hills and push things into the danger zone. I rushed into the building, made the pickup and headed for the destination. Good couriers glide through their days. They make it look easy. Sure, they move, but they never make it look like they're in a hurry—Zen and the art of bike messengering. If professional messengers are greyhounds, I was the Saint Bernard of the industry.

"Yes?" she asked. The receptionist was dressed like there was a cocktail party in the next room. I clicked my shoes louder. Decked out like I was she had to know this was the courier standing in front of her. "I have a tag, I mean package for you," I said, feeling out of place in her coiffed-and-manicured presence.

But therein lay the problem. I was not in possession of the delivery. Had it fallen out in transit? Damn. If it had slipped out of the bag en route it was gone for good. Rifling through my pouch, I began imagining what sort of valuable information I'd let slip into the wrong hands. Cashier checks? Payment schedules to the IMF? Diplomatic treaties between warring nations, plans for the economic recovery of a third-world country? Surely this was going to go down in my permanent bike messenger record.

After searching the bag for the third time I began to feel less like a hip young courier in the city and more like a clumsy pedestrian in a funny hat and loud shoes. Just then her phone rang. She put up one finger to silence my stammerings, like her slender digit was more than I deserved.

"I'll let him know," were her only words into the receiver. Her smile was forced. "The package was left back at the other office. Another one of you guys is bringing it over."

That was a relief. Embarrassed, I turned to leave. But since this was only a short-term gig I just had to ask what line of work she was associated with that would cause her to act so snooty.

"What is it you folks do here at . . . GCS?"

Her smile nearly collapsed under the weight of its own superficiality. "We distribute greeting cards."

As I reached the street, I had to wonder what could be so pressing in the greeting card world that would call for a courier service? Holidays are announced well in advance, have been for years. Maybe a breakthrough haiku for Father's Day? Or some free verse for the Fourth of July that was going to stop the presses?

When I wasn't dodging delivery trucks, forgetting packages, hopping potholes and scaring pedestrians, I hung out in Golden Gate Park. A pretty good juggler, I would watch and sometimes join some of the regulars, guys who made a living as street performers. We'd toss pins or I'd learn new moves with rubber balls and beanbags. A couple of years later I swear I saw one of those guys tossing bowling balls and knives into the air on the *David Letterman Show*. He was a Muslim gentleman with the biggest hands I've ever seen. You don't have to have big hands to go far in the juggling world but it doesn't hurt. He taught me how to claw four balls and demonstrated the flaming sticks. He had this great way of blowing starter fluid out of his mouth while juggling. He'd light the sticks in mid-air with his mouth. I felt kind of foolish when in return all I could do was eat an apple I was juggling.

We stopped our activities one afternoon so that he could pray.

"There are more than a hundred words in my language for God. It's a way of reminding us that it is more than anything we can conceive."

I gave him a set of really nice pins on what turned out to be the last time we juggled together. I'd spotted them at a yard sale. They had a certain Barnum & Bailey Circus feel about them and he deserved a token of my appreciation for all the moves he'd taught me. He would only accept them if I would allow him to take something for me from his collection. When I refused he pushed ornate pins on me—works of art, really.

"I don't want to take something of yours," I said.

He looked at me with the slightest hurt in his eyes. "You must," he whispered. "A gift which is not exceeded tenfold by the receiver is . . . a little death in the heart."

Each time I tossed those perfectly balanced, hand-carved pins into the air I thought of all the names for God . . . as many names as there are moments of kindness and seemingly small acts of humanity.

My week as a messenger ended in style. One of the messengers had a friend of a friend who got us swimming privileges, under false names, at a private club. We soaked our tired bones and put a couple of drinks and appetizers on the club's tab. Messengers get so few benefits, and each day, no matter how skilled a cyclist you might be, is a definite risk. I felt not one ounce of guilt as we enjoyed our momentary luxuries. Lounging in the hot tub like a pair of record executives, we noticed a trio of staff members headed in our direction.

"Gentleman, we are going to have to ask you to leave."

I chugged down my martini and ate the olive before they could take it away from me; a couple of savages on palace grounds. We tried dropping our friend's name but it only seemed to make the man in the most expensive suit more determined to escort us to the door. When we hit the sidewalk I tossed a bunch of those mint chocolates in the green wrappers to my cohort.

"I pinched them from the front desk when you were trying to get our rain jackets back."

We saddled up and rode toward the local pub—where a couple of bike messengers belonged at the end of the work week.

"I think I'm gonna miss this gig," I said, getting all sentimental after a few days on the streets.

"No you're not," the seasoned messenger responded. "The only thing anyone misses about couriering is the idea of the job."

He was right. Every now and then though, when I see a messenger zipping through traffic, I tip my helmet, whisper a quick prayer, and think, "There goes another one, living out every kid's daydream—to make a living in the saddle, going fast and furious on a bicycle."

THIS STORY IS DEDICATED TO THE MEMORY OF JOHNNY PACECAR, A PORTLAND, OREGON, MESSENGER WHO DELIVERED HIS LAST TAG.

Black Range Riding

SOMETIMES YOU HAVE TO WAIT FOR THE ADVENTURE TO COME TO YOU. With the Black Range, a daunting stretch of mountains in the southern corner of New Mexico, it's never a long wait. All sorts of trouble, good and bad, spills over those passes.

Snow and rain, hail and hippies, ranchers and renegade cows, and plenty of retirees in oversize RVs make the journey through the Black Range, pulling everything but the kitchen sink.

The real Butch Cassidy and his own gang of young riders came roaring over Emory Pass, with lawmen on their heels. They hid in the tight spots of Whitewater Canyon until the posse gave up, drank all the beer at the Blue Front Cafe, and went home. Billy the Kid wasted some of his youth in Silver City, the town on the west side of the mountains, before crossing the range on his way to the Lincoln County land wars and eternal notoriety. And let's not forget mountain man Ben Lilly, a pious fellow who loved children, the Sabbath and all of nature, and who for half a century shot any critter that moved in those deep woods—until someone told old Ben that would do and sent him back to the swamps of Louisiana.

The Black Range has seen them all.

Cyclists also tackle these mountains; the endless switchbacks and steep grades are part of the official southern cross along the transcontinental bike route. When I talk to people who have made the ocean-to-ocean crossing, they offer a nod of recognition and get rather quiet when Emory Pass is mentioned.

My first time pedaling over the range, I had no idea it was there until I smacked up against it. Coming at the end of a three-month odyssey from Idaho to New Mexico, it turned out to be my last real test. Some runners hit a wall near the end of marathons, I hit the Black Range in the closing miles of a ride I now refer to as the last chapter in my "wandering years." The morning I struck out from Elephant Butte Lake my map got little more than a passing glance. I noted that it was seventy-five miles to Silver City, stuffed the worn and tattered navigational device away, and predicted I'd be eating a late lunch in some café downtown.

Three months of nearly constant cycling will make a man cock-sure, strong, and reckless. I cycled the dry, windswept mesas and rolling foothills leading up to the mountain with happy abandon-ment. The pancakes in Hillsboro hit the spot, and dunking my head in a little creek outside of Kingston refreshed me. It was only then that I noticed the looming shadow those big rocks to the west were casting.

"It looks like I've got a little climb ahead of me," I said with a buoyant tone in my voice.

Soar, the proprietress of a shop of the same name, smiled at me out of the side of her mouth. The store was packed with an eclectic inventory: wood carvings, anarchist postcards, hardware supplies, New Age crystals, tractor blades, and horse feed. When she wasn't smiling in that strange way, Soar was a beautiful older woman—long, graying hair and muscles that belonged on a track star. We were the only people in the store.

"Nobody told you about the Black Range?" she asked. It was obvi-ous she'd seen this sort of thing before. Soar shook her head and straightened a picture of Pee-Wee Herman. I set down one of the yard gnomes that seemed to be the featured items on the counter.

"At least the weather's nice for your trek. The leaves are changing up there and it's not too hot. We had a couple women come through here on bicycles last December. I told them a storm was getting ready to dump and they'd never make it over the pass in one day. They went on anyway. Search and Rescue brought them back here. I warmed the pair up and slept them in the bunkhouse. The ambulance picks up a couple dozen riders every summer . . . heat exhaustion, sometimes stroke, dehydration, that sort of thing. You might want to purchase an endurance crystal for the journey."

Soar waved as I pedaled off. Quite a storyteller, that one. But her warnings seemed a bit drastic.

It was the last time my heart rate dropped below two hundred beats per minute that afternoon. I sweated, and groaned, and inched my way up the mountain, thankful that when I finally reached the summit, Soar had mentioned the little pipe the forest service had hidden off the side of the road at the mouth of a spring. "God bless you, Soar," I babbled out loud, then practically bathed in that icy water, ignoring the shock that might stop my taxed and overheated heart in its tracks. The climb had been an ordeal, plain and simple. At one point I slowed to a crawl and observed little spots gather across my vision, wondering which way my body and bike would fall when I lost consciousness. Into the road where it would be flattened by traffic, or over the cliff where it would . . . fall over a cliff?

Halfway up the mountain, a couple from some Scandinavian country stopped at the picnic table I was stretched across. We understood not a word of each other's languages, but this didn't stop them, after I got up, from setting a place for me at the table. I rallied long enough to bring out some of my meager supplies, and we ate in complete silence under the pines, heat, and changing leaves. The menu was pâté with a nice salmon flavor, crackers, and delicious but very stinky cheese. Before remounting my bike, I pressed that stinky cheese right up to my nostrils . . . an unorthodox but effective form of smelling salts. To their credit, the Scandinavian pair pretended not to notice.

Maybe it was that climb, but when I arrived in Silver City I didn't leave for the next five years. Okay, I ventured out for vacations, family reunions, and shorter tours, but I took up residence at the bottom of that range, and settled down for the first time in my adult life. Might have been my love affair with the West, could have been the right time in my life, but I'm sure that no small measure was my need to see just what the mountains would toss over next.

I was rarely disappointed.

"Yep, both retinas detached at thirty thousand feet and I stumbled about the cabin wondering who had turned out the lights."

Nobody likes to feel their eyes pop out of their sockets, especially on an eighteen-hour flight back to London, but if anyone was trained to handle such a challenge, it was Chris Fenn. A lively athlete from Scotland, Chris had advised top climbers on nutrition during their assaults on mountains such as K2 and Everest. In her spare time Chris went along for crossings of the North Pole.

"But when I lost my sight, that shook me to the core," Chris explained over lunch at my favorite little dive. Most of the cyclists found me, one way or another. People pointed them in my direction, word spread along the route, or I'd spot the really the really worn and beaten ones, scrape them off the road, and pop them in the shower. We became an unofficial hostel during the warmer months. Sometimes I would write articles about them; most of the time I just soaked them for tales of their favorite adventures, eating up each story up like it was a delicacy. Even though I had an address, these comrades let me extend my wandering days a little farther.

"It was a combination of the high altitudes of Everest and the blinding sun bouncing off the snow that led to my retinas slipping from their moorings," Chris said. "Emergency surgery was performed minutes after we landed but I had to wait in a hospital for five long miserable days to find out if I would ever see again."

Chris's eyes, clear and vibrant, teared up a little when she got to that part in her story. "It really was like coming back to the world, that first moment I saw again."

Some people would shake it off, count their blessings, maybe feel some empathy, but ultimately return to their old life. Chris, who has never done anything halfway, couldn't let go of the idea that she was a blind person.

"After I regained my sight, the doctors confided that they hadn't held out much hope for my recovery. They said it was so messy that medical wisdom said I would probably need a smart dog and a cane from that day forward. I think I'll always feel like a blind person who has been given my sight for back for a while. So I wanted to do something to raise a few dollars and lots of awareness."

The answer Chris came up with was to ride across the States telling her story and collecting pledges along the way for a small non-profit organization that provided services, including talking newspapers and computers, for the blind.

"I never pedaled a bike longer than a day at a time before this trip, but it's brilliant. Now, I'm completely addicted—the utter freedom," she confessed. "Besides, the hills, the rain and wind, are nothing compared to being blind every day!"

Chris, like so many of the rebels, renegades, and dreamers who popped over the Black Range on bicycles, spent only a few hours with me. But if you have the right conversations, a few hours allow you to see straight into each other.

Linda and Steve finished each other's sentences, but not in an annoying way. Sitting atop their tandem bicycle, this pair of school-teachers from Chicago presented the illusion of being one creature. A boisterous, playful entity. When I offered them a place to stay, their first question was whether we had kids.

"It's not that we don't love children. It's just that we teach at a junior high during the year," Steve said, almost apologetically. "We get a little burned out, by May," Linda added. "These rides help us love the kids again."

They were not being melodramatic. After hearing them relate, in animated tandem, anecdotes from an average week as an inner-city public school teacher I kept flashing to scenes from the chaotic unrest of Indonesia depicted in *The Year of Living Dangerously*. Metal detectors, drug busts, threats, and recriminations. Colleagues on autopilot or, worse, in league with some of the disenfranchised youth. Budget cuts, bomb threats, archaic textbooks, cold food, long hours. . . .

"Steve was jumped in the bathroom before a basketball game—a couple students with baseball bats," Linda said with a shrug.

"I recognized their voices. Had them in fifth period Earth Science. Why would you rob a schoolteacher, is my question? If I taught economics this might never have happened. They got seven dollars and a frequent shopper card. The card was back on my desk the next morning."

I saw for the first time that Linda's smile was tainted with fatigue.

"Sometimes it gets so hard we feel like just letting it go."

It wasn't *all* about child abuse, incest, and guns going off accidentally in ten-year-old hands, or the ghosts of boys and girls who would never get to grow up.

"We do manage to squeeze in a fair amount of teaching each year. I guess we just want to save them all; from themselves, their hormones, their peers, television. . . ."

"From life?" I asked.

The couple looked up, silenced by my comment. We enjoyed the strong New Mexico sun for a few tranquil moments. "Now you see why we had a good laugh when you talked about the challenges of the Black Range. We're teachers. Every day is uphill."

So teachers use the big climbs to clear their heads. Maybe the Tour de France organizers could add a category just for public school educators.

Tomoko and his wife, Kazunari, bowed repeatedly in my driveway, their helmets gripped politely in front of them. The couple were en route to Mexico City. The flight from Japan had deposited them in Anchorage, Alaska, four months earlier and somehow they'd managed to ride over the Black Range from the east, instead of pedaling into town via shorter climbs from Arizona.

Tomoko shrugged, "All our maps are in English, a little confusing. And the West is so big."

When I told them that my nickname was Metal Cowboy, Kazunari's face broke into a smile.

"People back in Japan call us cowboys," she said. "Some of them mean it as . . . compliment? Some say it to hurt."

Tomoko explained that in Japan it's honorable to use bicycles as transportation, and to go vacationing on one is perfectly acceptable, but to leave your job and set off on a quest around the world branded you as selfish and a bit crazy, at least by the older folks.

I thought about the looks I sometimes received during my tours, and my own father making one more effort to bring me into the fold, asking me to reconsider a fast track through business school.

"We don't care . . . I have enjoyed cycling since I was very young. It will be hard when we return, but. . . . " Tomoko trailed off.

"Who's to say it wouldn't have been hard if you stayed?" I told the pair.

He patted my shoulder lightly as we stood in a semicircle. "Then we are a pack of cowboys standing in the Wild West!"

Giddy up.

The recumbent bicycles kept coming, one after another over the pass, until there were about a dozen or so lined up in Gallenia's Canyon Campground like Harleys at a rally. The group of older men broke out cigars and lawn chairs, one of them began assembling a remote-control airplane, while another talked to someone from Europe on a ham radio. The bunch didn't go by any official name.

"Bent and Crabby," offered a tall man cutting heads of red lettuce at a picnic table.

That brought forth a chorus of chuckles.

"The Recumbent Dozen, or are you too young to get that movie reference?" another guy said.

I listed off the cast from memory and instantly improved my standing with the group.

"We've had to be official this or that for much of our lives. When it comes to these tours we keep things pretty loose."

I asked about wives.

"You didn't see any wives in *The Dirty Dozen,* did you?" the lettuce chopper said. I thought maybe I'd hit a bad chord, but they explained that some in the group were widowed, but many called home regularly . . . the trips never lasted more than a few weeks, and some of the gals met the boys in bigger cities along the route.

"It gives everyone a break from their routines around the house," the guy with the airplane said in a conspiratorial tone. "And it gives me a chance to fly these babies whenever I feel like it."

The plane took off, banked hard to avoid a wall of rocks, and buzzed toward the heavens.

This group held to the scantest of schedules. It had taken them several days to work their way over the pass, not because anyone was in outrageously bad shape, but because no one in this group saw the need to rush.

"If you want to make touring a sprint, you're probably not going to choose a recumbent bicycle to begin with," a man with a pair of binoculars around his neck said. "But they really get moving on the downhill," he added with a devilish grin.

As I was saying my goodbyes the ham radio operator pointed out that their adult children approved of the tours.

"They must figure we can't spend their inheritance as fast while riding around on bicycles."

From behind a cigar, one of his cohorts added. "What they don't realize is we're gonna live a lot longer with all this blasted exercise."

The chorus of laughter followed me down the canyon.

There were others, so many others who graced my life with their laughter and stories. Along the road less pedaled, I discovered that I didn't always have to be the traveler to enjoy the adventure. Often, I pedaled with them as far as the state line; and though it was nice, still, sometimes it wasn't enough.

In the words of Langston Hughes,

De railroad bridge is a sad song in the air,
every time de trains pass I want to go somewhere!

When my new friends' loaded bicycles dropped over the horizon and out of my life, I caught my breath and sighed deeply. . . .

Every time de bicycles pass I want to go somewhere.

Breakdowns and
Other Blessings

One should count each day a separate life. —Seneca

THE DREADFUL SOUND OF SOMETHING VITAL SNAPPING, LIKE A BONE, registers in the mind of the injured party even before that wrenching pop reaches the rest of the world. It's the same thing when an important component fails on your bicycle, which, when you've ridden it long enough, has really become an extension of your body.

Cover enough miles and there's not an inch on a bike that won't let you down in some way. The laws of nature cannot be reasoned with. There's no getting around entropy.

My first Raleigh gave up the ghost, finally, less than fifteen miles from the completion of a two-thousand-mile journey between Canada and Kings Canyon, California. The frame snapped apart at the seat post braze-ons. I'd just checked my tires for air pressure at a little garage, and put a solid downstroke on the right pedal to get my rig, overloaded as usual, rolling up a rather steep hill—a little bump in the road known as the Sierra Nevadas. Bang.

I cursed myself for adding that extra squirt of air, but when I listened for the horrible trill of a tire rapidly deflating, there was nothing. I was still rolling along. Oh well. Thinking someone's car had backfired and I was just off balance, I compensated by leaning in the other direction, then attempted another pedal stroke. This maneuver nearly launched me into the dirt. It was like balancing on a tightrope. The seat no longer connected to the back part of my bike, which I can attest is critical to safe forward progress.

I've faced a number of tough fixes along back roads and remote locales when a bike shop was not a fallback plan. I pride myself on being something of a clutch player when others toss up their hands and throw in the greasy towel. Derailleurs have been stomped back into commission, pedals held together by abundant quantities of strategically placed duct tape, and once I fashioned a brake pad out of the thick end of a discarded windshield wiper. But when a bicycle frame snaps, it's all over except for the hitchhiking—not that I didn't pull out the stops. I went straight for the duct tape the way a paramedic reaches for the defibrillator paddles. It looked pretty good ensconced in all that sticky silver, but didn't last ten yards. When duct fails that miserably and fast, you need to stick a body tag on a spoke and call the next of kin.

But this had been my bicycle for half a decade, my trusty steed.

Maybe if I used a couple of Allen wrenches to shore up the places where the frame broke, like inserting steel rods in a shattered leg, then the duct tape would have a fighting chance. This repair lasted long enough so that I had a good head of stream built up when the tape tore. Unhurt, I remained on the ground for several minutes before a wilderness ranger in an old Subaru took pity on me. We drove in peaceful silence. And here I had been looking so forward to pedaling right up to the gate of the summer camp I'd been hired to direct. There's a certain level of confidence a leader who has just completed an unaided solo bicycle tour from Canada instills in his staff by pedaling casually through the entrance.

The ranger dropped me on the other side of the road. I could still stage my big debut.

"You should get Raleigh to replace that frame," my new sports director noted, after looking over my setup. "This shouldn't have snapped from normal wear and tear."

I mumbled something that led him to believe that I agreed, but the truth was a little more complicated. I'd put tens of thousands of miles on that bike, burdened it with outrageous loads, and let the poor thing topple over more times than I could remember, including that unfortunate incident with a set of railroad tracks and a faulty bike rack on top of a Suwannee Country Tours van. It had been submerged in oceans on both sides of the continent, manhandled by callous Greyhound loaders, and ridden into the ground one morning by a crazy German racer who pointed out that you had to wreck a bike a few times to show it who was boss.

But the final blow might have been that hill—okay, that *small cliff* along the Pacific Coast Highway it rolled—okay, *toppled* down. Still, the sports director was so enthusiastic about my writing a letter to Raleigh that by the end of the summer I had complied.

"You must have really let them have it!" he said when I rolled up on the new touring bicycle the company had authorized a dealer to hand over to me. I had to tell him the truth.

"And they still gave you the bike?"

My expression revealed that I was just as surprised as him.

"Said if I got that much out of my first one it was worth it to them to have me riding their latest product all over the globe." I spun the freewheel. "Check out this funky new index shifting, just came on the market. Yeah, they threw in new components, the works. It's designed so you can convert the wheels for off-road riding."

I took an oath that day to treat my new rig with respect and care, reverence and sanctity, for truly, had this not shown me the error of my wretched ways? I'd been given a second chance—saved.

That lasted about a week.

Several years later, surrounded by an ocean of red dirt in the remotest reaches of the outback, I was confronted with another grave breakdown. This time it wasn't the bike, but the rack. Any sane individual would have spent a few bucks on a new carrying device before crossing a couple of thousand miles of desert, especially as it was the only rack I'd ever owned—no spring chicken in anyone's book. But I subscribed to the "If It Ain't Broke, Don't Fix It" philosophy at the time. This little nugget of wisdom has been sparring with "Better Safe Than Sorry" for eons. That afternoon in the absolute middle of nowhere, I got caught in their crossfire.

Nothing dramatic this time. No shearing of metal or crunching of moving parts. I simply came out of my pedaling meditations to observe my gear dragging behind the bike like the day's catch in a shrimp boat's netting. Yikes.

Some of the stuff sacks sustained cursory scuffs, which I felt blended nicely with the other stains and abuses they'd endured over the years, and though I wasn't happy about losing one of my gallon jugs full of precious water to a dirty gash the size of a thumbnail, this repair project looked like a minor setback. I dug around in the bags for my trusty duct tape, planning to be on the road in short order. But I soon discovered there was nothing left to tape. Parts of the connecting joints had disintegrated. As I tried to jam the rack back in place it fell apart in my hands, reminding me of an erector set I got when I was ten, played with once, then left out in the rain.

This was bad. I picked up a few of the pieces, like a dazed soldier gathering body parts. The train wouldn't be by for days. I managed to pile my gear across the front bag and, with my head poking above the unbalanced mess, wobble forward. Even when I bungeed the tent and sleeping bag to my back, the front wheel felt the burden of too much weight hanging over the handlebars.

I blamed my troubles on water, the heaviest substance known to man. Okay, it only tips the scales at about seven pounds per gallon, but it might as well be granite to the touring cyclist; it's bulky and cumbersome, but a necessity. And I was carrying more full jugs on that trip than any other adventure I'd taken; a veritable distillery in motion. My filter pump usually allowed me to avoid the extra weight, but the Sugar Train didn't carry tanker cars of water for show. This country was bone dry. The ailing rack, on top of eveything else, hadn't been able to handle all that liquid jostling about, pulling it in every direction. I found some waist-high bushes and waited for the heat of the day to pass and my fortunes to change.

Buoyed by a slight evening breeze, I decided to limp along, cover a few miles in the darkness. Animals came out at night. I had to be alert for kangaroos, boars, and dingos, among other things. Scanning for watchful eyes peering through the dim light cast from my headlamp occupied my attention. I'd never been attacked, but there was a first for everything. I'd never had a rack come apart in hands until that day.

I thought I was seeing things when a pair of headlights loomed through the darkness behind me. There hadn't been a vehicle sighting in four days. A driver would have mistaken me for one of the animals the way I stared, frozen, into the headlights. The Range Rover slid to a halt just feet from me. The truck had to be a prototype for a new lunar vehicle the way its exterior was dotted with solar panels and the top rack loaded with all manner of equipment, some of which resembled small, homemade speakers.

"Aren't you a sight, mate," said a lanky man in Buddy Holly glasses, a short-sleeve white dress shirt complete with pocket protector, dark slacks, and standard-issue wing tips on his feet.

I could say the same about him. If not for the Foreign Legion–style hat he wore, this bloke would have fit right in at an MIT research lab. We shook hands. A hefty gal with stringy blond hair and bushy eyebrows waved from the passenger seat.

I waved back. Had they been sporting six arms, blowholes on their foreheads, and told me we were going back to their mother ship, I wouldn't have cared. Their arrival meant I wasn't going to perish in the desert after all.

"I'm Thomas and that's Hattie. We were on our way to the test area for an evening's work," he said, straightening his glasses. So maybe the mother ship *was* hovering somewhere in the distance.

"Looks like you've had a spot of trouble," Thomas stated in a matter-of-fact tone. We stood over my gear. The remains of the rack had been discarded miles earlier.

"You could say that," I replied.

"No worries," he added cheerfully.

Of course not. He had a big old Range Rover to cart his stuff around in. Thomas and Hattie were kind enough to give me a lift. Thomas said that when we got back from the test area he thought he could fashion a new rack out of some stuff lying around the homestead. Fashion a new rack out of a few odds and ends? Who'd he think he was, a rocket scientist? Not exactly, but I hadn't missed the mark by much.

"I invent things," was all Thomas would say. It was Hattie who filled in the rest of his résumé for me. But that came later. We bounced and rambled to a stop at the edge of a dry lake bed. It was about the length and width of a football field and had been ringed with small speakers spaced at twenty-five-yard intervals. You had to look hard to see them, and there were no visible wires.

Hattie took up her position in the center of the lake, microphone in hand. A spotlight attached to the hood bathed Hattie in light. After he made a few calculations, Thomas asked if I could help him situate a new speaker. His preparations were deliberate and meticulous. I took a place beside him while he fiddled with a small electronic gadget in his hand. I felt like one of the extras on *Star Trek* standing next to Mr. Spock.

"I never liked going to outdoor concerts because I always ended up behind speakers the size of small houses. I couldn't see the band, and my ears bled by the second set," Thomas said.

Somehow I had trouble picturing this guy, lighter in hand, screaming at some band for an encore. People keep surprising me.

"The question then is: Can one develop a transmitting device that will deliver the same amount of sound in a much smaller package in open spaces? It must be wireless and pack the punch of the big equipment or no one's going to buy it. Behold."

Thomas threw a switch on his little box. The speakers hummed to life. When Hattie started to work through a smoky blues number it felt like a miracle. She had a very nice voice, but that wasn't the half of it. Standing inside all that sound was an absolute thrill, orgasmic. The clarity was amazing, but more than that it felt as if you were wearing headphones—no, as if the music was originating inside your brain, allowing you control over it.

"Whew," I said when Hattie took a break. "How did you do that?"

Thomas pointed at a bulky generator device on top of the truck.

"That way it's mobile. Designed it so that no matter where you stand inside the circle you hear everything in equal proportions in each ear. Did you notice that?"

Thomas began speaking in code, peppering his conversation with talk of computer chips the size of fleas, radio transmitters everywhere and digital sequencing. "It's the future, mate." His face lit up. "I was working on this sort of thing in England at the beginning of the decade when I . . . when I went into business for myself." That was the first time I noticed a little twitch near his left eye. "This technology won't be on the market for years, not for years."

I had to sit down while Hattie belted out "Piece of My Heart" by Janis Joplin. Watching this big woman with the stringy hair become the music was too much. When she broke out a harmonica I forgot everything: my nonexistent bike rack, what decade it was, even what continent I was on. This setup was going to revolutionize the industry someday. It was like really good drugs.

When I turned around Thomas looked pleased. "Honey, I'm gonna add some backup, now. Let's see how far we can push it."

He punched a button and the entire E Street Band joined Hattie in a rousing version of "Spirits in the Night." I wondered if The Boss would get a kick out of knowing just how far his influence reached, and that he was being channeled at the moment by a big-boned Aussie in the desert. As the song was kicking into overdrive, a silence fell abruptly across the desert.

Thomas started talking to himself. "No, that's good. That tells me something. The cooling system still needs work. It trips the shut-off before it overheats. We'll be masters of the universe when we really learn how to control heat. Cold fusion, next stop, the stars."

He wandered off, his firing synapses the only thing in the entire world to him at the moment. I sat in the half light wishing I could feed my head with more music.

When Thomas returned from the darkness, they decided to wrap things up for the night. I started to ask if the equipment would be safe just sitting out there, but that was the knee-jerk reaction of a city boy. The possums and kangaroos certainly had no need for an extra woofer or tweeter, and it hadn't rained since the dawn of time in those parts. Somehow, despite the bumpy drive, I fell asleep against my scuffed stuff sacks in the back of the Range Rover, vapor trails of music drifting inside my head.

It wasn't until the next morning that I got a good look at the compound that I'd stumbled through on my way to bed. It was a cross between a commune and mission control. A collection of geodomes and windowless concrete buildings, across which every homemade invention and gadget had been strung: gray-water collectors, solar panels, pulleys, ramps, and things about whose purpose I had no clue. A space-age windmill-looking device stood at the edge of a garden of organic vegetables. Animals wandered about the piles of raw material —junked cars, scraps of various metals, and heavy machinery which I had no doubt Thomas kept in working order.

I received a tour of the place. We ended up in Thomas's lab. A mad scientist's playground if there ever was one. And here I'd been worried he couldn't possibly fashion a new rack for me. Given enough time, it wouldn't have surprised me to see a space shuttle towed from behind one of the geodomes.

While I helped Hattie pick some vegetables for lunch, she explained that Thomas held degrees in half a dozen disciplines and had worked for a technology consortium in Europe for some time.

"They wanted to box him in. Keep him focused on one thing for too long. That's not how he operates. He's an artist, really."

I flashed on her belting out Joplin. There were a couple of gifted people in the family by my count.

"Thomas was wrapped so tight during those years. He just had to completely unravel . . . to get back to what he wanted."

A breakdown.

Hattie's smile couldn't hide the burden it must have placed on their relationship at the time. But here they were, doing what they wanted. "He still dresses for work every day, and he's made some amazing progress on certain projects."

They funded their little desert headquarters with several patents Thomas secured during his college years. Projects that garnered more than college credit. I laughed thinking of my senior paper, which compared the film *Blade Runner* to biblical crucifixions and resurrections. No patents pending on that baby.

After lunch I enjoyed a solar-powered shower in an immodest outdoor facility. Standing naked in the desert, drops of water evaporating moments after hitting my body, I wondered if sometimes a breakdown wasn't a blessing in disguise. A chance to pause and ponder, rest and unravel, before turning back into the wind.

It took Thomas a few hours to build me a new rack. God, did it look awful. Thick tubes spot-welded onto a rectangular plate of metal. But surprisingly light and functional.

"Notice that when you attach your panniers to this rack, they point at an angle, offering less surface area, which creates less wind resistance as you pedal forward."

There was another patent waiting to happen.

On the drive back to the "road" Thomas wanted to hear all about my plans. We talked literature, which of course he had a more extensive knowledge of than I did. He quoted a few of his favorite poets.

" 'Nothing will come of nothing. Dare mighty things!' " he recited, grinning in my direction. I shrugged. He had me, which wasn't hard to do.

"Shakespeare!" He laughed. "When in doubt, mate, always go to the Bard. He said just about everything at one time or another."

Thomas wanted to help me secure my load on the new rack. Meticulous and exacting, this scientist had my ballast balanced down to the gram.

"I've got one I know old William didn't say," I announced when there was nothing left to do but offer our farewells. "One should count each day a separate life."

Thomas met my eyes and something was exchanged; a recognition of something, of everything, maybe.

"Who said that?" he asked.

I started pedaling.

"Can't remember. . . . I heard it so many lifetimes ago."

Traveling Companion

THE FIRST THING I NOTICED WHEN CHAD PRICE PEDALED INTO THE campground was not his Teva sandals—a somewhat unorthodox footwear selection for distance biking—or the loaded backpack he shouldered rather than bothering with additional panniers. Nor was it the young man's compacted stature or big, winning grin. It concerned the family-size Styrofoam picnic cooler he was towing in a two-wheeled carrier behind his mountain bike. Toddlers rode in such devices, and a few long-distance cyclists who simply couldn't part with enough gear used them to haul various supplies—cameras, extra water. Hell, I even rode with one ingenious entrepreneur for a few days who packed a small sunglass business inside one of those things, setting up at a moment's notice wherever a crowd might gather, or pedestrian traffic was ample. "Better than Ray-Bans. The ultimate in UV protection and any degree of tinting you preferred, at a fraction of department store prices!" he was fond of telling anyone who would listen.

The tinting on those shades held for about forty-eight hours before flaking like the window of an old sports car. The actual amount of UV protection I received during the product's short tenure was suspect, and, like a leper in a light breeze, one of the arms dropped off my pair without provocation. At least he knew enough about his merchandise to stay mobile.

But my reaction when I spotted that oversize cooler hitching a free ride behind Chad's bike was that this shaggy-haired traveler either had a wicked drinking problem, or . . . what? He was conducting some sort of scientific research? His John Lennon glasses did give him a graduate student appearance. Nobody would use such a bulky container just to store camping gear. Maybe he had some specimens on ice? A significant amount of space in the carrier was wasted because the cooler had straight, boxy dimensions.

Chad gave me a wave before sliding that chunk of Styrofoam inside his tent. When he emerged a few minutes later he was holding neither a beverage nor scientific gadgets.

He strolled over to my campsite. I liked Chad right off. Open and inherently funny, with a healthy admiration for Jerry Garcia that did not stray into the realm of obsession, Chad was also a whiz at plant identification.

"It's not even a challenge anymore, the flora here in Colorado, you know, growing up around it and all. It's still beautiful, but I'm working my way down near the equator on this ride."

We played hacky sack and talked about his route as well as nearby hikes I might want to take. It was like having my very own wilderness ranger and bicycling guide around the campfire. His dog came up in conversation a couple of times during the evening. We had a family pooch while I was growing up, a poodle of all things, but I never had my very own mutt to pal around with. Fetch with a poodle is a losing proposition. By the time I was old enough to go out and find one of man's best friends for myself, riding a bike around the globe had taken over my life.

"You can't play hacky sack around Whistle, unless you include him in the game," Chad noted.

Later, when we were talking about a hike, he said, "You'll like that stretch of country. My dog chased a bunch of range cattle damn near off the cliff."

Chad seemed pretty attached to his pooch. He said he hated to leave the mutt home for the ride. I asked him why his dog was named Whistle.

"Got him as a birthday present when I was twelve. My dad told me to whistle whenever he started running away. Sad truth is I suck at whistling so, as a joke, I yelled the word *whistle*, instead. I was gonna call him Rex or something like that, but Whistle just stuck."

I showed Chad my own whistling prowess.

"Oh man, you suck, too."

After dinner I suggested Chad break out a few beverages from his kingly supply.

"I've got nothing but tap water," he stated, sounding genuine. "The cooler? That's . . . just some stuff I have to drop off near the border."

Fair enough. But I needed more than that.

"Stuff?" I asked.

Chad shrugged casually.

"We could ask around the other fires, buy a couple beers off someone," he suggested.

After our little shopping expedition proved mildly successful, we sat around laughing and got into a little contest over matching song titles with the one-hit wonders who recorded them. I forgot all about the cooler until I was tucked into my bag for the night. It's strange what you'll ponder alone in a tent far from the street lights and television screens of modern life.

When I wasn't trying to remember all the top ten hits from the Bay City Rollers, my mind would drift over to the cooler. Hadn't I seen some water dripping from the little plastic release valve when he pushed it into the tent? What sort of stuff do you drag around in a carrier and keep on ice? Hadn't he heard of UPS? Chad didn't strike me as down to his last penny, yet.

Now I really wanted to know what was in the cooler. That, and just what sort of deal with the devil the group Air Supply made so that all those people bought their albums.

"I've decided to show you that hike personally," Chad remarked the next morning. "That is, if you don't mind the company for a few days?"

I was more than happy to have him join me, but I was headed north, planning to loop the state on this shorter summer tour. Last time I checked, the equator was in the opposite direction.

"My timetable is pretty loose," Chad explained.

We shared a knowing look. Few solo touring cyclists have a stack of responsibilities waiting back on some desk.

The cooler was already loaded in the carrier. I noticed that the lid was taped down, preventing me from taking a quick peek.

What did it matter? Old laundry soaking in cold water, slabs of Polish sausage on ice, maybe?

Truth is, blind and reckless curiosity has always been a character flaw of mine. I search the house for Christmas presents starting in July. If friends huddle, talking in whispers, I have to know what is being said, even if it's mundane gossip. And if there's a cooler with tape on it, I need a look.

"I know this great spot for lunch," Chad said. "Cheap, with big portions."

This time I'd driven by car to Colorado from Florida with my sister and started the bike tour right at the front range of the Rockies. I was in decent shape but my insides hadn't fully adjusted to the elevation change. Even though I wasn't at full throttle, Chad was a decent cyclist. Considering he wore that damn pack on his back and had to haul whatever it was in the cooler, he kept up admirably.

Chad encouraged me to order a piece of pie, then begged off dessert himself after I'd made my selection. When that triangle of à la mode goodness arrived, Chad said he'd meet me at the bikes, then slipped out the entrance. The boy didn't know what he was missing.

When I met him at our rigs, it was obvious by the large circle of water on the cement and empty bags of party ice in the top of the trash can that my new friend had given me the slip so he could add fresh cubes to the cooler in private. This was starting to mess with my head.

"So, what *is* in the cooler?" I said playfully.

Chad smiled, but just under the surface he looked like someone had punched him in the small of his back.

"It's nothing really." He shook his head. "It's stupid . . . and a little personal. You don't mind, do you?"

Of course I did! What the hell's in there, Chad?

"No, it's cool," I heard myself saying.

Chad's shoulders relaxed a little.

The voice of Mr. Sheraton, a drama teacher I had in junior high, popped into my head.

"People have layers, like an onion. You can't just peel them back all at once—unless you're ready for the tears."

To Mr. Sheraton, every afternoon he had us in those tight little desks was another chance to deliver a soliloquy. He wasn't bad, a frustrated actor who did a little summer stock, but exhausting on a daily basis.

Still, Chad wasn't an onion and this cooler business had to end.

As we rode along I conjured up hideous images of body parts packed in ice. Maybe Chad had the head of his best gal along for the ride. What else could it be?

I looked over at him pedaling along in the summer sun. This was crazy talk. A kid barely out of his teens, naming off different species of plants as we rode along. The kind of guy I'd pick first when dividing up teams for a game of ball. Not for size, but for his attitude. Then again, wasn't Ted Bundy a charmer? I played it cool. Late in the afternoon, we pulled over at a small store.

"Can you get me a Baby Ruth?" I asked Chad. "I'm gonna top off my tires."

When he came out, I took the candy bar.

"That's Whistle in there, isn't it?" I said quietly.

His good cheer collapsed like I'd kicked the legs of the chair out from under him. We sat down on the curb. I put a gloved hand on his shoulder.

"Hey man, I'm really sorry."

I don't know if he heard me. An RV with a couple of retirees pulled away from the tire pump.

"How'd it happen?" I asked as gently as possible.

Chad took a deep breath.

He'd never have left Whistle at home for an adventure like a ride to the equator. I should have guessed as much. The carrier usually held Chad's backpack, some equipment, and Whistle.

"Last weekend I met this girl at an afternoon concert out at Red Rock. Whistle and me were headed for the equator right after the concert, but Joan was so sweet, and Whistle liked her."

"I pedaled us all back to her place. She lived on this sweet ranch in the foothills. Told me she was in college and her parents weren't due back for a couple days. Turned out Joan was seventeen, it was her uncle's place, and as her legal guardian he didn't like it one bit when he walked in and found me in his easy chair."

Chad shook his head, probably wishing he could go back in time.

"The guy was out of his mind. Joan told him nothing had happened, but he kept ranting about how this crap had gone on long enough. I said we'd just met and that I was leaving. Then he pushed me back down in the chair. Now that scared me. I broke for the door and was getting on my bike when he stepped to the railing with a gun."

"Did he take a shot at you?"

"There was some gunfire, but I think he was blasting into the air. I pedaled for the woods like some sort of lunatic, and waited. They argued on the porch. I could barely hear them at that distance, and I was all out of breath. Whistle was off playing somewhere. I called his name a couple times but got worried that I'd bring the uncle in my direction. Must have drifted off at some point."

Chad's voice started trembling.

"I thought . . . thought I'd dreamed those last gunshots. It was really late . . . and Whistle . . . he must have come back to the house looking for me. I found him . . . the next morning after they drove off somewhere."

He kept back the tears by pinching the the bridge of his nose and holding his head down. I'd also located Whistle. His white, lifeless eyes looking up at nothing from inside the cooler. This was bad. People were heartless and cold and I couldn't do a damn thing about it.

"No way I was going to leave him out there," Chad said. Anger crept in now, under the pain. We looked over at the cooler. "I stole it from the porch. What I wanted to do was kick in the son-of-a-bitch's door and ransack the place. But I just got my dog and. . . . It's been like he's still here, kinda. I'm okay as long as I . . . I just don't know how to do this . . . I can't—"

Chad fell apart. We sat there for a long time.

My candy bar tasted like chalk. It found a place in the trash. When I came back, Chad was pulling himself together.

"Listen," I reasoned. "We gotta do something. A proper burial. Maybe—"

Chad stood up, nodding. "I was taking him down to the San Juan Mountains, for a nice send-off. But when we got talking about that hike last night, I thought of a perfect spot for him out there."

It was another full day's ride to the trailhead, and then what? The ground in Colorado is hard and, well, rocky. It would be a shame to have some forest creatures dig the body up while we were still out there. The cooler was sweating and drippy. Whistle wasn't going to keep much longer.

I went to the pay phone and looked up funeral homes. I asked Chad how he felt about cremation.

A solemn man, overdressed for a postcard-quality day in Colorado, placed a container, not really an urn, into Chad's hands. After I explained the situation a couple of times over the phone, they had made some exceptions. I sat under the shade of some tall pines while Chad said his goodbyes to the intact Whistle. A few hours later we walked out of there with the remains. Chad was handling it better than I expected. He seemed to appreciate someone else making the arrangements. As we tossed the Styrofoam coffin into a dumpster, his face radiated relief. Carrying the shell of your best friend around in a cooler is no picnic.

"So we'll take Whistle on that hike," Chad said as we pedaled for a nearby campground, his voice tired but steady. "It's a good place to scatter him, you'll see."

The next day was pure cycling enjoyment. The sort of carefree riding reminiscent of childhood jaunts with good friends, when it was just about riding as fast and far as your legs and daylight would allow. I could have cycled to China on days like that. No plans or rules, just turning the pedals clean and true.

Chad talked out his memories of Whistle as we rode along. Not a morbid conversation, but something akin to an Irish wake. He recalled many things he'd nearly forgotten over time, and others he rarely thought about because Whistle was always something in the present tense. I really enjoyed hearing about when he took Whistle tubing and the dog decided after a few minutes to swim to the bank and run along, refusing to come in; just barking and having a grand time on land. Whistle would dart off, to chase something or follow a scent, then show up a quarter mile later.

At one point the river split around a small island covered in reeds and brush. Chad was behind his other float buddies, so he hadn't seen which route they took. He drifted down the path that had a fallen tree blocking forward progress. By the time he realized there was no way to squeeze through, it was too late. Water was being pulled under the hulking tree with no small amount of force. The sucking action held Chad's tube in place. The branches hidden below the surface would act like the screen on a door, trapping anything drawn under against them. Chad tried to climb onto the trunk of the tree, but it was too big to find a secure purchase and he didn't want to chance a fall into the water and be pulled under.

"I called to Whistle. When he finally got there I told him to go get the others, like in a *Lassie* episode," Chad recalled, shaking his head and laughing. "So what does he do? He comes running onto the log like I want to play or something. Not only did I have to claw my way up the damn trunk, but I had to make sure he didn't fall in."

We cruised along.

"He was a good dog," Chad said.

The hike was everything Chad promised, with a dazzling vista at the top of a ridge overlooking a mountain lake. I stood in the sun and wondered how the sky could be so blue. We were more than a few feet above sea level. I tried to force a little more oxygen into my lungs while Chad retrieved the container of ashes from his pack.

I thought my friend might offer a long speech, but he stepped forward, shook the ashes into the breeze, then stood back.

Chad handed me an old Frisbee, chewed along the edges, and kept the worn rubber ball for himself. We heaved them off the ridge as far as we could.

"Fetch, boy. Go get it," he whispered.

Then Chad tried to whistle.

I struggled to maintain the sorrow I'd been feeling only moments before, but he really did suck. I started to chuckle, then added my pitiful tweets to the chorus. Pretty soon we were laughing so hard it's a wonder we didn't fall off the mountain.

Chad was headed for a distant spot on the map where everything feels different. Exotic plants crowd the jungles, the piercing heat of the sun beats down year-round, and the sky is a pale and hazy blue. For all his good cheer, it was a long way from home. And for maybe the first time in his life, Chad would be completely alone. Made me want to throw my lot in with the ebullient young man from Colorado.

"Thanks, for everything," Chad said.

All I'd done was stand around while he let go of a friend.

"Wind at your back, man," I replied, searching my thoughts for something a little more useful to impart. But the mysteries of the road would show themselves in good time or not at all. Best we can manage sometimes is to find the strength to laugh, and keep moving forward.

The Day Before the Best Day of My Life

THE BEST DAY OF MY LIFE?

Some people have trouble with that one, but the answer rolls from my lips swiftly, with the easy confidence of someone speaking about certainty in a world full of too many questions.

It was when Beth Biagini stepped out of a truck parked high in the mountains of Bryce Canyon, Utah. My life opened up right then, like the greatest novel of all time, an epic story full of promise, redemption, laughter, and a peace I'd always wanted to believe could exist between two people. Clueless, I leaned against my bicycle eating pistachios while the key to my happiness walked up and introduced herself.

It would take a few years for us to tie the knot; the story of true love had a detour or two, outside complications, and its share of logistical bumps before takeoff. But from that day forward a hole in my heart filled in and the world has made a certain amount of sense no matter how cruel, bizarre, or downright crummy things get.

I found my Juliet, my place of worship, my true north, and like the lunch-cart poets say, the rest is gravy.

Lucky me.

But the story of true love must wait.

Instead, let's focus on the day before the best day of my life. All that stuff about it being darkest before the dawn, that a storm's rage is strongest before it passes? What they should include in the fine print is that it can be a very long night, and once in a great while storms will actually circle back for one more devastating blow.

It was around five o'clock, quitting time at most of the industrial facilities, mines, and gravel pits dotting Utah's stark desert country. I was thinking about retiring for the day myself. With close to a hundred miles of pedaling under my belt I'd earned the right to relax at a reservoir recreation area I'd noticed a heads-up sign for a few miles back. If my computer counter was working properly the reservoir was over the next rise.

Cycling in the desert, it's easy to achieve a trancelike state. The sun, wind, and sweeping vistas are similar to the ocean in many ways. Tracer lines of heat radiating off the pavement take on the appearance of waves if you stare at them long enough.

I was in one of these states when an oversize white truck powered dangerously close to me. I snapped to attention and veered to the right, hugging the edge of the pavement. The truck dropped back for an instant and when it came roaring forward the passenger opened his door, brushing my handlebars and knocking my mirror out of joint. Harsh laughter could be heard from the truck's cab. I braked hard, screaming obscenities as I slowed. The truck barreled over the hill, spewing a thick mix of monoxide juices in its wake.

When I'd recovered enough to continue, the reptilian section of my brain went on red alert. Senseless acts of cruelty, and even close calls, remind a person that we're still apes with better wardrobes much of the time. I felt a little sick with adrenaline. At least they hadn't knocked me to the ground, or worse.

I tried to shake it off, thinking instead of the sweet, satisfied feeling that would engulf me once I stepped off the bike for the night. That's when I noticed a loathsome sight—the white truck idling at the base of the descent, less than a quarter mile away.

Damn.

I scanned in vain for the reservoir turnoff but it was just me, a straight road, and a pair of edgy rednecks waiting at the bottom of the hill, rednecks who had already demonstrated a propensity for violence. Maybe if I didn't look down there for a while they'd go away.

Of course when I sneaked a peek they were still there. I heard the engine shut off and tried to remember whether I'd seen a gun rack along the back window when the truck tore by. I couldn't make one out with any certainty from this distance, but there *was* something there.

Controlling fear is a nasty business. Mine threatened to swallow me. That sort of intense longing to be anywhere but where you are makes a person feel rather small and bite-size. But in the middle of nowhere, surrounded by dirt and a few fist-size rocks, I was going to have to meet this situation head-on. It was doubtful my communication skills were going to come in handy with these boys.

One of the guys walked to the back of the truck and leaned against it, casual, patient. He opened a can of something and downed it in one steady pull. Wonderful, now alcohol was part of the equation.

Okay, first things first, where was my Mace? I carried a small cylinder of debilitation for this type of circumstance, but it had been such a tranquil journey I'd packed it away miles earlier. If it was going to come down to do or die, I needed an edge, or at least something to give me a sporting chance.

Taking a few deep breaths, what a Buddhist roommate of mine once called cleansing breaths, I dug into my pannier. Maybe it fell out when I repacked in Salt Lake City? More breathing. Now I was on the verge of hyperventilating.

I finally located the cylinder tucked under some Minute Rice. The trouble with Mace is, it's a hand-to-hand combat type of weapon. You realize this in no uncertain terms when it comes time to use it. I wasn't ready to ride down there, yet. But as I pulled the slender black tube from the bag, its silver tip glittering in the sunlight, a twisted plan began to form. It was time to see what sort of card players these guys were.

I brought the tube of Mace over my head with both hands, pointing it toward the sky, then I pantomimed the motion of cocking it—like a big handgun. Don't ask what came over me. Maybe it was the way the cylinder gave the appearance of being a gun at a certain distance. Maybe that was simply wishful thinking. Nevertheless, I found myself leaning over the handlebars in the Utah desert pointing five inches of plastic at a pair of rednecks.

How quickly life can turn ugly and raw.

In my favor, I was shirtless, with miles of exercise ridden into my muscles and two months worth of untidy beard covering my face. I could be mistaken for "unstable" under the right circumstances. I was praying these were the right circumstances.

Stacking up against me were the facts that I was not really holding a gun, there was no escape if this bluff failed, and my opponents probably had actual firepower. Welcome to Utah; joker's wild.

My arms began to shake a little.

Steady. . . .

The rednecks hadn't moved except to accumulate more empty cans on the ground below them.

"Come and get a piece of this," I screamed over and over. "I wish you'd come get a piece of this."

Spit leapt out between my threats. I was nearly hysterical. Howling. I remember howling at one point. When I was done, the desert seemed more quiet than usual. The rednecks conferred by the back of the truck, then headed for the cab. Raise and call. I tasted a rancid, metallic burn at the top of my throat. I'm not much of a gambler.

The truck's engine gunned to life, then revved a few times before rolling away. When it didn't turn around and power up the hill with vehicular homicide as its goal, I let out a weak sigh of relief. It was a good ten minutes before I took my eyes off the horizon and relaxed.

Sitting on the ground, I studied the can of Mace. Could I really press that button in defense? More to the point, did the container even work properly after sitting dormant for so many bike adventures? Carefully, like a member of a bomb squad, I extended my shooting arm as far from my body as possible, aimed the Mace away from me, and squeezed.

Wind direction, damn it! I forgot about wind direction! Though I wasn't hit with a direct burst of chemicals, enough of the Mace drifted across my face to cause pain and suffering. I had to waste a nearly full water bottle bathing my eyes and washing the burning sensation off my cheeks and neck.

The coughing tapered back after a few minutes. Now I knew the Mace worked. I thought about putting a label on the cylinder. "This product has been tested on humans."

You know things aren't that bad when you can still laugh at yourself. I went in search of the reservoir turnoff, still keeping one eye peeled for a white truck, and trying not to cough too much so I didn't give myself away.

But there was no truck, only a big hole in the ground filled with water. It appeared I had the place to myself. I dumped the bike at the bottom of a long dirt path and collapsed on a dock that extended some distance over the water. After setting up my tent, I shuffled back to the dock, flopped down, and stared at the billowing clouds for a while. I began to feel lazy, and almost sane again.

Clouds?

In Utah clouds don't just drift by on their lonesome. They run in large packs, the puffy white ones being the leaders, followed by hordes of darker, fast-moving thunderheads. Clouds in Utah mean walls of rain and flash flooding. The very last place you want to be is in an arroyo. I looked around. The reservoir met that description.

Calm.

I scurried up the gravel of the closest rise. A warm blast of wind smacked my face. The sky was so dark in one direction it could have been night. The storm was closing fast.

Sliding back down the hill, I ignored the scrapes and splinters received along the way. The tent flapped out of control in the wind as I tried to pack it. For a moment I stood frozen by exhaustion, indecision, and my old friend, fear. Flash floods come out of nowhere. I knew the clock was running.

I bungeed onto the back rack everything that wouldn't fit into the panniers, then struggled for the pavement. It actually felt better to be on the bike. The first drops of rain were like the crack of a stagecoach driver's whip. I wanted to outrun the worst of it, not certain if even the highway was immune to flooding. With the storm nipping at my heels, I forgot about my exhaustion for a while. Realizing I'd beaten the worst of it, I yelled and taunted the clouds like a schoolyard bully. I definitely qualified as unstable at that point.

But exhilaration turned to misery shortly after reaching for my water bottle. Not more than a swallow or two was left at the bottom of the container. I'd never gotten around to filtering fresh water at the reservoir. I opened my mouth to catch a few errant raindrops, but the storm was well behind and to the left of me.

Now look who was taunting whom.

I just wanted to stop, but my instincts told me storms can change directions. I needed shelter, rest, and water. I needed to find a town, or even a farmhouse.

A road sign indicated the existence of a settlement called Fishkill seven miles ahead. Though I couldn't find it on any of my maps, I was hopeful, even drinking the last of the water as I fought a crosswind with the dregs of my energy.

I set in motion a litany of swearing that spiraled into a series of grunts while I slumped beside the sign for the mythical Fishkill. There was absolutely nothing that could be construed as civilization. And worse still, I couldn't even find a puddle of dirty water to filter into my water bottle. I threw my helmet down and wondered if I had the strength left to cry.

That's when I remembered Candy.

Many miles ago, before things went south, I had pulled over at a small house bearing the words CANDY HERE! painted by hand onto giant pieces of plywood.

Never underestimate the power of advertising.

Nobody answered the door but I thought I heard a hoarse voice shouting something so I chanced it. Another door, with the top half open, forming a counter of sorts, was visible on the other side of the room. An old man peered out. He was sitting right behind the door, which made his head appear to float without a body.

Nothing fazed me anymore. "Do you have any Crunch Bars, or Baby Ruths?" I asked cheerfully.

When he laughed I could see he was toothless. Eventually he popped his dentures in and swung the bottom half of the door open. A full bowl of snap peas was in his lap. He expertly worked the legumes free of their pods while we talked.

"Candy? Candy's my daughter! She does hair, and people's nails. She's really good with that airbrush art, too."

A Crunch Bar was not in my immediate future. Like a chipmunk on speed, a small dog shot from around the corner and ran figure eights through my legs.

"Wait a second, son. I'm gonna call Candy."

Candy said she was busy at the stove so we made our way into the kitchen. She thought my mistake a riot as well.

"You mean people don't pull off the highway a couple times a day asking for chocolate and other sweets? Your sign is the size of a bill-board."

"The road's not really a tourist corridor. We put that up 'cause Candy was a pretty famous hairdresser in the city. Had quite a follow-ing. When she opted for the country life her customers kept trying to find her way out here. They all know where she is now. Maybe I should think about taking that sign down," the man said.

We chatted for a bit. I even helped snap some peas.

"Look, you've got to take some of the harvest with you. It's more than we'll be able to eat or freeze," Candy noted. "It's the least we can do seeing as we don't have any Crunch Bars on hand." She began loading my arms with radishes, carrots, ears of corn, and vine-ripe tomatoes.

I protested, claiming I couldn't carry that much on my bike, but it all looked garden fresh. The old man wobbled out to my ride and strapped a bag of potatoes here and a bushel of radishes there. He jammed a Ziploc full of apples into my front bag.

I rode away heavy with produce but appreciative of the gesture. I'd forgotten to jettison most of the weight and now, in Fishkill, Utah, I gave thanks to Candy and her dad before chomping into a plump tomato. I reasoned that the tomatoes had more liquid in them than the apples.

Gunnison, Utah, was fifteen miles away. Even with the tomatoes I felt dehydrated. The last of it was uphill, which nearly finished me. I was like a prizefighter looking around in desperation for someone, anyone, to throw in that damn towel. I could only pray that Gunnison was an actual place. A sign for a state prison gave me hope. If those prisoners had anyone who loved them, who cared enough to see them, maybe Gunnison built some hotels and restaurants where those visitors slept and ate.

"Come on you wretched sinners," I pleaded in the fading light. "Someone's gotta love you."

The streetlights of Gunnison were flickering to life when I coasted slowly down the main strip. There was a diner with booth seating available.

"You okay, mister?" the waitress asked, visibly shocked by my appearance. I spotted myself in the mirror behind the counter. Sweat and dirt clung to my face while tomato juice hung in my beard. Where the Mace hadn't irritated my skin, the day's exertion had sucked the life out of it. My shorts were ripped, and nicks and cuts dotted my arms and legs. I looked frightful, and I'm usually a charitable critic of my own appearance.

"Not really," I mustered the strength to say. "Water, in that booth . . . bathroom?"

When I emerged, slightly more presentable, she offered a motherly smile. I drank a pitcher of water before ordering a king's feast. The second piece of pie was even better than the first. If heaven doesn't include pie, I'll pass.

"You hit a rough patch out there today?" the waitress asked knowingly.

All I could do was nod. It was too fresh in my mind to talk about.

"Happens to all of us. Well, tomorrow's another day, right?" She eased the bill onto the table and went to refill somebody's coffee.

As it turned out tomorrow was the best day of my life, and all the more delicious for what I had to push through to get there.

Rarely do you win big; more often you fold, or you lose your shirt. I walk around most of the time just hoping I'll break even, and feel really good about it. I fell into a hotel bed that night, a tired smile on my face, and called things even.

Just Trying to Make It Home

"I CAN'T TAKE YOUR MONEY," THE FORTUNE-TELLER SAID WITH A LOOK of chagrin as she pushed my fingers gently back into a ball.

Not much older than me, this would-be mystic had a nice smile, smelled like honeysuckles and Ivory soap, and, truth be told, the fact that she wasn't wearing shoes is what really attracted me to her services. In my book, the power of a winsome young woman's bare feet is so much stronger then the pull of the stars.

Maybe I hadn't heard her correctly. I did have to keep peeking outside the entrance of her colorful, makeshift tent along a busy midway at the Renaissance Festival. You want to trust these playful folks from the Middle Ages. Still, someone in medieval garb could ride off with my touring bicycle faster than a person can say Friar Tuck.

"Are you telling me this is on the house?" I queried.

She pushed herself back from the table. A plethora of wrist bracelets clanked and two long earrings twirled.

"I can't take your money . . . because I can't read you," she said. This admission seemed to rattle her a bit. The young seer drank deeply from a can of Mountain Dew. But then she followed up her concession to failure with a smile so light and disarming that I knew I was about to be conned.

"Okay, what do you propose we do about this?" I said, cringing inside because I'd had voluntarily wandered farther into her web, but part of me still wanted to know how her sales pitch would go.

"I could try the cards," she said, placing a hand on a Tarot deck to her right. "Or maybe tea leaves, but I've only seen this one other time. When you can't read someone, it doesn't matter what method you use."

She was setting me up for something big. Had to be. It was flattering in a way, to be singled out for the deep score.

"What are you trying to say, I don't have a future?" I asked, a little defiantly.

She produced a smile meant to indicate everything was all right.

"I should probably just go," I sighed. "I think I've been on the road too long."

There's a point in every journey when you should turn for home. It doesn't matter how amazing the sunrises have been, how many mornings you've woken up alone, stunned by your good fortune and left to ponder what you did to deserve another priceless day of adventure, or the number of times you and a collection of hardy, knowing souls laughed together along the side of the road until it hurt. Home always beckons.

When you begin to think weekend fortune-tellers are trying to run scams on you for a few extra pieces of silver, it's time to head for the comforts of your little cave and recharge the batteries.

My guess is that when the boys in the lab coats have finally wrestled out all the mysteries wrapped so tightly inside each of us, they'll find something called the carrier pigeon gene. Most travelers have it, or had it at one time. It's what keeps us from allowing an adventure to unravel into a lifetime of aimless wandering.

Conversely, the thirst for the unknown, that giddy, driving desire to pedal, climb, hike, or paddle until you've experienced it all, is what I've dubbed the "trying to swallow the ocean" gene. If these internal forces don't work in concert, the results can be dire.

I remember a children's book in which a boy tried to swallow the ocean. His head, filled with all that water, those waves and sand and seaweed, had swelled to many times the size of the rest of his body. The boy was in such pain. For pages his head continued to grow until you just knew he was going to burst. Then, red-faced and eyes bulging, he finally, begrudgingly, hurled the ocean back.

When I meet people on the road who never went home, never

stopped to rest their head and heart and examine the journey until a sense of place became mythical, the one adventure beyond their grasp, I think about that ambitious little boy, and I realize that standing before me is his real-life alter ego. Someone who swallowed instead of spit.

I often feel a twisted sense of pride for the untethered seekers. At least they aren't cowering in the corner with the blinds pulled waiting for the end. Could be that I recognize myself in there somewhere. I've been that little boy.

"Don't rush off. It's been kinda dead all morning," the fortune teller said. She flipped open a small cooler that had been tucked under the silk-clothed table and offered me a soda. We walked to the entrance of the tent and took a look at my bike.

"Where do you live, anyway?"

How is it that fortune-tellers can explain your future in detail, but don't know where you're from?

"I've got places all over," I replied, smiling.

Even without the tricks of the trade, she knew this wasn't true.

"You've covered some miles on that thing," the fortune teller said. It didn't take an oracle to see this.

I gave her the grand tour of my rig. We talked about camping, how much weight I was carrying, some of the places I'd been, and how to fix a rear derailleur with a paper clip and a rubber band. She revealed that she'd been working the Renaissance Festival circuit for the better part of a year, enjoyed it for the most part (except the food), really believed she could guide people toward a better future, and grew up outside of Baltimore.

We talked a while longer and watched a falcon perform aerial tricks for a crowd in the courtyard across the path. If this young entrepreneur was going to fleece me, she certainly was waiting until the last possible moment.

"It's not that you don't have a future," explained the fortune-teller. She was holding the handlebars of my bike while I saddled up. "Some people kind of set their course early in life, so you can see where most things are headed. Others say they don't know what's going to happen but the indicators jump right out when you turn the cards, open their palm, or look into their eyes."

It was coming, I could feel it. The advice that was going to cost me.

"Then there are the people like you . . . who color too far outside the lines. If you're most likely to do anything," she nodded at my bicycle, "then the future is a complete mystery."

That was years ago, and most days are still a mystery. I was wrong about my fortune-teller, though. She didn't have her sights set on my money clip. I willingly handed her the going rate for her services. It's the only time I've been to a fortune-teller, and not having my fortune told was more than worth it.

"Hey, let me ask you something," I said. "Can you read your own fortune?"

She laughed. "I've never tried. Don't get other people to read me, either. I guess I'd . . . rather be surprised."

I waved, then rolled back onto the highway . . . with absolutely no idea where I was going next. Truth was, in geographic terms I was without an address at that moment. But contrary to what Dorothy learned at the end of the yellow brick road and what the IRS requires for documentation purposes, home doesn't have to be a place. It need only be something or somebody that keeps you grounded, focused, and, well, sane. A spot you fill up with passion and don't mind putting a lot of work into. One true thing that you can reach for at day's end that connects you to the world. Roots.

Though I held no mortgages during my travels, and often received my mail General Delivery at whatever post office was along the route, for years I'd been the proud owner of a nice little abode. A familiar place that had sheltered me through some rough patches. I acquired this real estate back in fifth grade. Pretty young to own property, but all it cost me was sixth period and a solemn commitment to become a lifelong storyteller.

Mrs. MacCumber asked me to stay after class. Judgment day had arrived. She wanted to know if there were any family problems. I wasn't the sort of student to start blowing off assignments. Sounding like some overworked executive, I leaned across her desk, hands clutching a collection of worn ring binders.

"Something had to go, Mrs. M. You see, last summer I started writing this mystery series . . . I call it *The Sunshine Boys.*" I held out exhibits A, B, C, and D, and the first chapter of E, basically a rip-off of the Hardy Boys, on bicycles, with a Florida setting, and three friends instead of two brothers, but I was so proud of it. I carried those binders everywhere I went.

"When school started, I just couldn't stop writing. And what with classroom work, my favorite television shows, playing with my friends, and keeping up with my comic-book reading, I . . . I let some of my English assignments slide—only because I knew I could catch up whenever I wanted."

If you're going to skip assignments, conventional wisdom says things will go easier when you have a binder full of stories to toss on the judge's desk. But what's a ten-year-old know about justice? Mrs. M took the entire series with her, saying we'd talk in the morning. She gave no indication of her feelings.

Nearly in tears on the bicycle commute home, I had to drown my sorrows at the local convenience store with multiple games of pinball (exercise), bags of Funyons (comfort food), and Issue #114 of *The Incredible Hulk*, one I already had (a familiar friend).

My sentence was handed down at the beginning of sixth period. Mrs. M called me to the front of the class. Ah, public humiliation. Mrs. M was a smooth operator. But the ax never fell. She gave me time each day to work on the series. In exchange I had to read it to the class on Friday afternoons. A tough time slot. *You* try holding the attention of sweaty ten-year-olds jittery for the weekend, in a school that had yet to discover central air-conditioning.

This actually improved the work because it forced me to bring in new characters—my fellow students—and keep things hopping. When I teamed up the classroom troublemaker and the resident popularity queen, making them a clever, criminal duo, my audience went crazy.

The Sunshine Boys became a Friday ritual, and a cult classic. Then Mrs. M edited a few of the tales, submitted them to a kid's magazine, and handed me an excerpt. It was right there in black and white. I felt the roots taking hold. Something solid and worthwhile slowly grew up around me. Writing became my first home and a life-long refuge.

It should come as no surprise that I consider my bicycle another of my residences, a mobile home for sure but a place with all the amenities I could possibly need for an extended stay. It's not a place where I can live indefinitely, but in that little rolling space I've found friendships, thrills, freedom, adventure, sore muscles, plenty of material to write about, and . . . the time my life.

You'd think a couple of emotional homes, little shelters from the storms of life, would be enough for any man, but my Taj Mahal, a palace of laughter and joy that would give me some real grounding, pulled into a Bryce Canyon campground. Beth was her name, and we would not have met if I weren't riding a bicycle. She backed her truck into the campsite next to mine on the basis that a guy touring around on a bike couldn't be that bad. Thank God for my two-wheeled wonder.

My arrival in that campground almost didn't happen. The near-death experiences of the previous day encouraged me to skip the long climb into the park. I'd convinced myself that Bryce Canyon was more than likely Zion National Park on a smaller scale, so I could head down the road and not miss much. The owner of the little hotel hooted at this statement.

"Yeah, you can think that if you want."

He said this it with just enough dismissiveness in his voice to get my wheels pointed up that long and winding hill. I still had most of those vegetables from Candy's Beauty Salon in the Utah desert, so when she got back from a hike, I cooked Beth dinner, something I called "bike pannier surprise."

We stayed up late talking about everything and nothing in particular until we couldn't keep our eyes open, but wanted to keep going. The next evening she cooked me dinner.

When I rode out of the park the following morning, I felt like someone had gone inside me with one of those fishing knives and demonstrated the proper way to gut and dress a full-grown man. It wasn't a dramatic, heartsick moment of confusion bred by lust and superficial attraction, though she is a beautiful woman. When I rounded the curve and could no longer see Beth's face, I felt lost and completely empty. Like leaving home for the first time.

We were married two years later, and lived like nomads for a while after that. The proposal was made on the top of a mountain and the wedding held New Year's Day in a friend's little adobe home just outside a national forest boundary.

"Never marry a girl who won't pick up an ax and chop wood with you," Gordy, the seventy-eight-year-old cyclist, had told me.

On our wedding day, amid the fallen snow and the high-mountain blues of a New Mexico sky, we chopped and stacked a cord or two for the fireplace. The light in Beth's eyes as the sun dipped behind leafless trees and the temperature dropped made all things seem possible. It felt like the start of my greatest adventure.

We still lacked a permanent address, but I had finally, unequivocally, made it home.

The Blind Leading The Blind

Like leaves and kings, all things must fall. —Josh Ritter

Of all the characters in *Metal Cowboy*, it's the blind old rancher at the opening that everyone wants to know about. The fact that I perform our encounter in my stage show has something to do with it, but I think there's more. He left something unfinished hanging out there in the cold Idaho morning light.

Even then, young, wild, living as fast as my legs and the vaguest of dreams would carry, the man stopped me in my tracks, reached right in and stirred things up but good. That weatherbeaten face, the way he held himself just so, proving force of will can prop up bones turned to balsawood by the hands of time. When he worked his cane over my rig like an insect's antennae, then christened me the Metal Cowboy in a voice that exposed a thousand miles of busted gravel behind it, well. . . .

With his very next breath he quested me on a fool's errand—to find where the innocent sleep. I've been on the job, with varied success, ever since.

But whatever happened to that relic, half-sage and half-apparition ambling back into the mist? I wanted the rest of his story too, but if the road has taught me anything, it's that answers come in their own time if they come at all.

For years I've shrugged my shoulders, let my mind wander and wonder, before putting my head back down to take my turn out front.

Then a letter arrived.

It wasn't completely unexpected, but let's call it a long shot. During boys' day out, a cross-country summer ride with my two sons in tow chronicled in *Momentum Is Your Friend,* we happened upon a robust gathering of rowdy folks in one of Yellowstone's campgrounds. What I thought was a company picnic gone rogue, or an annual retreat after the boss has departed, turned out to be just one family— one grande Irish Catholic family. It took them three full-size RVs and several chase vehicles to transport their crew from Pocatello, Idaho for geyser-inspired fun in the national park, but by some twisted logic they were impressed that I was carting two boys and gear by bicycle across America.

We got on like peas and carrots. The boys learned how to sing a round, discovered why brothers with large waistlines and suspect coordination should not attempt to riverdance around a campfire, and just who had purchased most of the chocolate and marshmallows west of the Continental Divide.

When we parted—to pedal over the highest point in Yellowstone— the bulk of the Irish were sleeping it off, but the patriarch of the family, he looked to be stirring coals for a batch of wake up coffee, saluted us as we rolled out.

I remember that moment clearly. It was the last time my heart beat at a normal pace for the next three hours. I hammered the bicycle train out of the campground into morning tourist traffic in the wrong gear. This is a catastrophically successful way to slow your pace to a crawl and break your spirit in one motion. After some swearing and chain slippage I located a level of punishment I would have to live with.

A midday stop at Old Faithful let me inventory what remained of my strength and gather my reserves. When the Continental Divide sign came into view, indicating the high point had been reached, I nearly wept with gratitude. An RV roared by, coming to a halt behind the sign, brakes still stinking. A preposterous number of folks spilled out of its doors. The Pocatello Catholics had caught us.

Everyone gathered around, heroes of the gridiron style. If we hadn't been so sweaty they'd have hoisted us on their shoulders. As it was, the Patriarch pulled out a silver flask from his back pocket and offered the boys a nip. "Absolutely not," I announced; then I took a swallow or two before handing it back to the big man.

To a person, no one could get over that we'd pedaled all the way from the campground to the Continental Divide sign . . . in one day, less than a day. There was still time for a late lunch. The Catholics brought out enough food to feed a small country. Over short ribs and Gatorade I got around to the story of the blind old rancher. The big man kept smiling long after everyone had gone back to their ribs.

"I think I know who you're talking about." he said.

Of course. They lived in Pocatello, where the whole thing had gone down years before. People in a small town would have to remember a blind rancher tapping around their streets. The answers had finally found me. But there wasn't time. The shadows were lengthening and food was going back into the RV. I handed him a card and asked him to follow up with the rest of the rancher's story. He said he'd try to nail it down for me. We hit the flask once more time, for St. Patrick.

Pictures were snapped—on the wide angle lens setting—in front of the sign. Then we pushed off, down a steep hill, into the other half of a country and the rest of our lives.

No return address, no preamble, just a typed letter. Somewhere between the mailbox and the front door I felt myself slipping into a John LeCarré novel. Virgil, no last name, but it said everyone knew him as Digs. He'd moved from Montana to Pocatello after serving in WWII, bringing his high school sweetheart with him. Reunited after the war. In my mind's eye I saw the famous fountain photo of the GI kissing the love of his life in that deep sweeping dance move.

They raised a family, built a successful business, but lived modestly. A law degree courtesy of the GI bill. Friends, state fairs, fishing in the creeks, church on Sundays. Civic duties and a small ranch purchased about the time the kids went off to college. Summer evenings on the porch gazing out at shoulder high corn and watching the red tailed hawks circle the thermals.

His eyes went bad after his wife passed. But he was often heard to say that was Okay because they'd held up long enough to see beauty leave this world. Digs was a regular sight in town, until he ran out of fight in the early 90s. Not long after our encounter. But not before he wrote out checks to many local institutions.

I sat on my own porch, letting it sink in. The blind old rancher could count himself the backbone of "the greatest generation". He'd measured out a life, what he needed rather than trying to horde the whole thing or pouring it out in all directions. I sighed deeply and allowed myself think there was a time before reality TV, social networks and the sickly sweet sound of desperate hands grabbing at the last straws of a go-go culture. There was a time before . . . this.

I was about to add his uplifting postscript to my stage shows when another letter arrived. There's always another got-damned letter isn't there? Another shoe, miles that weren't listed on any map. The rest of the rest of the story, Mr. Harvey.

The Digs of the second letter had shadows and hidden sides. As much as I fought it, for better or worse, the guy in this letter felt like a real person. I bit my lip reading this missive. I'd bought the first version, played in major chords and closed out with a crescendo, a twenty-one-gun salute and a flyover. Is it childish of me to feel homesick for that version after only a paragraph of Digs' new life?

Same guy on the surface of it, but the sweetheart he'd brought with him from Montana was not the woman who'd waited out the war. She'd died in childbirth. The math may or may not have worked out as his offspring, but he married her older sister, they claimed the child, and moved to Pocatello.

His life played out along the same lines, law school, successful practice, ranch. Only in the second version there were corporations trading on his services to build highways and dig up resources sans red tape—the origin of his nickname—and the ranch was said to be a payoff for keeping word of back room deals from getting out the front door. His first son could do no wrong, while the younger boy took the brunt of his expectations and at times the back of his hand. He lost his sight to a painful disease that causes vision to go myopic until it's gone. If there's any question that the universe has a twisted sense of humor consider this; Monet, the painter, suffered this fate. Painting until the last of his vision left him, then sitting in the gardens he'd shared with the world, incapable of seeing them anymore. The condition takes years to reach closure, so it's a safe bet Digs' wife was around long after darkness fell.

Both letters were typed. Neither had contact information. I tried to let the whole thing go. Then I got booked to play a show in Logan, Utah. It had been fifteen years since I'd been that close to Pocatello. Whether I'd make the side trip was anyone's guess, but the letters found their way into my bags just the same.

A corner cafe at the intersection where the old rancher worked his cane over me was now a hip coffeehouse. I looked from laptop to laptop, searching for a cluster of old timers, but they wouldn't be caught dead in a place with a dozen different ways to order coffee and clever names for a plate of eggs.

I tracked them down at the feed store. Easy laughter from a clutch of five or six guys in no hurry to get back to wherever they'd come in from. Some had merchandise in hand. I stepped into the breach.

When I'd finished my dog and pony show, even playing out the blind old rancher encounter complete with cane I improvised from a yard stick grabbed near the counter, the men stood in silence. Maybe it was a comfortable silence to them, but I was anything but.

"Shhhiiiiiiit . . ." one of them put me out of my misery with, playing the word long and slow. "That Virgil *must* have been blind. He thought you were a cowboy."

None of them knew my man. I handed the clerk the yard stick and left. After a morning of inquires that went nowhere, I consoled myself with some pie and ice cream at a sidewalk table down the block from the coffeehouse. One of the farmers from the feed store took a seat next to me and asked if I happened to have those letters with me. As he read, I watched his face for a tell of some sort. Let's say I wouldn't want to play poker in Pocatello.

"You really want to know who this Virgil was?!"

I nodded.

"Wait here, I'm gonna pop in for a cup a coffee."

When he came back the letters weren't with him. We sat there. Him sipping and watching the lunch hour traffic while I studied the last of my vanilla ice cream soup up on a small plate.

"My letters?"

He set down his cup. "Every town had Virgils and Digs, or did at one time." He shook his head and gave me a tight smile. I knew my letters were gone. "You want to know someone, you got to be there, shoulder to shoulder. The rest is just talk."

I stood up. "Were you there?"

He liked that question. "Let me ask you something. You think someone could put your whole life into a couple of letters?"

Kick it up, Cowboy. Schooled proper over a cup of coffee before noon. I was five books into my life and had barely broken the surface. I picked up my bag and walked.

The blind will have to continue to lead the blind. My rancher's story remains in the wind and I'll keep pedaling through this wicked world, trusting my inner Virgil to help me rise above and trying not to cut too many deals with Digs to get by.

The Mother of All Tailwinds

Bringing one hundred miles in under three hours on a bicycle is akin to breaking the three minute mile on foot. Maybe the pros do it all the time; I'm not one of them so I wouldn't know, but if you don't have a resting heart rate below 50 and a fat-to-body mass index of 5 percent, charging past the 100-mile mark in three hours is a pipe dream.

Monks could use the climb out of Yosemite as a form of self-flagellation. Once on top though few places outside Vegas pay off as big. I pointed my wheels toward Pinedale and never looked back. Feathering the brakes as little as possible on a steep descent is a dodgy proposition. Pressing hard on luck, relying on muscle memory and the lines I was choosing coming down that mountain road resembled extreme skiing.

I have no idea what it looked like from the cheap seats—a fully loaded touring bicycle and rider blitzing off a mountain, leaning into the curves, defying gravity and common sense, yelping a primal howl into the morning light, but with 1500 miles of West Coast up-and-down riding behind me, I was capable of doing things on a bicycle which would have me in traction if I tried them now.

One of the feel-good philosophers said that life's a sliver of light between two infinities of darkness, and I say that within that, it's a few precious moments of grace and daring that let us see it through and offer something beautiful to talk about in the closing scenes.

The downhill run off Yosemite makes my best-of list, hands down. Something unexpected happened at the bottom of the mountain. I didn't encounter a series of rollers to break my spirit or throw off my rhythm, I didn't turn directions and head into the wind, I didn't experience a slight tilting of the earth in favor of the away team. Instead, I kept going at a breakneck pace aided by the hint of a downhill, something almost undetectable by the naked eye, and a tailwind that grew stronger as the miles dropped away.

When a gift as big as this comes your way you jump to it no matter what your body did the day before. Mine had climbed Half-Dome and should have been putting up siren wails of protest, but my systems seemed to be on the same page. I ran through all the reasons to slow down, but came up wanting.

Let's do this.

A spot of yellow in the distance kept growing until it became a school bus. I closed in on its back end the way a torpedo does in war movies. I assumed it was because the bus was making stops, but when I got close enough to see the faces of middle school kids in the very back seats, I was doing 38 mph and it was rolling steady. That's when they put up the sign. No, not the one that would have, by law, forced me to come to a complete stop—something I don't think I could have done, either physically or emotionally. This was a handmade sign done in magic markers: NO MORE TEACHERS, NO MORE BOOKS!

Another popped up: SEE YOU NEXT YEAR, SUCKERS!

And one more: SCHOOL'S OUT FOREVER!

And then the one you couldn't get away with these days even in middle school; SCHOOL'S BEEN BLOWN 2 PIECES!

I did the math as I hummed Alice Cooper's anthem to summertime anarchy sung from coast to coast this time of year. It was indeed the last day of servitude and those signs were the smallest act of rebellion, maybe their first; hiding out in the back of a bus, showing off over the release from indenture just a few hours before it really happened. Hell, what can they do to us now?

I gave them a nod and a smile as I got within spitting distance—it was like looking through a fun house mirror back at my middle school self. I'd have bet the farm that half the bus was carrying silly string or cans of shaving cream, and that seeing a bike going 40 miles per hour in the sunshine of a June morning was a glimpse at what could be . . . possibilities. Hang on, kids, the world is waiting for you on the other side of the glass.

At first they were making faces and trying to be fierce, but once the sign holders saw that I was keeping up with their bus, their expressions changed. Remarkable as it sounds, I began to overtake the rig. Drafting it at first, a la that scene from the film *Breaking Away*. The sign kids were fist pumping me on to victory. Maybe it was when the rest of the busload of kids urged me forward with high pitched cheers and the lowering of those undersized windows, but I found myself halfway to the front mirrors, then even with the passenger door. Cheers grew as I gained ground on the front of the vehicle. In my mirror I saw children's hands and heads wedging out the side windows now. The driver looked stunned. We made eye contact through the glass of the passenger door. I gave a little shrug and kept going. At least he had an answer to why his cargo had suddenly morphed into *Lord Of The Flies*.

At some point the bus turned off Highway 41, but not before I had a quarter of a mile on it. That should have been enough. I'd outpaced a bus for godsake, but it only fueled my need for speed. We're not even talking about speed here, but a desire to break from everything that binds us to ourselves. I wanted to time travel, to find a place inside the ride that doesn't exist anywhere else. World class surfers, when asked if anything compares to catching the perfect wave, have said they've felt the edges of it on long bike rides.

I put my head down and went all the way inside. When I came out, my Cateye had clocked 102 miles. It was 10:20 A.M. I'd been at it for 2 hours and 57 minutes. My legs and lungs were brand new.

The silence by the side of the road felt complete. I looked back for the first time. A breeze blew hot on my face. The three hour century was part of my personal history now. Done. The only part of it that would come to matter would be the memory of how it made me feel. I owned the stopwatch now.

There was a turn-off for a recreation area 200 yards back. I pedaled slowly at first, then something took over, I fought into the wind, stood and hammered to get my pace up, before realization washed over me. I geared down and dug for it, struggling by the campground at under 10 mph.

Call me the king of pain, I'd decided to double down. A place 25 miles back had caught my eye in the split second it took to rocket by the first time. A place where you could pan for gold and sleep in a replica of a prairie schooner.

Speed's tricky, we try to harness it to serve us, to save us, but when we realize it's taken over the show, it's often too late.

Those 25 miles ate up another three hours, but I'd be damned if I was going to put up a tent and call it a day at ten in the morning; not with wagons and the lure of gold waiting back up the road. Not with blacktop and daylight in front of me.

Besides, since conquering time and space, I'll set the pace from here on, and do things that matter to me with what remains.

Updates

Chapter 2: Finding Sanctuary In a Wild World. Oh the places I've slept on bike adventures since then. My head has rested against such improbable locations as the inside wall of a port-a-potty in Botswana due in large part to the hyenas who had the shitter surrounded. I mistook their calls for my fellow riders laughing at the unfortunate sounds I was making in the darkness. I'd taken one dose of malaria pills—an unnecessary precaution since it was the dry season. It did not agree with me. But that was no reason to laugh. Imagine my surprise when I glimpsed a circle of those crazy hyena eyes through the half-opened potty door. Fell asleep in the seated position.

From hammocks in the Costa Rican jungle to cave ledges in Northern Mexico; from snuggling my family in sleeping bags while stargazing and watching for summer meteor showers on a Vancouver island beach to parking our mountain bikes in front of John Houston's villa for a stay in the electricity-free hideaway high above the surf of Puerto Vallarta; from just off the path of a rail trail across Missouri to high above the ocean on the Cabot Trail in Nova Scotia—the world has allowed me and mine safe passage and peaceful slumbers.

The one thing that has changed in regard to sleeping arrangements is that I now have a home to welcome the weary riders of the world. For years now I've been returning the favor for all the doors that opened to me along the way, all the kindnesses that didn't have to be shown, all the laughter and sanctuary. By feeding and bedding down the cyclotourists of the world, talking shop and sharing stories over desserts and beers, we've kept ourselves from closing up as we get older. Instead of fear we choose community and it's made all the difference.

And the truth is we get so much more out of the deal. A bed and a meal pale in comparison to the stories, craft projects taught to my kids, wild berries pedaled in on bike, home improvement projects volunteered and wisdom shared.

So the next time you're looking for sanctuary in a wild world I hope you find it. And if you're in the neighborhood, ride on over. We'll leave the light on.

Chapter 3: If You Can't Run With The Big Geese . . . Seems like you can't go more than a couple chapters in one of my books without something chasing me—dogs, geese, bears, moose, neckless jocks in Camaros so there's nothing to update here, except . . .

How to Outpedal an African Elephant

I know what you're thinking. When will I ever need this information? But the world's an unpredictable place—just ask any childhood star of a TV sitcom. Around the next corner could be a bag of money or perhaps a worked up pachyderm. Statistically you may think instructions for outpacing a twelve thousand pound African elephant charging your mountain bike in deep sand are on par with Eskimos sending out for party ice at the annual potlatch, but you'll wish you had some skills when it all goes down. Think of this as my public service announcement to you.

It was the second day in country and first full one in the saddle. We numbered 300 riders on a South African fundraising bike adventure with Children in the Wilderness. Divided into groups of about twenty with two guides, the plan called for 100 plus kilometers per day through remote bush on full suspension bikes. Ride of a lifetime. By the end we'd pedal through six private game preserves and four national parks in five countries. From warthogs to water buck, this was unfettered country with no fences and very little back up. ATV or helicopter if you couldn't keep going under your own power, and in years past the guides rode with guns strapped over their shoulders messenger bag style. But the practice was discontinued when a guide accidentally discharged one into his foot. Now they carried something called elephant bangers, meant to scare off a charging bull with a loud noise. Eyes rolled every time it made an appearance.

I'd love to say that I followed the suggested training routine for six months leading up to this adventure on wheels, and I did, in a way, if chasing three lively boys through playground sand, sometimes through the thicker grade found on the beach, counts. Then there was the assistance I offered my pregnant wife—let's call it the family man's form of pilates. My training schedule is the same year round; GET ON YOUR BIKE! rinse, repeat.

So no, I didn't take their formal training schedule seriously, and I laughed off the part of the application that asked for blood type. I wasn't laughing at the end of the first day. This was billed as a tour, but many folks didn't get the memo. I'd been misplaced in one of the lead groups full of former cricket players and type-A personalities with something to prove. Mostly, that it's possible to pedal a bicycle across a stretch of Africa without looking up.

When our guide, who was riding a tandem mountain bike with his wife like it was about to become a new category in the Tour de France, yelled "Tighten up!" for the millionth time that morning, I decided to drop back with the game-viewers group. These were my peeps. Their idea was to strip down and cool off at watering holes, to point out the flora and fauna along the way and take full advantage of the rest stop offerings. The only downside of being with the game viewers is that sometimes the game has had enough.

I swore off the malaria pills after the first dose, but it had me in a weakened state for pedaling a bike 100 kilometers, even weaker for outpacing an elephant. When the massive creature finished waving his ears at me and charged, I had to dig deep. It's amazing when a lifetime of riding allows muscle memory to take over. If I'd leaned into the handlebars and pushed down I'd have gone over in sand that deep. Instead, some reptilian part of my brain remembered to sit back behind the saddle, go loose on the handlebars, pedal fast but feel light, floating over the sand.

I'm told that it was a mock charge, elephants only mean business when they tuck their trunks up and in, leading with the tusks. You could have fooled me.

Some people think I make this stuff up, but the elephant encounter was caught on tape. To see the whole thing go to:

youtube.com/watch?v=jnUWSSe69YI

To get in on the fun, take the ride of a lifetime and raise funds for a great cause that gives local children a chance at careers in eco-tourism, go to childreninthewilderness.com

Chapter 4: It's a Good Day to Ride Gordy, that stripped-down-to-the-bike-frame retiree, bear of a cyclist, is the second most asked about character from *Metal Cowboy* behind The Blind Old Rancher who gave me my name. As a cyclist, Gordy made me look bad, tired, and downright spastic on a bike, and for that I will always be in his debt. He had the true heart of a cyclist—to go go go, no matter the equipment, the conditions, the obstacles or the odds. I imagined Gordy battling on and on, beyond the end of time, but it saddens me to report that Gordy took his last ride in 2003. I called the number for the truckstop where Gordy said he worked between rides. They gave me the sad news. I asked if he'd died on a bike but learned it was nothing so romantic. He just didn't get up one day. And I never got a chance to tell him how many people he inspired through the pages of my book. But, and I'm projecting here, but I'm guessing he'd have smiled, nodded and said, "Then we'll probably see them on the road, won't we? Just try to keep up, Cowboy." It's a deep-seated goal of mine to become Gordy as I get on in life. What always stayed with me was that while he was on the back end of things, seeing the end of the line not far in the distance, it didn't faze him. It didn't make him regretful or melancholy or nostalgic. Gordy showed me that it's not about worrying that this is all going to end one day, but being amazed and overwhelmed and grateful that we here at all, for whatever time is left on the clock.

Chapter 5: Heartbreak Hotel The hotel in St. George is gone and Elvis may have left the building, but really, isn't he everywhere, and the B team of impersonators must be out there chasing the dream along with him, or some incarnation of them, though I haven't caught up with that band of merry men and women since. Which just makes the few hours spent with them years ago all the more mind-blowing. You can keep all your pitch-perfect Elvis impersonators, playing the strip for the big money, I'd pay hard cash to party with oldest Elvis, karate Elvis, Comeback Elvis, and of course Animal Elvis, in a heartbeat.

Chapter 6: The Button Boy of The Delaware Water Gap An encounter like that can't be repeated, nor should it. One take, shattered hearts and that's a wrap. He reminded me of John the Baptist of the bike world, or Marley with buttons instead of chains from A

Christmas Carol. A roadside prophet on the edge of the wilderness that was part of my education, one as important if not more than any schools I attended. Oh, and sometimes when I'm feeling really beat up by the world I'll hum the melody to that gospel diddy "Deeper River," and it lights a little corner of the dark.

Chapter 7: The Touring Cyclist's Diet: Anything That's Not Nailed Down   Much like being chased by animals, food's a recurring theme in my books. I feel sorry for people who eat just to fuel the machine, those empty souls who fill up their bellies but don't appreciate food on a viscercal level: the smell, taste, texture. I have a good friend in New Mexico who feels that eating is a burden. "I won't miss eating when I'm dead." Are you kidding me? The lure of good meals prepared and shared with friends is half of what gets me out of bed in the morning. An instant classic when it comes to cyclist's strapping on the feedbag is my "Trucker's Dream" story in *Mud, Sweat and Gears.* If you don't have that book, run out and buy yourself a copy. . . .

Chapter 8: Cutting Corners   I still haven't landed a better haircut than the one I got from my Tour De Barber. At some point I threw away my comb and declared my helmet the winner.

Chapter 9: Rough Road   Here's the hardest stretch I've run into lately:

Never again will I whine about pushing silver into a Northwest winter—griping about a chilly little bike trek down to the library in January or slogging my two-wheeled steed into the barometrically challenged elements for St. Patrick's Day party supplies.

Few realize how good we have it here on the Left Coast. Only a handful, in my estimation, have the appropriate appreciation regarding the flat out luxury, the absolute joyride that is a Pacific Northwest rainy season by bicycle. That, or maybe I'm the last slow learner who needed an object lesson in the relativity of suffering. Consider me schooled.

There will be no more bemoaning the many ways in which rain is ruining my morning commute or that, with the wind-chill factor, it feels like 20 degrees along the river during the Sunday morning loop ride with my club pals.

You see, I went to the promised land one February and came back a changed man—the cycling equivalent of Bill Murray's character reborn in the film *Groundhog Day* . . . only the backdrop for my deep freeze drama wasn't Punxsutawney, Pennsylvania, but Perry, Iowa.

"Cold enough for you?" This became the traditional greeting echoed by every taxi driver, waitress, and desk clerk during my four day stay in Des Moines. As the entertainment for the Iowa Bicycle Coalition Summit and Bike Night Auction (thankfully, held entirely inside the climate-controlled confines of the downtown Holiday Inn Conference Center—love that Midwest buffet tradition, but people, three full troughs of breakfast sausages cannot be FDA approved).

I could have laughed off the multiple feet of plowed snow along the roadways and icebox temperatures, if not for the fact that I had agreed to pedal as their B-list celebrity cycling author on a weekend ride in neighboring Perry. I'm told they phoned Lance first but he was off living strong and warm in the saddle somewhere near the equator. No doubt an umbrella drink sticking out of his water bottle.

Here's the *Des Moines Register*'s quick take on the ride:

"About 500 cyclists from around the state braved below-zero temperatures to participate in the 30th Annual BRR Ride, a 30-mile bike ride from Perry to Rippey and back. (Bike Ride to Rippey forms the event's initials.) With the temperature around minus 5 degrees, negative 25 with the wind-chill, riders pedaled through one of the coldest organized rides in the country."

What that sound bite neglects is that up to 3,000 people often turn out for this event, the unofficial kick off party of RAGBRAI. Cyclists—racers to commuters and everyone else in a 1,000 mile radius who decides to dust off a bike that morning—digs out some sort of wheeled contraption to "pedal and party" around Perry. This year most of them stayed inside church basements, gyms, and bars, waving while the stark-raving foolish in search of frostbite took to the wind.

What was I thinking? I haven't been Catholic for several decades . . . and still I can't refuse requests involving voluntary acts of suffering with no good explanation . . . beyond the carrot of "character building." I'd rather build a fire over here for potential survivors, thank you.

The facts on the ground felt more like an assault on Everest or a suicide mission than a bike ride. A few miles out of town, those who had thought it would make a great bar tale, were already turning around. I nicknamed them The Mensa Club Contingent. Shortly thereafter we noticed stray winter clothing and bike wheels littering the snow, people doing their best imitations of the Michelin Man in massive parkas throwing in the towel, or "resting" along the shoulder while their lungs thawed out enough to call out for help.

My friends at Bike World set me up on a TREK 520, that was one of the lucky rigs not to have its lube and chain grease freeze, locking up the freewheel like a bank vault. I was sporting no less than eight layers—long johns, multiple River City Bicycle winter tights, bibs, and jerseys. Brian Duffy, the editorial cartoonist from the local newspaper took pity on me, not only lending me an extra ski mask—the one with a name that sounds like an expensive dessert, but allowed me to sit in his shadow for the headwind push to the turnaround spot—a spit of buildings and three large silver silos gleaming in the morning sun. Less helpful was the number of times he told me we were almost there. Note to self: A grain silo in Iowa appears to be one mile way from anywhere—Houston, Montana, anywhere.

A local farmer took one look at my gloves and dug out a pair of camouflaged hunter's Gore-Tex models from the back of his truck.

"What's with the index fingers?" I asked. While still insulated, this digit cover was thin and offered more mobility.

"That there is your trigger finger, son." He mimed a shotgun blast motion.

Of course the only animals not holed up inside were us, so a bit of hunting was probably out of the question.

Another bit of advice: never wear metal rimmed eyeglasses in arctic conditions. At least they kept my eyes from freezing shut, but visibility was reduced to periscope level. Which was all for the best because I missed the Iowa Girls Gone Wild lifting of shirts and opening of parkas. I'm a married man. Besides, the roadway, while plowed and salted, was dangerous enough without those kinds of distractions.

Every time I threatened to turn back, my posse from the paper and bike shop formed a protective paceline membrane around me. When I fell off the back I would make the sound of a llama during childbirth. This caused them to slow just enough so I could latch on again.

I tried busying myself with a swallow or two from a shop-provided water bottle. That futile act of kindness had frozen solid a few moments outside the town limits.

At the turnaround we were treated to "pork on a stick" and firehouse chili.

"It's been dead this year!" the cute Tyson Foods volunteer said as we purchased our charity meat popsicles. "I don't think more than a hundred of you . . . you guys . . . braved it the entire way."

I noticed a woman trying to rub her feet back to life in the corner of the room, sobbing softly. Another rider was drinking lite beer served in a quart milk jug. Some of it had frozen to his beard.

That could end badly.

But foolish behavior has its privileges. Upon my frosty return, like a survivor from the Shackleton expedition hollering into my cell phone for directions to the church basement gym party, I realized something.

Reflecting upon my ordeal while gazing across a silent little community, all glistening and angel-wing white from snowfall, a weak winter afternoon sun, and a cobalt blue sky, here's what I concluded.

I'd found my below-zero frozen field of dreams while pedaling through that frat boy dare-sized nightmare ride . . . and I'd never, ever bitch about bike fender season in the Northwest again.

Chapter 10: Trying Not To Miss the Boat   I've never had luck with ferries. See Chapter 14 in *Mud, Sweat and Gears* for the gory details.

Chapter 11: Mistaken Identity   No longer am I mistaken for Mr. Sutherland. These days it's . . . basketball great Bill Walton. They did a split screen of us recently at one of my events—it's uncanny, if you discount that fact that I'm about two feet shorter. Mini-Walton. These days I'm just happy to be out and about to be mistaken for anyone.

Chapter 12: Complications   Like a good detective, Sherri slipped into the shadows and I haven't been able to track her down.

Chapter 14: When The Going Gets Tough   Toni and I stayed in touch. She married a state trooper and moved to Vermont, about as far away from the beaches of Aruba as you can get, physically anyway. She runs the Vermont Marathon and can more than likely still do more pull ups than me.

Chapter 17: Yo Ho Ho and a Bottle Of Rum   I still love to sail, though I don't get out on the open water enough these days. Clark's been a no-show at our high school reunions but I hear he's still out in the world looking for a safe harbor. And we'll always have that summer on the edge of childhood when we flew the Jolly Roger and lived unfettered, like proper pirates, doing as we pleased.

Chapter 21: The Next Parade   I still love a parade and I've ended up in more than a few since becoming something less than a household name in the literary world. My favorite parade story involves leading a procession of 7,000 happy-go-lucky cyclists through the streets of Portland, Oregon at midnight for the World Naked Bike ride. You don't have to bare all but most people did. And yes, I wore my helmet.

Chapter 25: There's A Little Bit of Greg LeMond In Every Touring Cyclist   These days, they're trying to keep up with me. . . . Read on.

"Yellow bracelet?"

Two racers on a training ride flank me at the light. We're at the top of the hill. I passed them coming up, but traffic laws allowed them to pull even. As we wait for the green the one on my left, executing a decent track stand, rephrases the question. It sounds like something closer to an accusation this time.

"You're with Lance's fight against cancer, right?!"

I look at their wrists, yellow plastic loops are on prominent display. I'm down with that, with all my heart really, but what's throwing me into a state of stunned confusion involves guys in that much spandex and wraparound eyewear speaking to me in the first place. Normally, racers talk only amongst themselves, like ants in a colony (if you look closely you can make out their antennas). They'll occasionally acknowledge my existence with a slight nod if I happen to be wearing one of my sponsor's jerseys and forget my panniers at home. Barring that, I'm dead to them.

But I did just pass these svelte gents on a hill, with loaded bags . . . on a tandem . . . attached to a trailabike . . . which is hooked to a trailer . . . with three sons in tow. Might this have caused a tectonic shift in our lines of communication?

What I want to say to them is this; "Hey, if blowing you guys off the back on that hill doesn't count as living strong, I doubt a yellow band of plastic is going to tip the balance."

But you don't diss the yellow band and live . . . long.

I stay mute while they look over at my sons naked wrists. Quinn models a shark's tooth necklace we searched out in Hawaii and Enzo fashions a Pokemon decoder ring the size of Delaware on his pointer finger, but no canary-colored bands of courage.

Oh, the shame.

The racer on my right points at his bracelet, nods, then gives me the thumbs up.

Now they're creeping me out. A bit too evangelical about their bracelets for a Saturday morning.

If you haven't seen the ubiquitous yellow plastic on every third wrist in America by now, either you're colorblind or about to walk into traffic due to a chronic lack of attention.

Allow me to recap. Lance Armstrong achieved his victory against cancer through powerful treatment and daily hard work, luck and an ornery Texas death match attitude. I can speak to his attitude because I once interviewed this young and improving, cocky racer after the Tour DuPont. The kid showed the right combination of brash self preservation and enough hutzpah to scare the bejesus out of the most experienced racers that day. Cancer didn't stand a chance. But it did change his physical make up and softened his out-look on his fellow man, seven Tour de France victories gave him the platform to help support other cancer victims by creating the yellow Live Strong wristband. With help from Nike, the bracelet was launched in 2004 and became an instant, worldwide success. Money went to research—and almost 60 million bracelets have been sold so far.

An amazing story, I stand for, around, and behind it . . .

I just don't like jewelry, or accessories of any sort, stowing away on my person. Hats I like. Hats I would wear, if I didn't look so foolish in hats. Put any make or model on my noggin and immediately it takes 20 IQ points off my appearance. Ballcaps are the worst. Pop one on me and I feel the need to chew gum with my mouth open, make change for a twenty and top off your tank.

I wear a helmet because of gravity and velocity, but I won't be offended if you look away. It's almost too scary an image to force upon the world. The addition of bracelets and I would be absolutely hideous. My only choice would be to go completely over the top; piercings, a tall bike, large tattoos. Or pull a Liberace—glitter, owl glasses, platform shoes and rings on every finger. No one wants me to go there.

I'm about launch into a discussion with my sons about the pros and cons of overzealous missionary work when a stream of cyclists pedal past. Then more, and more still. All of them sporting yellow bracelets, some wearing yellow t-shits announcing the event. My world began to make sense again. Without realizing it, we've turned onto the route of a Lance Armstrong Foundation Live Strong Challenge Ride.

The next time you see me, I just might be wearing yellow, black, AND Jacamian flag colored bracelets. A hat, even. Perhaps a fedora.

If you look away, I'll understand.

Chapter 27: The Flesh Is Willing   I've ridden with my brothers-in-law a number of times since that New Year's morning ordeal, and my performance has never embarrassed me again, but in Italy I took them to the cleaners. Something about pulling 450 pounds of bicycle, boys, and gear on a 16-foot tandem across Canada puts you in good standing. Hell, when it's just you, a mountain bike, and a hill—child's play.

Chapter 31: The Tree Huggers   I've never met anyone else named Whisper, but I have come across more than a few Crickets. Also, I haven't loaned my U-lock to anyone who went on to chain themselves to a bulldozer, but these days I feel like chaining myself to a few offshore drilling rigs and raging against anyone who thinks the fight is over. We're still destroying the planet at an alarming rate, smiling for Capitol Hill hearings, denying responsibility for everything as long as the profits keep rolling in, and the only chance we have is not in changing a few habits but an entire way of living. I try to walk my talk, and fail some days but speak my mind, clearly and without malice and hope it helps put a few people on the good foot. Maybe we can turn this thing around before all the beauty I found out there and brought to life in the pages of my books is gone.